Sir Frank Fraser Darling, 1977
(photo: Douglas Stronach)

Fraser Darling's Islands

J. MORTON BOYD

EDINBURGH UNIVERSITY PRESS

© J. Morton Boyd 1986

Edinburgh University Press
22 George Square, Edinburgh

Set in Linotronic Plantin
by Speedspools, Edinburgh, and
printed in Great Britain by
Redwood Burn Limited,
Trowbridge, Wilts

British Library Cataloguing
    in Publication Data
Boyd, J. Morton
Fraser Darling's islands—
    (Island biology)
1. Darling, Frank Fraser
2. Environmental protection—
    Scotland—Biography
I. Title   II. Series
333.7′2′0941′1   TD171.5.G7
ISBN 0 85224 514 9

Preface

Frank Fraser Darling had a gift of writing scientifically in a biographical way. His books revealed a great deal of his own character as well as his biology. It is the aim of the Edinburgh Series to give a precise account of scientific results within a biographical framework, similar to the writings of Fraser Darling in *A Herd of Red Deer*, *Bird Flocks and the Breeding Cycle* and *A Naturalist on Rona*, and to tap the rich field of biological research using islands as natural laboratories – again like Fraser Darling, starting in the Scottish islands and extending in interest to other parts of the world.

This inaugural volume is not intended to be a biography; it is a portrait of Fraser Darling as I knew him and from his books, journals and letters. I have attempted to let Sir Frank tell his own story. He was an industrious and lucid writer of journals: fluent, lyrical and precise. Much of the text from his journals of Priest Island, Treshnish and North Rona has already been published in *Island Years*. However, I have preferred the original hand-written text to the published and have included much unpublished material. (This means that I needed to follow his fairly free way with Gaelic spellings.)

The book deals with the Scottish period of Fraser Darling's life which is comparatively unknown to his international public; just as most of his international eminence went unsung among the Scottish people for whom he felt great affinity. The Prologue gives a sight of him at the peak of his career and the Epilogue the same in retirement and declining health. My decision to write the book in this way springs from a promise I made to Fraser Darling that I would edit and have published his African journal after his death; this book prepares the ground for the fulfilment of that promise.

In this writing, I have been aware of the sensitive areas of

v

Fraser Darling's life. He was married three times, divorced by his first wife Marian Fraser ('Bobbie'), became a widower for a short time following the untimely death of his second wife Averil Morley, before marrying Christina Brotchie,the present Lady Fraser Darling. Frank is survived today by both Bobbie and Christina, by Alasdair (son of Frank and Bobbie), Richard, James and Francesca (children of Frank and Averil). I have not dwelt unduly upon sensitive matters, but, nevertheless, I have been determined that essential facts be included without which there can be no true appreciation of this great man.

I have been greatly helped in this by the members of the family. Christina has been my friend over all the years since I first knew and began to work with Sir Frank. She enhanced greatly my understanding and appreciation of him and his motivations. However, it is Bobbie and Alasdair to whom I owe a particularly deep debt of gratitude, for this book is also about them. Bobbie's first-hand description of her life with Frank was charming; her recall of events spanning fifty years or more was clear, with a thrill to me in her telling. I am also grateful to her for allowing me to photograph her. Without the help of Alasdair (and Mary, his wife) the book would have lacked reality, richness of detail and illustration; he made available to me personal letters from his father to him at crucial stages of family life. He also let me have press cuttings and many photographs from which to make a choice. I am the more grateful to him and his mother for enduring any anxieties to them which this work may have caused. I never knew Averil; she died before my collaboration with Frank began. However, I have had the encouragement of her children: Richard, James and Francesca. James and Francesca have provided most important information and insights into the mind and character of their father. Francesca has given me a particularly sensitive and candid appreciation of Sir Frank in old age and has lent me photographs. I dedicate this book to them all.

I am honoured that Professor Sir Robert Grieve agreed to write the Foreword and I am delighted that he has done so with that touch of personal reminiscence for which he is so well known. His recollections and appreciation of Fraser Darling are in themselves a substantive contribution to the book.

Many have helped in providing information from personal papers, experience and knowledge of Sir Frank. I am most grateful to Mrs Celia Kendon, who made available to me crucial letters between Frank and her husband between 1938 and 1952; without them I could not have described the state of Frank's mind in these troubled years. I am also grateful to Dr Russell Martin for allowing me to quote a letter he received from Frank; to Louis K. Stewart for his recollections of Frank during the Red Deer Survey; to Lt-Col. J. P. Grant of Rothiemurchus for his comments on the manuscript and his recall of Frank during the years of the *West Highland Survey* and the official discussions on red deer in the Highlands; to Richard Balharry for his comments and for suggesting the quotation from Aldo Leopold; to Niall and Bruce Campbell for their recollections of Frank at Kilcamb Lodge and for consulting the papers of their father, Col. Ronald Campbell; to Professor R. V. Short for discussions on the genesis of the book and the series; for information and advice to Dr John Berry, Dr and Mrs I. L. Boyd, R. D. Cramond, Charles A. Fraser, Donnie Fraser, Sandy MacLeod, Mrs Abie Muir, the Royal Society of Edinburgh and the Hon. Lord Swann.

I wish to thank all those who have provided photographs and whose names are credited in the captions, but I am particularly grateful to Tom Weir, who has admired Fraser Darling and written of his achievements over many years. Acknowledgement is given of kind permission to quote from Fraser Darling's and others' published works, from the Cambridge University Press, Oxford University Press, G. Bell & Sons Ltd, British Broadcasting Corporation, Athlone Press, Victor Gollancz Ltd, the Royal Society of Edinburgh, *The Countryman* and the *Glagow Herald*

My close association with Sir Frank owes much to the Nature Conservancy (now the NCC). Successively, as Regional officer for the West Highlands and Islands and Director for Scotland, I was able to maintain contact with him both officially and personally. In writing the book, I used the library of the Nature Conservancy Council and thank the librarian, Mrs A. Easterbee, for her help. Rawdon Goodier lent me books and papers. I owe a special debt of gratitude to Mrs Helen G. Forster for giving unstintingly of her time and effort in the production of the book; without her help it might not have been written. The skill, patience and perseverance of the staff of Edinburgh University Press have been much appreciated.

Lastly, I have been sustained in this task by the support of my wife, for whom Frank had considerable affection and who has been my counsellor on many aspects of the book and helped with the index which includes references to all birds.

J. Morton Boyd
Balephuil, Isle of Tiree

Contents

Foreword by Sir Robert Grieve

To most people at the end of the Second World War Fraser Darling was known for his account of the Summer Isles experiment; the courage and toil and hardship shared with his first wife stood out strongly and vividly. He often talked about it to me; and said that, if he had to do it again, he could not wish for a better partner. To the general reader of *Island Years* and *Island Farm*, this undoubtedly was the atmosphere generated. The ecological and professional aspects of the books were not really understood generally by most of his readers, affected as they were by the romantic Highland literature of the 'way of life' kind. To the end of his life, he himself regarded the Highlands and Islands as his 'laboratory', and I had the opportunity of observing in him (as in myself) the difficult mixture of attitudes in the period in which I was closest to him.

This book, therefore, is an illuminating one; it shows the whole man both as regards the Highlands and Islands and, very importantly, the growth of his knowledge and experience of the world-scene of conservation. He, like most intelligent and constantly learning human beings, had his spiritual and intellectual troubles, his discrepancies, his changes of attitude, his faults. The book deals fairly with all this but has an understandable warmth and respect for a genuinely great man. It matches such knowledge that, as a regional planner, I had of him and which I conveyed to the author in our discussions.

I am therefore glad that Dr Boyd asked me to write this Foreword, because I regarded Fraser Darling as a big man in every way. I knew him most intimately at a crucial period of his life and career between 1944 and 1950 when he was taking what was probably the most important step in his

x

progress towards world recognition of his reputation in the conservation movement. During this period the word 'conservation' and other cognate terms were used by us a great deal in discussing the immediate post-war struggle of ideas about the shape of our society and its environment. Today, however, the word 'conservation' is becoming less clear as, in some important ways, it moves away from the human creature. Almost certainly, there were subtle differences in the way in which we used it; and, to him, the emphasis was on nature conservation.

A very wide range of important Royal Commission and other Reports had been published dealing with matters ranging from the problems of our million-mark conurbations (Barlow Commission Report, 1940) to rural land utilisation, greenbelts, national parks, the administrative and financial handling of land values, and the acquisition of land for the purposes set out in these Reports. Also, and overall, a new national planning legislative system was proposed; this, later, had issue in the Town and Country Planning (Scotland) Act (1947), the basis of all subsequent national planning legislation.

All this was in train; a vigorous discussion of principles and consequent action was going on. It was an exhilarating period, and Fraser Darling was involved specifically in two main outcomes, the West Highland Survey and the Scottish National Parks Committee. But he was unquestionably interested in the whole flux of ideas about the quest for an improved environment, physical, social and economic; and it was in this connection that we first met, through his membership of the National Parks Survey Committee which preceded the Scottish National Parks Committee. I had submitted evidence from the Clyde Valley Regional Planning Advisory Committee, making the case for the Loch Lomond–Trossachs area as a national park. He had of course read this and wanted to see me and this pioneer regional planning organisation. We found much in common in our belief that, by taking real thought, much could be done to improve our whole approach to land-use planning. But what was 'land-use' planning? In the national park context, what proportion of the 'land-use' should be recreational, i.e. largely for urban man as tourist or visitor, mountaineer, naturalist (to use the older word), pony-trekker, angler, hunter, etc.? In the event, I found myself on the Scottish National Parks Committee [SNPC] which had to deal with the administrative and financial aspects of the five areas designated by the Survey Committee. It was clear that he had been impressed by the synoptic view of the new kind of regional planning going on in the Clyde Valley, much influenced by Patrick Geddes' writings as a planner-biologist. However, subsequent events showed that Frank perhaps somewhat over-valued the new tool, furnished by the powerful Town and Country Planning (Scotland) Act 1947, which came into effect on 1 July 1948. It slowly became clear that it was only applicable to urban areas, and in a negative manner to lowland rural areas; it did not fit the Highlands and Islands where his and others' developing ideas of synopsis were searching for an effective administrative system. But it was not till the creation of an 'ad hoc' planning-development organisation like the Highlands and Islands Development Board (and certainly not wholly in that) that the mechanism which could make an impact on such an area came into action twenty years afterwards. Of course, the Tennessee Valley Authority – part of the USA's New Deal Programme of the thirties – had inspired many of us; it certainly had more than a minor effect on the discussions revolving around our National Parks drive before and after the war. It was inevitable therefore that the National Park idea, when applied to the Highlands, raised big socio-economic questions; and there can be no doubt that, in the wider balance of conservation and development, we are still a long way from an administrative solution.

There was a difference of opinion on the National Parks Committee as to the role of a national park in the Highlands of Scotland. Some of us – eventually the majority – believed that the preservationist wildlife aspect had to be played down; that the Highlander who believed he had been exploited in the past for trees, sheep and deer would almost certainly now say he was to be exploited for scenery. He, we thought, had to be in the game this time, and manifestly so, through some kind of unified resource development in which recreation in its widest sense would have an important role. In the event, this was expressed in the final Report by the Glen Affric Appendix (a synoptic plan) which was signed by the majority. Fraser Darling did not sign it, along with three

xii

others; they constituted one-third of the total membership. All members signed the main Report; the Appendix was the compromise device, then, in 1947 – a kind of minority report signed by the majority.

My last meeting with Frank was in 1970 in Inverness when we discussed the work of the Highlands and Islands Development Board, which I was just about to leave. At that discussion, I was not left with a clear and specific impression of his contemporary view of what was happening in the Highlands, but I detected a movement in his slow and careful words of changing opinions. One thing seemed to be clear enough: that his overall attitude in 1945 that improved agriculture was the key to Highland rehabilitation had changed. He was thinking that the kind of urban society, mobile and better-off, which we then saw growing rapidly, would put a much greater emphasis on recreation in Highland terrain; and that that might be a better national economic solution. This was in direct line with his comments in the past of the lost opportunity to acquire and administer the five designated park areas for £3.5m (as recommended in the Report); the land in these areas could then have been bought for about 50p per acre.

There is, of course, a paradox in all this. In essence, in his earlier days in the Highlands, he was regarded as a 'laird's man', a denigratory, upper-echelon man. He believed that the only hope under the existing system was the enlightened landlord, since he alone had the power to achieve a proper land-use balance – if he did not always have the resources to carry it out in practice. Many Highlanders were hostile to him and quoted his gaffes with relish; his Yorkshire directness sometimes led him into trouble. Yet, today, one could reasonably point out that there is the growth of an almost universal movement of ordinary folk towards the view of the sporting people of the upper classes in the last few generations; in short, the curious effect of the contemporary conservationist movement (or some interpretations of it) is to make the preservationist Highland landlord more acceptable, to urban people at least, for the first time in five or six generations.

Fraser Darling is sometimes described as the defender of the crofting way of life. That is not how I remember him at all; his anecdotes in this field, whether right or wrong, were

xiii

anything but complimentary and his general contentions about agricultural improvement were not likely to lead to retention of the system as commonly understood. But he admired the very conservatism of the crofter he criticised. Like most of us who have been involved in the Highland mythology, he could be muddled.

I saw Frank really angry only once. That was a curious episode, illuminating his assessment at that time of the conservation movement. In the summer of 1947, as we were walking up a glen in Morven, he pointed out to me the incipient erosion caused by sheep on the steep hillside. He regarded sheep as an anathema and was not quite balanced on the subject. During the course of a consequent discussion on land-use, I pulled out a recent paper I had written and read what I thought was a relevant extract in the context. I had said that it was clear that we were moving out of the exploitative phase in our industrial civilisation and entering a conservation phase. He suddenly became angry. 'I don't agree at all', he barked out in a voice I hadn't heard before, 'if anything we're becoming more and more exploitative and stupid and criminal about it all.'

We walked back to his ancient Rolls Royce in a gloomy silence. I had never seen him so passionate. He was, of course, taking a much wider view than me – a world view.

That is the note for me to end on, the world-view to which Frank introduced me; and how he helped me to form my opinions, my knowledge, my grasp of synthesis in those wider countryside matters about which we talked and debated most. I can see and hear him now, an impressive, wise, large homely figure talking slowly and reflectively in his Yorkshire voice as we walked through the Highland glens.

Prologue: Shefford Woodlands House

Coat and briefcase in hand, I hailed a taxi from the steps of the Nature Conservancy; I barely had time in the rush hour to catch my train at Paddington. The tedium of a day-long meeting in the bemirrored and corniced conference room in Belgravia was suddenly over and I plummeted into the maelstrom of Knightsbridge. Gone was the world of talk; in its place the world of reality. Within that rather gracious room the state of Britain's wildlife has been mapped and remapped. All who have made an effort in the cause of conservation have at some time or another pondered its grandeur, imbibed it intellectually, and issued forth feeling the drastic contrast between the metropolis and the subject of discussion, the 'haunts of coot and hern'. To a naturalist like myself there returned the puerile joy of release from school to the sweet liberty of the river valley. I was off to meet Frank Fraser Darling at his home in the Berkshire countryside near Newbury.

After the War I was in a quandary about what I might do. I felt it a considerable come-down from the life of a Station Adjutant of a large RAF station to that of a student, and soon grew to dislike my original choice of becoming an engineer. My feelings were running not towards the disruption or harnessing of nature, no matter how well-intended, but towards its care and freedom. This was borne upon me when, as a student apprentice, I worked for six months on the Loch Sloy hydro-electric scheme at the north end of Loch Lomond. Try as I might, I could not develop the conviction and enthusiasm which characterised my mentors on the site and at the University. The pull of the natural sciences and the gospel of conservation were too strong, and I decided to become a biologist instead of an engineer. I cannot say that I had a 'Damascus Road' conversion, but I am certain that without the solitude and beauty of the Loch Lomond hills and woods, the writings of Fraser Darling in mind, and the encouragement of a few good friends, I could not have made the change.

My first contact with Fraser Darling came during my undergraduate days in Glasgow. I had to carry out a scientific investigation and provide a report as part of my Honours examination in zoology. I wrote to Fraser Darling about an idea in his recently published *Natural History in the Highlands and Islands*: the inter-specific competition between species of snails in the sand dunes of the Hebrides. Partly through the writings of Fraser Darling, Elton, Leopold, Seton Gordon and Robert Atkinson and partly through my own love and fascination for islands I made up my mind to read ecology and to use the Hebrides as my study area.

The reply was brief: inter-specific competition in snails was not at all suitable for an Honours study; why not simply describe the communities of plants and animals on a line drawn from the fore-dunes of the upper shore to the heath-land of the interior as a succession unbroken by cultivated land. He recommended Tiree as a place, and there I went with three botanist friends in 1952 to begin ecological studies which I continued in the Hebrides until 1957. Fraser Darling's advice contained the germ of my life's work in ecology and conservation from which grew the efforts of the late fifties and sixties on sea-birds, seals and Soay sheep, and the deep affinities which my family have for the islands; his example was also before me in later work in the Middle East, USSR, Africa, Aldabra and Christmas Island (Central Pacific).

I corresponded occasionally with Fraser Darling during the fifties. I did not know him well enough to be quite sure what he thought of me and my ideas. At that time he was travelling widely in North America and Africa, had his home in England and was seldom seen in Scotland, though he did still have official connections through a Readership at Edinburgh University and as Director of the Nature Conservancy's Red Deer Survey. I always felt that he still hoped to make a come-back to the Scottish scene and that he wished very much to have his place kept warm by a younger man of his own cast; this was later borne out by events.

2

On 27 April 1961 I received a letter from Fraser Darling; he was in New York working with the Conservation Foundation and was at the height of his popularity in the international conservation scene. Collins had asked him to produce a new edition of *Natural History in the Highlands and Islands* and would I like to help, with himself as senior author?

> I would now like to suggest to you what I have suggested to Collins, namely that you should help produce this second edition and take your place as second author. My notion would be that being so near the literature and the sources you should summarise the new knowledge which has arisen since 1947 and present it to me in such fashion that I can incorporate it in a rewritten edition.[1]

I realised that to say 'yes' would probably land me with the whole work (as it did), but to say 'no' would be to lose the chance of a lifetime. Since its publication in 1947 I had used the book continuously, knew it well and admired it both as a working tool and also a source of enjoyment. I wrote to Fraser Darling words which today, in hindsight, have lost none of their feeling of thrill, privilege and delight.

> Your offer of second authorship in the revised edition of *Natural History in the Highlands and Islands* I take up with both hands! I feel that it is not only a wonderful opportunity for me, but also a compliment. I hope that I will be able to do it well and to your complete satisfaction.[2]

The Fraser Darling I knew before I became his collaborator was the man of the islands, of the red deer and the grey seal. The greater impression of him as a man of international reputation had not come through to me by reading *A Pelican in the Wilderness* (1956), *A Naturalist in an African Territory* (1960) and his many articles; my interests did not then lie abroad and were concentrated in his former haunts in Scotland. I was unable to meet him personally for twelve months after receiving his invitation, and then only for a few moments in Edinburgh; almost two years had elapsed before I was able to take to him the revised manuscript, on 25 March 1963. There had been much writing and inevitable entanglements with many people and deadlines set and over-run. On 29 September 1962 he wrote to me:

> Don't worry about what you have not managed to do. This is one of the things you will have to learn, that the older you grow the busier you get and you do not get things done to the

3

same deadline as you used to do when you had nothing else but one paper to write following your bit of research. Think of me at this moment concerned with half a dozen research projects in Africa, conservation of snow-line grazings in the Rockies as sieves of radioactive fall-out, examining the situation facing us in the next two or three centuries through the rise of CO_2 content in the atmosphere, doing a survey of the National Parks system of the United States for the Department of the Interior, and trying to establish myself from January 1963 at the Desk of the (Conservation) Foundation for International Studies: I do not get through much more work than I did as a young man when I took the precious attitude of being immersed in my own bit of research. You are just at the beginning of administrative responsibility in addition to research and writing commitments. Do not lose heart but revel in the exhilaration of it all.[3]

At Paddington I bought a bottle of Manzanilla for the sideboard at Shefford Woodlands House. I had already visited the Fraser Darlings and knew how happily they lived, and though this prologue is a narrative composed in the form of one visit, it contains in hindsight the recollections of several in the same pattern without regard to date.

A warm welcome would await me and this would be matched by the comfort and beauty of a well-proportioned, very well-kept and well-lived-in Georgian house. What a contrast, I thought, to the old fishing station on Tanera described in *Island Farm* or the hut and tents on Priest Island, Lunga and North Rona of *Island Years*! The Brae House at Dundonnell and Kilcamb Lodge at Strontian were primitive compared with Shefford Woodlands, upon which the Fraser Darlings lavished their affections and individual tastes in building, landscaping, objets d'art, books, food, wines and a variety of pets. Above all there was the discussion; I was eager to hear of his journeys abroad, which did nothing but whet my appetite for travel; the following extract from his African journal of 4 March 1956 in the Luangwa Valley in Zambia might have been taken from that of Livingstone almost a century before:

Eustace blows his little horn at 5.30 a.m. and the camp is moving very quickly. Our pint of tea and slice of bread are eaten and we are marching by 6.30 o'clock. We descend the last 250 feet of the escarpment foothills into the valley of the Munyamadzi. The country changes immediately to lushness

4

Plate 1. Shefford Woodlands House, Berkshire.
(photo Dr A. Fraser-Darling)

and moist heat of over 100°F. To me it feels pretty good and
I sweat like a bull as we march along. The grass is 8 feet high
. . . On and on with the Munyamadzi River occasionally
visible on the left. And then we come to it, a 50-yard river
running at 3–4 knots, browny grey with suspended silt.
Below the steep bank is a dug-out canoe, the craziest thing
you ever saw. It paddles across to us by going up the river
pulling on the foliage and then coming down and across the
current, the paddler at the stern. I am sent across first and I
kneel down and crouch as low as possible. We pull up river
by the grasses and then off we go. The dug-out log rolls to
one side and the river pours in, bringing two little fish the
size and shape of sticklebacks. I lean the other way as quickly
as possible. We continue our crazy voyage and I watch the
freeboard. When I got over the river myself I was met by
several men and boys of the next village and greeted by the
cupped-hand clapping.

I now reply 'Mapulene' and 'mutende' which is the proper
reply. Soon one of the Messenger Corps arrives, a magnificent Bantu, and he stands to attention and salutes me. I reply
and he grins in appreciation. Then a group of women who go
down on their knees, ululate at me their fingers crossing their
mouths rapidly to and fro . . . I am being treated like a VIP.[4]

He was always keen to have my story of my latest visit to
North Rona and the scene in Scotland which he then seldom

5

saw and with which he did not wish to lose contact. The rewriting of the book did for us what it might not have done for others; it made us life-long friends.

I caught a fast train and was in Newbury in an hour, and there standing in half-light at the wicket were Christina and Frank, the former diminutive, the latter massive. I heard again the gentle voice, the deliberately and quietly spoken words, and felt the great, languid handshake which contrasted with Christina's incisive Scottish tongue and tight grip. In a few moments we were on our way in their landrover with Frank extolling the beauties of the Berkshire countryside and linking the aesthetic qualities with the ecological background. The impression is created that the scenery cannot be appreciated without ecological insight and that you expect beauty when man's ecology is right and ugliness when it is wrong. We might have been driving anywhere, the technique would be the same; Frank would in his mind be analysing cause and effect, and searching for the diagnostic signs of man's illwill with the environment, taking off the shelf of his personal experience an outstanding outrage of vandalism in some distant part of the world recently visited. Years later after his death I stood with others on a hillside in Java listening to the distinguished Venezuelan ecologist, Gerardo Budowski, describe the magnificent terraced country with enchanting thatched villages; he paused for words and found a quote 'here we see what Fraser Darling calls the wooing by man of his environment'.

When his third son James was a freshman at Williams College, Massachusetts, Frank was invited to give a seminar on landuse at the Centre for Environmental Studies in the College. Though James' studies were Ancient and Medieval, he piled into the convoy of cars which lurched up the dirt roads of southern Vermont. Every so often the convoy would halt, the troops extricate themselves with difficulty from their vehicles, and hear Frank discourse upon some nondescript patch of disused farmland. He showed how the farms were dying because of poor landuse – the New England countryside should never have been farmed; it was natural deciduous forest. With a certain amount of exultation he would indicate the reclamations of second-growth woodland. This was in contrast to the bitter, curt remarks of the local farmers, who seemed to suspect that something was fundamentally against them, that the land was cursed, that God was not helping such pious folk enough. Frank was not so tactless as to tell the worthy cultivators that they should not have been scratching about there in the first place, but it was evident to James and his fellow students!

In this matter of having an eye for country, Fraser Darling took up in the world conservation where Aldo Leopold left off, in 1948. Fraser Darling was too late to meet Leopold, but became great friends with his family in Wisconsin and collaborated with his son, Starker, in his ecological survey of Alaska. Leopold saw in a great deal of North America (mainly in Wisconsin) what Fraser Darling had seen about the same time in Britain (mainly in Scotland). Leopold's *A Sand Country Almanac* has no exact counterpart in Fraser Darling's writings; it is spread across several. Leopold saw the excesses of the industrial society of North America, as Fraser Darling saw them in Scotland.

In the introduction to his American journal of 1950 Fraser Darling wrote:

> Large fields of ecology can never be investigated experimentally, and we need to learn a good deal about comparative observation as a means of overcoming experimental difficulty. Furthermore, ecology must come out of its academic shell and help in the investigation of problems affecting our survival as a species on this planet. Ecology will lose nothing of its scientific spirit in accepting the problems of communities dominated by man . . . there is but one ecology: . . . a synthesis of soil conservation, resource conservation, pastoralism and agriculture, and wild-life conservation, together with a clearer idea of the natural history of the human being.
>
> It is sometimes difficult for an ecologist on this broader field to counter the view of absolute defeatism expressed by a character in Aldous Huxley's *Apes and Essence*. 'The relationship between modern man and the planet . . . has been that, not of symbiotic partners, but of tapeworm and infested dog, of fungus and blighted potato'. The phenomenon of accelerating devastation and increasing population has, in effect, been inevitable from the moment man began to break ecological climaxes and upset equilibria without allowing them to rebuild . . . Most of us are not prepared to defer to this final logic, that the very achievement of humanness dooms us, and that civilisation is an ultimate contradiction.
>
> In visiting the United States I wished to see examples of climax vegetation, forest, prairie, alp and desert . . . in states

7

of attack and repair, and in new situations what has been my principal pre-occupation in the course of the West Highland Survey, namely, the fundamental conflict between pastoralism and forest growth.[5]

Now such personal essays in human ecology have a difficult ride with students of environmental impact analysis, but there should always be a place for the philosopher who is willing to exercise his intuition and insight and describe in simple terms cause and effect in human ecology. Fraser Darling was one who chanced his arm continuously through his life with the exact scientist and though he occasionally came a cropper he had remarkable powers of recovery and intellectual innovation.

We swung through the big gateway and drove the hundred yards to the brilliantly lit house with reflections in the long fish and lily pond which was encircled by the drive. Six large windows of similar size faced the front with a smaller window above the front door, arched over with a modest, pillared portico. The door was half glass and half wood and possessed a fanlight. The public rooms on the ground floor, and the door with the window above, were dazzling after the dark drive and showed an elegant interior freshly decorated and handsomely furnished. What was not obvious at night was the fine red brickwork and the white pointing which set-off well the window arches and the white paintwork of the elegant windows and doors.

Fraser Darling's rebuilding with Bobbie, his first wife, of the old quay and fishing station on Tanera in the late thirties and early forties, and the chapel on North Rona in 1938, was repeated on a grander scale with Averil and Christina, his second and third wives, in their development of Shefford Woodlands House. Later still he built a fine wall in front of a house at Milton, Drumnadrochit, which they owned for about ten years. The major works at Shefford Woodlands were the landscaping of the garden with the construction of a large decorative pond and pleasance, the conversion of stables into a music room with Georgian-style windows, and the placing of another fine window in the staircase. All this was done to his personal specification and by craftsmen of his own choosing. The total effect was charming.

James, his son, saw Frank's attachment to the great country houses of eighteenth-century England as romantic; his

8

work as an agricultural adviser in Buckinghamshire in the twenties had brought him in contact with such estates. Shefford Woodlands House was a very small country house sitting in 1.8 hectares, but, comments James, in his own imagination his father could play the part of an eighteenth-century country gentleman, even down to using English furniture, glass and candlesticks of that period. He idealised the last era of pre-industrial England. The house had been knocked about a bit since the Regency period; a bow window and a chocolate-painted Victorian porch had been added. Frank eliminated the window, reconstructing the Georgian original with the old glazed bricks of which the house had been built. He designed the white classical porch himself, as well as the reflecting pool (1964) on the front lawn. But Frank had cultivated tastes for materials and craftsmanship which were well furth of Regency England; of a hotel in Mexico City he wrote:

> I went to an hotel on the Paso de la Reforma as the Maria Cristina was full. It was not very expensive, though good, but what struck me immediately was the quality of materials and workmanship about the place. Doors to all the rooms were beautifully panelled, the tableware was Mexican and beautiful to eat from, and a good deal of Mexican tiling, each tile coloured by hand, gave a remarkably civilised feeling. The patio with wrought iron grille completed the sensation of Renaissance Europe not being far away in time.[6]

Two hours after leaving Belgravia I was deep in the country, and being with Frank and Christina Fraser Darling brought an extra thrill to that transition. There was, after all, a close link between the day's debate at the Nature Conservancy and the reason for my being with Fraser Darling. In my quest for an understanding of the relationship between man and nature, I felt that the scientific and professional operation in the Nature Conservancy provided only part of the answer. The other part was provided, it seemed to me, by the expression of the human spirit in the creative arts and crafts. Frank confirmed this in the way he was able to articulate nature and human nature in a piece of sculpture, a sleeping leopard cub curled in a polished lump of serpentine. The work displayed at his hand and described by him acquired a double dimension; the magnificent cat and the magnificent stone are separate, completely unconnected

9

works of nature; their combination is the work of human nature: the substance of both genius and beauty. The sculptor was a fisherman's daughter from Portsoy; she used the natural colours and spots in the rock to enhance the likeness of the sleeping, camouflaged animal. Later, I recall him taking the youngest of my small sons into his arms, and with great gentleness placing the little boy's hand into his own – creating a moment of wonder for us who watched on the frontiers between man and nature.

My host had a remarkable sensitivity in handling things. In speaking about it – or to it, in the case of a living creature – he would pass his huge hand over it to enhance one's appreciation of shape; and find words, often with a flicker of his natural stammer, which superbly expressed its qualities and roots in civilisation. For those which he possessed, through either their material or design or both, he could provide an authoritative commentary, all of it well grounded. He was particularly proud of his collection of Chinese jades and ceramics, English and Jacobite glass, Persian rugs and bronzes, French clocks and clarets, and handled everything with great care and an affection which seemed to me to be far beyond the pleasure of possession. Each piece seemed to be a passport to another time, place and people, bringing a sense of triumph as in the case of the jades; heroism in the equestrian bronzes from Persia; prosperity in the air-twisted drinking glasses; extravagance in the rococo clocks; pomp in the peafowl by the pond; warmth of sun and richness of soil in the claret; peace in the cat curled upon his lap. But, as James remembers, there were snags to living among such beautiful things: 'I remember that we were to have supper around the fire in the library. I overloaded the tray as I brought things in to set the table. In the hall the cheese platter fell off and broke. Father looked at me mournfully and said, "It is only a hundred years old." I thought, "Why does everything in this house have to be an antique?"'

Dinner was informal, but no formal dinner was ever better prepared. Frank handled his claret as he handled his other treasures. Correctly cellared, it was always ready and was brought up in the late afternoon, decanted and placed by the chimney of Christina's big Aga. The kitchen table was of solid oak, made by Christina's father, Alexander Brotchie. Part of this table came from Donnington House. According to Frank, this wood was a relic from the table at which King Charles I had dined on the eve of the First Battle of Newbury. This story chimed, says James, with his father's dreamy romanticism about the old Stuart royalty. In a sentimental way Frank was a Jacobite. He had a glass with the Stuart rose engraved upon it, and explained that this was used to drink the health (silently) of James III.

Upon the table were placed polished candlesticks, two large and one small, with pure white candles. The little one was purchased for sixpence by Frank from Mr Gilhooly's junk shop in the Cowgate when he was an impoverished student in Edinburgh and was always on the table as a reminder that present comfort was temporary in time. The bread was homemade and Christina had a magic touch in serving the most delicious food. While carving the medium rare roast rib of beef on the sideboard, Frank would boast a trained eye for the best cuts, and made a special point of describing to his guests his visits to the local butcher in Newbury to discuss his precise needs.

By this time Frank was an elder statesman, and a maverick among his contemporaries in the world of conservation of nature. In the 1950s he had fallen from favour in Britain, partly because his views were unwelcome bureaucratically and politically and partly due to his spending too much time abroad and failing to meet binding commitments in Britain. Africa he often referred to as his great seductress and he was also infatuated with America far more than he had ever been by continental Europe, which he hardly knew at all by comparison. The United States became the *via principa* for him in the fifties and sixties, which provided outlets in North America and in Africa with a finale in Britain, capped with the Reith Lectures and a Knighthood. His introduction to America has all the excitement and romance typical of the person he was. In his own words:

> Looking forth over Manhattan from the 65th floor of the Rockefeller Centre and talking to Warren Weaver (Director, Natural Sciences Division), I had said I wanted to come to America to see. I wanted to see climax states of forest, deserts natural and man-made, and to sit and contemplate in various natural and human habitats. The Rockefeller Foundation unlocked the door (by a Special Fellowship in 1950), Fairfield Osborn (President of the Conservation Found-

11

ation) held it open, and the American people said 'Come right in'.[7]

My admiration for Fraser Darling which began when I was a schoolboy took a knock when, on my return from the RAF in 1947, I was to discover that the great romance of which I had oft-times dreamed as being closest to what I would wish for myself when demobilised, was at an end. I could not forget the pathos of the last few sentences of *Island Years* on return from their privation on Rona in 1938.

> . . . We reached Williamston (Aberdeenshire) on Christmas Eve to find a white world again and frozen curling ponds. Our hosts and Alasdair [son] came down the steps of the house to meet us and we were in a Christmas world of story-books.
>
> Three nights before, I had peeled off those hard-worn Grenfell clothes, let down my knee-bands, put on dry woolly socks and slippers and had a wash in preparation for one of Bobbie's Rona dinners. Now I had a real bath, climbed into my camphor-scented dinner-suit and boiled shirt and could hardly believe it was myself. I looked across the polished table, through the light of candles and the glint from silver and glass, to where Bobbie sat in her black evening-dress and Spanish shawl. Our eyes met and there was nothing to be said.[8]

With all the magic of their life among the deer, the sea-birds and the seals in the mountains of Wester Ross and the farthest Hebrides, this for me was stuff greater than the movies. I can remember a sense of personal let-down, but it was not great enough to kill the enchantment which Fraser Darling and his islands had for me. The personal tragedy in the breakdown of his first marriage did not touch the scientific challenge which lay behind his work with wildlife. However, though the science of *A Herd of Red Deer, Island Years, A Naturalist on Rona, Island Farm, Bird Flocks and the Breeding Cycle* and *Crofting Agriculture* still lives on as a wholesome pioneer-effort upon which others have built, the personal story of the island family is remembered by an older generation, for its sad ending.

Apart from these well-written books and also the *West Highland Survey*, which embodies a great deal of the spirit and knowledge of his island days, Frank wrote journals in his fluent accurate style and it is from these, as well as from his

12

books, that this work is compiled. His discipline in diary-writing, first displayed in his island journals, is repeated for his journeys in Africa and North America. His ability to write effortlessly, coupled with a boyish sense of wonder at nature, admirably equipped him as a diarist. The following are his descriptions of three incidents, one each from the islands, the African plains and the high Sierra of California.

On North Rona on 14 July 1938:

> Enormous waves broke against these cliffs [of Fianuis] and the water was churned to white foam for 75 yards from the cliff. The sound and scene were awe-inspiring. It was the sort of sea which people often say, 'nothing could live in this terrible surf'. So you would think, but there, close into the rocks and where the waves broke most fiercely, were our friends the great seals. They were not battling against the seas, but taking advantage of them for play. It was nothing but play, I am sure, which was keeping them there . . . They were keeping to the surface, nearly a hundred of them enjoying the deep rise and fall of the sea and the spray of the shattered waves. They were living joyfully and I in my way rejoiced with them. The sky had come a brilliant blue, the wind was dropping and, as usually happens, the surf began to get bigger. The whiteness of it shone in the sunlight and the movement and sound of it all were glorious.[9]

In the Mara, Kenya, 15 October 1958:

> We were among game, including lion and cheetah all the time, and when around 6 o'clock in the evening sun we sat on top of a little hill Temple-Boreham calls Roan Hill and looked over a valley to the Sand River and another wooded hill and lightly-brushed areas, we had a view long to remember. Down near the line of riverine vegetation was a herd of 50 elephant playing about; a herd of 93 buffalo slowly crossed the plain to the water; 8 roan antelope were just below us; there were 2 or 3 giraffe and eland in the landscape; a herd of impala; several knots of zebra; one or two old bull wildebeeste; several small groups of kongoni [hartebeeste]; a few topi and some Thomson's gazelles; warthogs here and there; two reedbuck and one lion a good way off. Where else could you see as much as this at one time? It was almost dark as we came over the plains and the wildebeeste in their hundreds were in silhouette, so deeply moving.[10]

In the High Sierra, California, August 1950:

> Our destination for a few days was the western side of the High Sierra, in the Emigrant Basin country of glaciated

13

polished granite, with little lakes and damp flats and occasional castellated mountain caps of basalt. John Muir called this 'the country of light' and I can think of no better name. It kept recurring to me as I walked over these polished, bare expanses of granite relieved by the beautiful Sierra junipers, white bark pines and blue spruces. The country fascinated me because I had not imagined quite such a habitat before. It is extremely rough, with very little soil left by the glaciers. The substantial trees grow in the cracks of the granite or in the peaty soil which forms round the glacier lakes. The 'draws' become luxuriant with an undergrowth of elder, dogwood, rowan, manzanita and huckleberry oak. And then in a few moments on the bare granite again. The trees are humanly inviolate up here and when they fall they gently rot, largely consumed by carpenter ants, and ultimately they accept the contour of the ground where they have fallen, finally becoming but a dim strip of dust. The sierra juniper is the oldest lived of trees, an age of three thousand years being moderately common. The trunk is a most beautiful warm brown, longitudinally striated, and the foliage is deep, rich bottle green . . .

I was loth to come out of this enchanted country like the 'great forest' of Arthurian legend, for Malory's forest meant a wilderness. Always the sun, the lightness and fantastic quality of the granite, the hosts of tiny flowers, little scarlet and blue pentstemons, castillejas and saxifrages. There were Steller's and Californian blue jays in the pines, some beautiful warblers and chickadees in the sierra junipers; bucks would start up from clumps of huckleberry oaks, and on the sandy shores of the lakes where we would camp there were tracks of deer and bear, made afresh by time we got out in the early morning.[11]

As the candles burned lower and Christina's meal advanced to the cheese and wholemeal biscuits, Frank would raise the second decanter of claret and look through its rich colour to the candle flame, reciting a eulogy to the particular chateau, vintage and the countryside of Bordeaux. Then, with dignity and care he would recharge the shell-thin glasses. The candlelight matched the feeling of relaxation created by the food, the wine and the scientific discourse embellished with anecdote and caricature of people of our common acquaintance.

Best of all we enjoyed sharing our natural history and would take our discussion after dinner into the brightly lit

14

hall and parlour with their pictures, clocks, ornaments and display cabinets. The house was invariably well heated and on one occasion we had dinner in what Frank called 'Kenyan style': in our pyjamas and dressing-gowns. Nothing can be more relaxing with the ambient temperature around 70°F!

In the course of these after-dinner walkabouts he, on three occasions, presented me with a small token of his friendship: pieces of jade and glass. The most beautiful and certainly the most memorable of these is an English wine glass of about 1837. He was recounting the illness of Averil his second wife and of her death in 1957 of cancer. We were standing in the hall beside the tall cabinet in which his collection of glass reflected the lights with startling brilliance and there returned to him the grief which is well recaptured in a short note written on a back page of his African journal:

> This batch [of the journal] is from last year's trip, not sent home because it would have taken longer than I would. And after getting home, my darling never had the chance to read it.[12]

Were it not that we were grown men we might have wept outright, but Frank, in a moment of pathos, found the key of the cabinet and without hesitation selected a glass with a large tear-drop in the shank. 'Here,' he said, 'take this tear-drop in memory of this moment and she whom you never knew.'

As I bade Christina and Frank 'goodnight' I could not help admire and appreciate how events had brought them together and of how devoted they were to each other in their fine home. By Providence, after Averil's death, Christina was there to look after the three children and the home, while Frank, having pulled himself together following his loss, continued his work in the United States. They were wed at St Cuthbert's, Edinburgh, on 2 July 1960, and went on together to a full and happy life which, in the 1960s, revolved on a New York–London axis with the big conservation job, the running of the home, the raising of Frank's and Averil's children Richard (born 2 March 1949), James (b. 23 March 1950) and Francesca (b. 22 October 1955) and the setting-up of a holiday home at Milton, Drumnadrochit.

On the stairs the Fraser Darlings had a collection of signed prints of Russell Flint watercolours of Spanish ladies. As I passed from one to another on my way to bed I could hardly

15

believe that it was the same day that I had sat through the discussion of nature-reserve management plans in Belgravia. The lunch in the Coal Board canteen was in another world and the rush-hour train was far away. Just outside my bedroom door was hung a small drawing of the old quay at Isle Tanera by Geordie Leslie. That, I thought, as I pulled up the sheets and doused the light, was part of another life not to be forgotten.

1

The Formative Years

The Spanish shawl which Bobbie wore on that romantic Christmas at Williamston in 1938 was an heirloom of Frank's mother's family from the Peninsular War. One of two brothers who went to Spain returned with a hidalga, and it was to her that Frank attributed the fire in the Darling temperament. He wrote in a biographical article in *The Countryman* in 1972:

> The hidalga persisted in my mother. Her temper was slow to rouse, but monumental and utterly awe-inspiring to me when it did emerge. [13]

In the course of writing, he makes references occasionally to his temper but always with a sense of resignation that it was inevitable. It was immutable in his chemistry, which was put together as far back as Badajoz, Salamanca and Vittoria. Having such a Regency pedigree a bad temper, however deplorable at the time, had a respect in history. Frank did not visit Spain, but his visit to Mexico in 1950 is full of an innate nostalgia. He wrote:

> I have a greater admiration for Spanish culture than most folk have. It is no blind admiration, God knows, but I believe I understand some things about the ways of Spain a little better than some of my fellows. The fact that many Spaniards fail to reach the standards of what Spanish pride and the aristocratic ideal impose in no way invalidates these qualities of a nation. Equally, I admire the English way of life though so few of us fulfil it. [14]

He loved what he saw in Mexico for the streak of Spanish which he knew to be in him. This feeling radiates from his writings:

17

Coming back to Tamuzanchale (a poor little town on the Rio Verde) that evening I found there was an upper village to the town, primitive perhaps, but well kept and satisfying. The houses as you pass them are clean and white-washed inside and almost always you see a picture of Our Lady. From several houses came the sound of a guitar, and singing would come, always sweet and low. The people sing a good deal in everyday life. That very night as I came back from the plaza and over the high bridge of the Rio Verde, a man was holding a girl by her upper arms a few inches away from him and singing to her in a soft, sweet voice. The flimsiest wattle hut will give forth music.

The people are so kind to their children here. You see man and woman walking out with their tinies as if that was what they wished most to do. The pregnant women have an air of pride and feeling as they do about children, what could be better?[15]

Frank was born at a farm near Chesterfield on 23 June 1903. His writings tell little of his childhood. Though his mother, Harriet Ellse Cowley Darling, was from a well-to-do family of cutlers from Sheffield, her affair with Frank Moss and the pregnancy which followed had sequestered her from the family home. He remembered his mother saying how, in these days of loneliness, pain and humiliation, she had drawn great comfort at night with him at her breast, while hearing the peaceful sound of the horses in the stable below. He never forgot his mother's decision to keep him by her and not to have him fostered. This single act of love was sacred to him throughout his life; more than any other, it determined his future. Frank never met his father, who went off to East Africa and died there in 1917 during the campaign against the Germans in Tanganyika. In a letter to Alasdair dated 24 January 1977, Frank wrote in congratulation to him on becoming an ADC to the Queen while serving as a Colonel in the Territorial Army :

It never occurred to me when a child that I was at the bottom of the social ladder, as I was, or that being born in a stable loft was in any way derogatory. Indeed in this latter I felt rather pleased when my mother used to tell me how she used to listen to the horses munching below and their head stall chains running through the rings in the manger as they reached up for the hay. Neverthless, I was soon aware that the climb out of the hole I was born in would be harder for

18

me than most. I think that feeling I was outside gave me the freedom I might not have had, and lack of conventionality being outside class and yet inwardly convinced that I was tolerably well bred. Whatever there might have been in me was helped by good luck, but I also have a feeling that fortune favours the one who can see his opportunities when they come, and take them. Many people can't do that. So in some measure I prospered and have done what I wanted to do in life, the most satisfying thing one could expect.

The military tradition is one which I admire though I would not have adorned it! You have done so well by the family name which I am so glad is Fraser as well as Darling. I have never felt a nobody though I started below scratch. Neither did my mother. In her younger days that I remember, even with her social handicap, she thought herself in the class of people that dispenses grace rather than receives it . . . By the way did I ever tell you that I got to the site of the battle in Tanganyika where he (my father) was killed in 1917. There was still a bully-beef can or two in the bush.[16]

The nostalgia which Frank had continuously for the English countryside he attributed to his mother. Later in life he developed the same for Africa and particularly the bush: the Africa of the pioneers which was that of his father's. Years later when he came to stay with me he brought a gift: Fitz-Patrick's *Jock of the Bushveld*, one of his favourite stories.

The mother and son bond was strong throughout life; even in adulthood, Frank felt himself accountable to his mother with whom he had to make his peace. The bond was of course rooted in his childhood when she would have him up at five on a May morning, across the meadows to the great wood which was his retreat, to find the nests of thrush and wren. Sometimes they went to the moors where he scented the heather and bog-myrtle and heard the 'go back, go back' call of the grouse and the song of the soaring lark. At other times he went alone to explore streams and found there a wonderland; if he remained still enough for long enough the tiny, almost transparent minnows were fairylike. Of these early days he wrote:

> I remember sitting on a rounded boulder in a tiny high-banked stream in the great wood. The foliage of oak and birch was far overhead, and directly above were ferns and woodrush. It was very private and the tinkle of the stream cut out all other sound. Cross-leaved mossy saxifrage, liverworts

19

Plate 1.1. Frank aged four. (photo A. Seaman & Sons)

and mosses were on a level with my eyes. There was just light enough to see the occasional spider, and if I parted the surface of the mosses I saw tiny collembolans, humble inhabitants of a smaller, more secret world than mine. When I peeled back the bark from a bit of fallen birch branch, there were more springtails – different ones I could tell, but going their own ways, silent and secret from me. I remember the moment of intense awareness, in different dimensions it seemed. The whole of that tiny environment was conveyed to me. And then one had to go back home and to school next day.[17]

School to Frank was happy enough at first when at the primary school he had the same teacher for five years. Later, at secondary school twelve miles away from home in a big town Frank became a rebel. His sheer awkwardness of attitude and behaviour arose from self-consciousness about his very large ears, dreadful stammer, birth and the hurtful comments and actions of his schoolmates. His nickname was Dummy, and a close friend from schooldays indicates that Frank needed greatly the protection and support at school of a trusted friend. He sang in the choir and it is interesting that, years later in Mexico when visiting a magnificent Romanesque church in Puebla he remarked that:

> The organ music was very fine indeed, but the choirboys did not sing as we understand it; they just shouted, which seemed to me a great pity . . .[18]

He was talking from experience. Yet, despite his affinity for the Church he refused to be confirmed. During confirmation lessons he read Darwin's *Origin of Species* (see p.240) and T. H. Huxley's essays, and rebelled in his boyish way against the fundamental doctrine he was receiving at confirmation classes which he could not reconcile with the truth of Darwin's theory; he was in conflict with family, school and church over the truth of creation as he had grown to see it. His mother accepted his decision without too much fuss; the lame curate was deeply hurt and remonstrated for weeks; his Victorian grandmother wagged her finger and declared 'Thou, God, seest me'.

Frank's religious stance did not seem to change throughout his life from the time of his failure to accept confirmation, to his death and Christian funeral. He saw God as a spirit moving in the whole of creation and himself as part of that.

21

Plate 1.2. Frank's mother, Harriet Ellse Cowley Darling, born 20 February 1877. A portrait dated about 1932. (photo Sweatman, Hedgeland and Dunk Ltd)

God was within him; there was no creature in Frank's universe in which God did not reside. He dismissed the image of a personal God to whom he would pray. God was to him the Unknown and the Unknowable, but the older he became the nearer to God did he move, finding contact always in nature. At the age of sixty-nine he wrote:

> I wish I had some notion of the nature of evil, but I have not. Is it the denial of God within us, or is there tangible evil? There have been moments when it has seemed so and very near, horrific and in the miasma of humanity. Yet evil cannot destroy the human being who meets it in the amplitude of vision and courage. The resurrection is of the quality of pie in the sky to me, but the crucifixion touches me ever more deeply as the human triumph over evil. It was no easy path. How brave was the Christ man who showed how human he was in Gethsemane and could then show the stuff of God which was within him and within the rest of us, more or less!
>
> More or less, for there is no equality of the stuff of God. We are born with our complement of genes and grow with the accidents of our environment. There is not, nor can there be, with all our political eagerness for doctrinaire notions, any equality of opportunity. I accept this and hold that in humility we should strive towards our potential. If we are favoured, we can practise the aristocratic ideal and show forbearance for those less fortunate than ourselves.[19]

Frank loathed school; even when the headmaster broke the news of Kitchener's death and with a voice full of despair said 'You can all go home', Frank had a feeling of joy at being freed from the interminable boredom of the classroom. His poor performance coupled with a nose and throat operation put him out at the age of fifteen to find work as a farm labourer and become part of the war effort. In fact he left school without permission and as he told his children in later life, 'I liberated myself on the night of my fifteenth birthday'. First he went jobbing from farm to farm in the good summer weather of 1918 and learned to scythe, load and unload a hay cart, build a stack, milk cows and gather sheep. Having been inducted on casual work he wanted a regular job and got one near Grindleford in the Derbyshire Peak District, through his mother's influence, with a stern, mean farmer who could be relied on to knock some sense into the young rebel. The farmer's letter said that Frank could stand or fall by work: 'Whoever is not a help is a hindrance here!' He complained that the only meat he was given to eat was rabbit, but, in due course, man and lad came to respect each other and Frank was on the way up. In later years he referred occasionally to the need of every man at some time in life to learn what it is like to be at the bottom, and that is where he put himself when he started with the 'Old Cock'.

> I immediately respected the 'Old Cock', as he was known for many miles around, because he never expected more of a man than he was prepared to do himself. I was determined to reach his standard and earn his respect. There were no such things as hours, only tasks to get done. Half a day a month was my time off, and that begrudged. The Old Cock's temper was choleric but I never got the worst of it. He taught me my job and was never contemptuous of my interest in natural history. Once when spudding thistles a lark flew up from his feet. He scratched his head and asked the lark why the devil she had to build her nest under a thistle.
>
> 'I canna' leave a thistle to seed and I canna' leave your nest without cover. Confound you!'
>
> So with infinite care and irritation he took out his penknife and cut the emergent flower-stalk from the thistle, leaving the lower leaves to shade the nest.
>
> During my second summer with the Old Cock I had changed from the lad who walked out of school. I had lain fallow in mind and now the bare fallow was ready to take the seed corn. Regretfully, for the Old Cock talked of my being his manager soon, he helped me to get into the agricultural college for a year's course. I was very sorry to leave the animals, for I had lived with them and for them.[20]

The bogey of an unhappy schooling was laid. The fire in the belly was well lit and shortly after going to the agricultural college at Sutton Bonington he applied himself intellectually probably for the first time. Fortunately, a friend of the family, James Walker, came to lodge with Frank's mother and grandmother. He was a scholar and teacher who tutored the lad, reviving his interest in literature and creating a new zest for learning which quickly redressed the leeway to be made-up in academic qualification for entry into the degree course. Uncle Jim, as Frank affectionately called his friend and tutor, following on the admonitions of the 'Old Cock', worked wonders in producing a young man capable of using both his brains and his hands to advantage.

24

Plate 1.3. Frank (centre of front row) with his classmates at the Midland Agricultural College, Sutton Bonington, winter 1922-23. (photo Fraser Darling Collection)

I am not sure how far satisfaction in using my hands has hindered me in life, and how far helped. The intellectual life has never been enough, and every now and then I have wished to withdraw and work with my hands. Drystone dykeing is like a soothing balm to me – the feel of stone, the intuition as I pick it up, where it is to go, that satisfaction of good alignment without using a line, and the strength of the wall which comes through into the man . . .[21]

At Sutton Bonington Frank fell in love with a tall, good-looking girl who was a fine tennis player. He admired her physique and her sense of timing and movement. Later when they went together to the islands he could never match the way she could leap ashore and scale the rocks, on split-second timing and with the grace of a trained athlete. Her name was Marian Fraser whose pet name was 'Bobbie'. She was studying for a diploma in Dairying and left the College a year before Frank to work on the Hope-Simpson Farm in Somerset. Frank obtained his diploma in agriculture and found a job as a Clean Milk Adviser in Buckinghamshire. They were married at Enfield, Bobbie's home, on 5 September 1925 and set up in a small poultry farm near Amersham. They sold their produce in the market and were comfortably close to Bobbie's parents who were concerned for their welfare. Bobbie's father, Mr Simon Fraser, was a successful printer and a keen freemason whose father had emigrated from Aberdeenshire, the land of the Black Frasers as distinct from the Red (Lovat) Frasers from Inverness-shire.

Frank had little respect for, or satisfaction from, his milk advisory job and reached for greater things in becoming the factor of a small estate owned by an autocratic lady of the country who was at first greatly taken by him. Later, following a particularly bad accident when cows were poisoned by licking empty paint tins jettisoned by a litter-lout, relations became strained and Frank was in search of a change; not simply a change of work but a job with a much higher intellectual and ideological challenge. Bobbie kept the home and the farm; Frank worked without spirit and found it difficult to settle with nobody to help him. They found it difficult to make ends meet and almost went to Tasmania.

Frank's life since leaving school and his choice of a partner had prepared him for a career in agriculture, but had left him confused. His high intelligence quickened by the tuition of Uncle Jim, the orthodoxy of the agriculture course and the desire to erase the stigma of his childhood from his life were the elements of a deep inner challenge. He wished to break away from tradition and attain a freedom both of action and, perhaps more important, of intellectual expression backed by his growing erudition. During his student days he came to know Scotland. His innate nostalgia for Edinburgh was created by an unsubstantiated belief that his mother's family were of that ilk. However, whether or not there was any historical link is immaterial; the important point at the time was that Frank felt there was, declared himself to be half-Scottish and saw a move to Scotland as a coming back to his genealogical roots.

> The Scottish people to which the half of me belongs has a traditional nostalgia, and sure in no other race are found at the same time such power for successful action and such nullifying defeatism . . . I also have suffered this sweet and bitter longing and have replied to it by coming back, shedding such worldly comforts as seemed good reasons for not coming. I wanted in those earlier days to live by my science, working as it wished to work, for to me science and art are not far from each other; each is creative and concerned with discovery. Would I work alone, or would I vegetate?[22]

In the maturing Frank a conflict had grown. It is a conflict which to some extent is common to all, namely the balance which has to be struck between the practical and ideological

26

sides of life. In Frank this was a hiatus, on the one hand he had in him the direct pragmatism of the Old Cock, the rough-hewn man of skills, and on the other the scholarship of Uncle Jim. This conflict persisted throughout life, though he became resigned later to being essentially an impractical man; yet he did not see himself as solely a man of erudition but one of action with a penetrating eye and mind in the life process. In recalling his time of break-out he wrote:

> These thoughts and many more coursed through my mind as half fears in early days when I had more or less accepted the idea that I ought to be a practical man. But this cloak of practicality never suited me, just as I find it difficult to get real boots and clothes to fit. When I became practical I was dead, and when I was impractical I lived and prospered. The day has come when I have shed the rose-coloured spectacles of my nostalgic longing and the colours of reality have withstood the change. I have come back to a real country where the joys and discomforts of living have given zest to my mind. Now I know that if I am to interpret life in men and animals it must not be from the attic or suburban study, but at the time and from the place where my life is lived.[23]

Bobbie and Frank had an Irish neighbour in the Vale of Aylesbury who had fine horses. He had a vile temper and one day Bobbie saw him thrashing a lovely stallion. She protested and for her efforts she was told 'Here, take him away; do what you like with him, he's yours!'. But their encounters were notable in other ways. Talks about livestock and mud invariably drifted into nostalgia for his County Clare and Frank's Highlands and Islands of Scotland. Looking back when writing on Tanera twenty years later Frank recalled the Irishman's words as having stayed with him through his island years:

> As you stand here, boy, in this sink of mud from which there seems no escape, remember this: if you want to reach your island farm, and you must get there while you're young or never at all, do something towards getting there every day. Never let one day pass but you save a penny or a pound or make yourself abler to live that life.[24]

It took guts to make the break when the time came. Frank admired the writings of F. A. E. Crewe, Professor of Genetics at Edinburgh University, wrote to him seeking advice, later went to Edinburgh to see him, hit it off and was offered a place to study for a PhD on the fleece characteristics of Blackface sheep. There was one snag: money. Crewe said that if Frank could support himself for the first year he would try for a grant for the second. In the end no money was obtained and they lived on £250 which Bobbie's father gave them for the first year and a number of small loans and earnings in the second. Throughout the period of their early married life Bobbie's parents provided great material and moral support; they found it difficult to understand what was going on in Frank's mind and what he would do next.

Frank saw his acceptance by Crewe as a great compliment and an omen of greater things to come. Perhaps, more than any other event in that uncertain time, it helped with the break and also convinced Bobbie about the move. During the two years of the studentship, however, Frank was happy

> . . . enjoying to the full and romantically the Edinburgh of my fathers, working on something new with the Mountain Blackface breed of sheep, and travelling the hill districts of Scotland about that work. I was working under a brilliant man who fired my imagination and opened for me new gates of the mind. There was a constant stream of new faces and stimulating personalities.[25]

The one virtue of the ground-floor flat in Portobello was that it faced the sea – that is the only good thing which Frank saw about the place and they were manifestly very unhappy in their impoverished life-style, which separated them for long-ish periods.

> She [Bobbie] had all the irksomeness of urban life which we had never known before. The baby was a skinny and nervous creature in the early months of his life; Bobbie devoted herself to him and made him a fine child, and she never let the baby and the work he caused impinge on my life. I think in the interest of my own affairs I grew unduly selfish and got farthest away from Bobbie in that time. She could not walk the Pentlands and Moorfoots with me nor spend the weekend bird-watching in Aberlady Bay.[26]

The news of the drowning at sea of an uncle of Bobbie's resulted in the loss of her milk in nursing the baby, which was a setback in hard times. Bobbie's parents also helped by introducing them to interesting and helpful people. In the early days in Portobello Mrs Denholm-Young, one of the Saxby family from Shetland, called upon them. She kindled within Frank's heart a great longing for the island life.

> Her nephew, Stephen Saxby, came from Unst to study in
> Edinburgh, and the island bond made us friends. I went to
> his home in the North Isles for one of the most wonderful
> months of my life, for it was May and bird time, but Bobbie
> was back there in the Portobello flat, half living.[27]

Frank wrote these lines in Tanera in 1943, some fourteen
years afterwards, and they appear to be a confessional to his
own selfishness but without much sign of remorse since, as
will emerge in Chapter 8, Bobbie was still in her selfless
setting and Frank as selfish as before. His candour about
Bobbie's unhappiness at a time of his own self-indulgence
during these days in Edinburgh shows a weakness in a partnership which seemed set upon two pillars – Frank's belief in
himself as a specially gifted and privileged person among his
contemporaries; Bobbie's belief in herself as the force of
family unity, through instant service to the needs of life.

The PhD thesis was submitted in the autumn of 1928
entitled 'Studies in the Biology of the Fleece of the Scottish
Mountain Blackface Breed of Sheep'. It is a typescript of
seventy-seven pages which describes the proportions of
wool, hair and kemp fibres in the different parts of the fleece
in different stocks of Blackface. The growth rates and moult
of the three fibres are recorded. The variation of all these
attributes by sex and age are also examined and Frank ex-
presses his sincere thanks to Professor Crewe 'who made all
things possible and inspired me to tackle this work'.

Their fortunes changed when, having successfully completed his PhD, Frank was appointed as the Chief Officer of
the Imperial Bureau of Animal Genetics in Edinburgh in the
autumn of 1930. They moved to a larger house in Broomie-
knowe but Frank was severely shocked by the loss of a great
friend which brought back again the great urge to go and live
in the islands. His job at the Bureau, though rather grand in
title, was little more than bibliographical work and the setting-up of an information centre in animal genetics by recording, abstracting and circulating all scientific publications
in that field. The work was routine, office-bound and lacking
in the creativity necessary to keep him happy. The wholesome life he knew with the Old Cock, with its practical skills
and commonsense objectives in life, returned to mind.

> Here was I, a fellow who had overcome much to be a farmer,
> living in the country where I belonged, sitting with white
> hands in a room in a town. It had all happened imperceptibly,
> losing sight of the goal for the sake of expediency.[28]

The new job brought more income and the new house
more comfort and the future looked brighter. However,
psychologically, Frank was unwell: a victim of depression.
The loss of his great friend whose identity is unknown had an
effect on him which was by his own account drastic. He
portrays himself as a lonely man full of self-pity in his grief
and seeking solace in the solitude of the islands away from
family and friends whose love he cherished nonetheless. He
went tramping alone in Mull and Iona and came across a
tinker pearl-fisher who showed him a fine pearl of such a size
and beauty that he could not resist buying it and bringing it
back to Bobbie as a love token, but perhaps also as a tear drop
of regret for the pain he had caused her. The pearl was later
set in a ring which Bobbie gave to Mary, her daughter-in-law.

Frank realised more than ever the sights and sounds of
nature which brightened his urban life – the shape of the
Pentlands, sparrows and starlings on the window-sill, flocks
of peewits wheeling and crying, birds' nests in Polton Park
and also the companionship of dogs and tame mice.

> Mice gave me considerable consolation, for the mouse and
> the elephant and the cow were my favourite animals. I took
> one tiny blue mouse from her mother at three weeks old and
> let her make my person and clothes her home. She was
> immensely rewarding, knowing inside out both my room at
> the Institute and the sitting-room at home. After a romp
> round the cupboards and desk she would run up my leg and
> compose herself in my pocket for a sleep. She was called
> Squeaky because this was how she would draw my attention
> specially. I learned much from Squeaky in the months we
> were together but she developed one bad habit, of deciding
> that the middle of my back between the shoulder blades was
> the most desirable resting-place. One evening I forgot and
> leaned back in a chair. I have never had another personal
> mouse, for the risk and the heartbreak are too great.[29]

His struggle, he recognised, was within himself and it was
similar to that which had made him desert his 'safe' job in the
south for the studentship in Edinburgh. Now it was as clear
as it could be to him that Edinburgh was but a stepping-stone

towards his heart's desire: the island life. One May morning he went out on to the roof of his institute to look at the Braids and the Pentlands and to listen to the song of larks.

> 'What's gone wrong?' I asked myself. Here I was in a library as my place of work, my private life a nostalgic, yearning, dreaming sort of whimsey-whamsy. When and how had I made the mistake?[30]

There were two other disheartening events which helped to confirm in his mind that the islands were the place for him and that he must make great efforts to find the ways and means. In co-operation with Sir Wilfred Grenfell, Frank put forward proposals for a reindeer ranch in Labrador, and, with his veterinary surgeon friend William Orr, proposals for a study of the behaviour and ecology of elephant in Uganda; both fell through.

Slowly but surely he was moving towards another point of break-out made all the more worrying in its financial implications and the damage it might do to longer-term prospects of a university job and the security that that carried with it for the family. His discontentment with his job in the Bureau and his known desire for a change estranged him from some colleagues. Crewe, who had been largely responsible for his coming to Edinburgh, and for his PhD, dropped him. When he did succeed in obtaining financial support for his work on red deer, which brought his resignation from the Bureau, J. H. Ashworth, the then Regius Professor of Natural History, shook his head and forecast that he would have great difficulty in obtaining a university post. In fact, twenty years were to pass before Frank was to obtain a university appointment, as a Reader in Ecology and Conservation at Edinburgh. He had the support of James Ritchie, whom he trusted and admired. However, despite all the pressures upon him to retain an orthodox view of his career, his thrust of life was changing direction inexorably. He seemed prepared to follow his instincts rather than his reason and to take Bobbie with him. His argument with himself was unrelenting.

> There was something wrong with my science now; it had lost the simplicity of the wondering child which I think is the approach of the greatest men of science. I did some work on animal behaviour for my own amusement but realised that if it was to be of permanent value and not just anecdotal, I must

31

get away from the artificial atmosphere of experimentation under laboratory conditions, and not place too much weight on what I saw of the natural behaviour of wild creatures in the short periods in which I was able to watch them. I began to see that if I was constructive enough in my thinking, the goal of the island and the life of the man of science need not be incompatible.[31]

A small legacy of £100 set them off in search of an island. In these days a houseless, uninhabited island in the Hebrides fetched £1 per acre; now, depending on location, the same might fetch over £100 per acre. They had an ideal in which were combined agriculture, fishing and nature conservation. However, even had it been available, it would have been far beyond their means to buy and manage by themselves and Frank had no mind to be a tenant or manager for another person.

The 150-acre island of Little Colonsay came on the market just when Frank and Bobbie were about to depart on a walking holiday – their first alone for seven years; Alasdair was cared for by Frank's mother in Maidstone. They decided to go to Mull and have a look at Little Colonsay and caught the early morning steamer to Tobermory where they breakfasted at the Mishnish Hotel on fresh herrings in oatmeal, before setting out on road and hill in fine weather, sleeping in the heather in advance of the midge plague. In due course they arrived at Ulva Ferry. Awaiting them was the boatman John McColum, known locally as Johnny Colonsay; of him Frank wrote:

> He was a fine man to whom I warmed immediately; his smile was slow to come, his look direct and his dignity and courtesy would have graced a king . . . The wind had been fresh before starting and had meant a hard pull out of the landing at Cragaig before John McColum could raise his sail. Then suddenly the boat was a dead thing no longer; she leapt forward, spray flying and gunwale down on the water. John McColum sat silent and unmoving in the stern, one hand on the tiller and the other holding the straining sheet. The two-and-a-half miles over to Little Colonsay, through the skerries and shallow channels that are characteristic of that stretch of coast, were all too short for us. Not only was the sailing stimulating, sea-starved as we were, but John McColum's skill was a thing to watch of itself.[32]

Unst

7°W 6 5 4 3 2

Sula Sgeir · North Rona Orkney Is.

59°N

Shetland Rackwick · · Gairsay
Hoy

Cape Wrath

Butt of Lewis

Lewis

Flannan Is. Stornoway 58

Scarp Summer · Achiltibuie
Is. · Ullapool
Harris Dundonnell

Kilda Wester Ross

onach Is. Forres ·

Uists Milton · · Inverness

Skye Aberdeen ·

Barra 57

Rum SCOTLAND
Mingulay

Coll Dundee

Tiree Tobermory · Crianlarich ·

Treshnish Is. Oban

Iona

Mull Aberlady

Colonsay Jura Glasgow · Edinburgh 56

Islay Moorfoot
Hills

Firth of Clyde

100 km

55

33

They camped a night on Little Colonsay, were greatly disturbed by rats and came away disappointed that the island possessed no sea-birds. In truth, none of the drawbacks ought to have been off-putting to such an extent. Little Colonsay might have proved to be the island farm they sought and an excellent base for Frank's studies of red deer (on Mull), sea-birds and seals (on the Treshnish Isles and Mull sea-lochs), but it was not to be and Frank's mind was already working on another scheme which came to light on the way home from that magnificent holiday. He could not bear to look out of the window of the train until it reached Crianlarich and buried his attention in a copy of *The Listener*. A long editorial on the new Leverhulme Research Fellowships caught his imagination and linked with ideas he had clearly fostered for a long time:

> Ever since childhood I had had the power of dissolving into a background of woodland and hill and of becoming at one with the creatures I found there, and now these moments were poignant. It was never difficult for me to stalk deer or to find weasels and hedgehogs whose lives I could watch intently for some short episode; and I have spent hours which were almost mystical in the bed of a woodland beck where the growth of fern and honeysuckle has met above my head, watching the passage of spiders and insects among the liverworts and cross-leaved mossy saxifrage. Tiny silent lives, but not passing unknown.[33]

These Fellowships were for senior workers who were kept from their research by routine duties by which they obtained a livelihood, and showing the paper to Bobbie across the compartment he said with pointing finger:

> 'I'm going to get one of those.'
> 'You never were blessed with initial modesty, Frank,' she answered with a smile that took the sting out of it, and would have dismissed the subject there and then but he said again:
> 'I'm serious; I tell you one of these Fellowships is going to set us free; it is the rising tide to be taken at the flood.'[34]

Frank's mind settled not upon the islands but upon the mountains. His idea was simplicity itself – to do something which had been awaiting science for almost a century and which no scientist had yet done – watch a herd of red deer on a Highland hill, recording in detail their movements and behaviour and providing a year-round description of their

34

social life with interpretation of environmental factors such as climate and pasture. Until then his notions of studying animal behaviour in the islands had been airy-fairy but the red deer idea gelled and he was back again in the fix of persuading Bobbie and his private and professional friends that it was right to desert the establishment with its good, steady job. When he had finally completed and submitted his application he had it in his bones that he would be successful.

> 'If you don't get this Fellowship and your application becomes known in high places, you'll lose your job,' she said . . .
> 'But after all, Bobbie, I'm not going to fail, and I would rather take the bull by the horns anyway.'
> 'Well, if you do, I expect I shall be following you.'[35]

Word came of Frank's success when he was in Cambridge and his feelings matched the background of classical science. Once more there returned that belief in his own gifted self which no doubt had visited him when Frank Crewe had brought him to Edinburgh. He walked the Backs and pondered the beauty of King's College Chapel. His romantic heart was deeply moved by the Evensong.

> The great organ, the high vaulted roof and impression of space and peace affected me in the same way as when I lay as a child under the foliage on the banks of a woodland burn. I became one with that great place in the chanting of the psalm and came forth humbled. There can be few moments like that in any man's life. And that evening I remember my host filled my cup of joy by playing a long Beethoven sonata on his piano. My sensitiveness was heightened; each bar and chord cut clear into my mind as it had never done before, and I was touched with the inspiration of the master.[36]

Frank's dream was that Rum should be his study area for the red deer, as he explained to Thane Riney and me thirty-five years later as we sailed under the ramparts of Eigg in the *Loch Arkaig*. Out into the sunshine we came rolling across the roost between the islands, drawing ever closer to Rum, its cloud-swept, mountainous mass possessing all the wild, rough character of the Scottish deer forest. All three of us were enchanted. 'Look yonder,' I said, 'the Dibidil bothy has the roof catching the sun.' 'Yes, that's one of the places I had in mind for my work in the 1930s,' said Frank pensively. 'You see, two of the great advantages of Rum over the mainland forest are the fact that Rum is an island and the

deer cannot move out and island isolation cuts down disturbance. I'd have given all I had to have been allowed to work
on Rum then.' In Rum the Fraser Darlings probably saw the
coming together of the 'island bond' as Frank called it, and
the great red deer study. He approached Sir George Bul-
lough, the then laird of Rum, but had his application turned
down, a rebuff which he remembered when, as a member of
the Ramsay Committee on Scottish National Parks in 1943–
4, he recommended that a large research nature reserve be
set up on Rum for the study of red deer and their environment. Later, as a member of the Nature Conservancy, he was
to see his aspirations fulfilled when, in 1957, the ownership
of Rum was transferred to the Conservancy by a Deed which
bore his own signature as a member of that body. Then the
Island became a National Nature Reserve and later Biosphere Reserve under the Man and Biosphere Programme of
UNESCO. Over the following twenty years Frank was to
admire the efforts of many young researchers on Rum following on from the work he pioneered in red deer with his
Leverhulme Fellowship, in the reserve which was his idea in
the first place.

The plans for the Leverhulme Fellowship took a severe
shock at the failure to obtain the study area of Rum which
was a complete deer forest in itself. Not only would he
require to find another but would require to involve more
than one landowner – the deer do not have respect for estate
boundaries. Where would he find such a study area in a
country where estates very much kept themselves to themselves? This was a problem which had not existed seriously
when he first conceived the study, but now stared him in the
face as disaster following his resignation in Edinburgh.

It was not the first time that Bobbie's father had come to
the rescue. Through his high office in Freemasonry, Mr
Fraser knew Sir Alexander Gibb the distinguished engineer
and owner of the Gruinard Estate and secured introductions
for Frank to Sir Alexander and three of his neighbours in
Wester Ross. Frank made the most of this opening and
succeeded in persuading the four contiguous lairds to allow
him access for his study; this in itself was no mean feat of
public relations and served to confirm what was known widely but never admitted among lairds and stalkers, that if the
deer are to be understood and managed properly the pool of

knowledge for work on one forest must be drawn from several. There is little doubt that despite his high-mindedness and off-beat approach to life, Frank was a positively exciting personality with the support of a good wife and a beguiling youngster, who cut an impressive figure and caused a lot of talk among the lairds and their retainers. However, this did not extend immediately to their being offered a house when they visited Wester Ross, but soon one came their way which was to be their home until they moved to Tanera in May 1938 and then as a second home for a further two years: a place to fall back upon if the going on Tanera was too bad. On first arriving in Wester Ross he wrote:

> We slept in the car that night well wrapped in sleeping bags and rugs, and the first thing we saw when we woke the following morning was the Brae House, Dundonnell. 'That is exactly the sort of house which has seemed ideal to me,' I said. 'Wouldn't it be perfect for our job here!'
>
> Strange to relate, it was empty. The floors were rocky and the walls terribly damp, but there it was, the house under the bruach, backed by trees of many kinds and looking across to An Teallach, the highest point in my new territory. By nightfall of that day we had arranged to rent the place, and that is how we came to live in the house from which we watched the deer and in a later time hatched our island ploys.[37]

About thirty years later he recalled these Highland days:

> The Brae House, Dundonnell, was for me the perfect home – four bare rooms and an open hearth, and the burn thirty-five yards away for washing and water. The great copper kettle I had bought years before from Mr Gilhooly's junk shop in the Cowgate now rested on the hob by the wood fire and was our hot-water supply. We looked southwards to the Teallach and I could spy several thousand acres from the doorstep. The house remained in our tenancy for seven years at an annual rental of £12. How could conditions be more felicitous? I had a new field of my own choosing and the work went well from the start. I had no intention of turning back from the Highlands, for here were not only animals to watch but a long history of land use to unravel, partly from books but mostly from observation.[38]

The freedom which Frank received through his Fellowship was quite new in the 1930s. Since then such freedom has been enjoyed throughout the world by thousands of research-ers. Scotland has had its share, financed through Govern-ment Agencies, Research Councils, learned societies and trusts. At one stage in my own career, some twenty-three years after Frank's first award, I was 'set free' myself for four years to follow a study of the soil fauna of the Hebrides, originating from an idea he had from his days with the West Highland Survey; thereafter my freedom to continue this work on island ecology, Soay sheep and seals was extended as the Nature Conservancy's first Regional Officer in the West Highlands and Islands and further to conservation projects abroad. Since then my freedom has been eroded progres-sively by administrative and public duties, but these lines in turn have been taken up by full-time research teams in the Natural Environment Research Council and the Universities among whom my second son, Ian, is numbered.

Frank lived to see his pioneer work on deer influenced greatly by his writings and his works in conservation. In the 1930s he called for a 'State Biological Service' taking in not only the idea that wildlife should be protected and managed properly, but that many young minds would have the free-dom to research the problems and in doing so develop a greater awareness of a spiritual relationship between the naturalist and nature itself. A number of his main aspirations are now reality.

2

Dundonnell

This song of the waters is audible to every ear, but there is other music in these hills, by no means audible to all. To hear even a few notes of it you must first live here for a long time, and you must know the speech of hills and rivers. Then on a still night, when the campfire is low and the Pleiades have climbed over rimrocks, sit quietly and listen . . . and think hard of everything you have seen and tried to understand. Then you may hear it – a vast pulsing harmony – its score inscribed on a thousand hills, its notes the lives and deaths of plants and animals, its rhythms spanning the seconds and the centuries.

Aldo Leopold, *A Sand Country Almanac*

Frank, the newly-minted Leverhulme Fellow, could have no greater freedom than to be as free as the deer on a Highland hill and this freedom he had for two years from his home at the Brae House. His life had the ingredients of the deer stalker (with notebook and camera instead of rifle), naturalist, philosopher, writer and family man. He identified with stalkers as men of honour and integrity far more than he did with their employers, and this friendship and respect was reflected to him by the stalkers. In the fifties he directed the Nature Conservancy's Red Deer Survey supported by three of the finest stalkers, Archie Macdonald, Philip Macrae and Louis Stewart, two of whom were later awarded honours for their outstanding work on red deer. Though travelling much abroad in these days he enjoyed nothing more than to be with his stalkers on the hill counting deer and in the bothy at night, dry, warm and full of talk about stags and hinds and the ways of the world. Louis Stewart writes:

My recollections of Frank are always of his gentle authoritative manner. During our nights in the bothy or days on the

39

hill he proved one of the easiest to understand on many of the more complex matters of natural history. He always had time to explain. In the rough bothy he would relax after a meal with either a dram or his pipe. For one who rarely indulged in either, he displayed the greatest enjoyment in both. Having charged his pipe he would light up and until it was finished he rarely spoke a word. He often stressed that the only way to smoke was in a state of complete relaxation.

When he started his work at Dundonnell he knew little of the country to which he had come; yet Frank, born and raised as a country lad from his earliest days as well as later with the Old Cock, knew the attitudes and sensitivities of country folk. He knew that the stalkers of Dundonnell, Letterewe, Gruinard and Eilean Daraich held many lifetimes' knowledge of their forests and that the key to his success lay in their friendship and co-operation. That he succeeded in his study speaks well of those friendships and to the knowledge which the stalkers shared with him without which he might well have been frustrated. One of them would kill anything and had a peregrine's head on the wall describing it as a Rhode Island Red! Frank kept at him about his persecution of the predatory birds. Finally he said, 'Well, I'll leave one egg!' Another said, 'I wouldn't mind poaching, if only they'd wait till the laird is out of sight.' Walter Boa was the shepherd at Eilean Daraich whose wife came from London and enjoyed Bobbie's company; their son and Alasdair (born 25 May 1928) played happily.

In the wider world of science within which he had found a secure place, Frank also had his friends. His three years in Edinburgh had established him as someone of unusual promise, for he had not long begun his deer study when he was elected a Fellow of the Royal Society of Edinburgh in 1934. His supporters were Professor F. A. E. Crewe, W. C. Miller, Alick Buchanan-Smith (the late Lord Balerno of Currie) and J. M. Robson. He also had contacts in 'Oxbridge' which were created and enlivened by his Leverhulme success. Julian Huxley was the doyen of classical natural history in Britain and Charles Elton had just become Director of the Bureau of Animal Population in Oxford. Frank admired both, and both were interested in his red deer project. Elton who, at the time, was awarded the other of the two Leverhulme Fellowships, later read the script of *A Herd of Red Deer*

40

before publication by the Oxford University Press in 1937. Though the journey of over three years from the Vale of Aylesbury to Dundonnell had been noted for its misgivings, when Frank first took to the slopes of An Teallach after the deer he did so in the knowledge that before him lay a wonderful experience and around him an increasing number of friends and admirers both at home and throughout Britain.

The red deer study area was about 21,000 hectares of some of the wildest, most rugged and remote mountains in Britain and consisted of parts of the deer forests of Dundonnell, Letterewe and Gruinard in Wester Ross. The area is without roads or inhabitants except for a few on the north and west along the coastal road. Only someone with an enormous appetite for the mountains, unfailing good health and with the physique and stride of a giant could contemplate such a task. Frank had all of these in the thirties and more, for he also had the necessary patience to await the unhurried pace of nature and the will to endure the discomfort and exhaustion in return for the fruits of a serene life in a stupendous setting, full of discovery and personal triumph.

> On certain days of the year – such as, approximately, July 15th, when the deer have gone up to stay; October 15th, in the height of the rut; November 15th, when only a few young stags are rutting and the harems broken up; March 15th, if the weather is good and the deer are wandering; June 15th, in the calving season – I have made special journeys through as much of the ground as possible in one day. I attempted no stalking on these occasions, for the aim was to see where as many deer as possible were at one time. By using the high ridges as much as I could time and distance were saved, and speed was essential. Such days mean 35–40 miles of walking and 7,000–10,000 feet of climbing, and they are among my most pleasant memories.[39]

Frank's description of the country leaves no mountain, glen, corrie, loch and stream unappreciated, not for what they are as individual features but for the contribution which each makes to the spacious canvas of his beat. The interdependence of the Torridonian sandstone peaks of Bidein a' Glas Thuill (1,061 m), Sgurr Fheoin (1,058 m) and Sail Liath (960 m) and about a dozen others of lesser height, with their great, galleried sandstone bastions walling round the corries of Toll an Lochain, Glas Thuill, Corrie Mor and many more

41

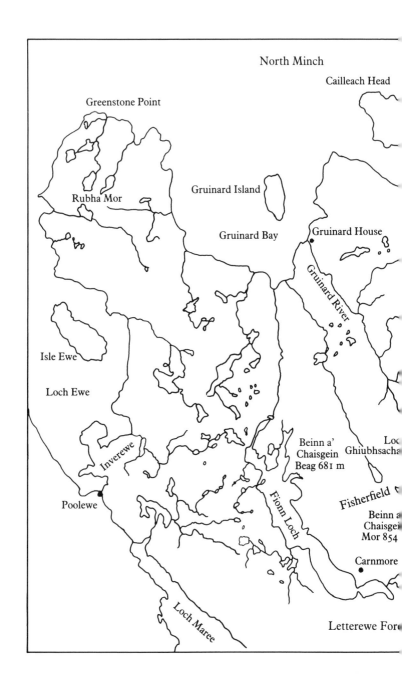

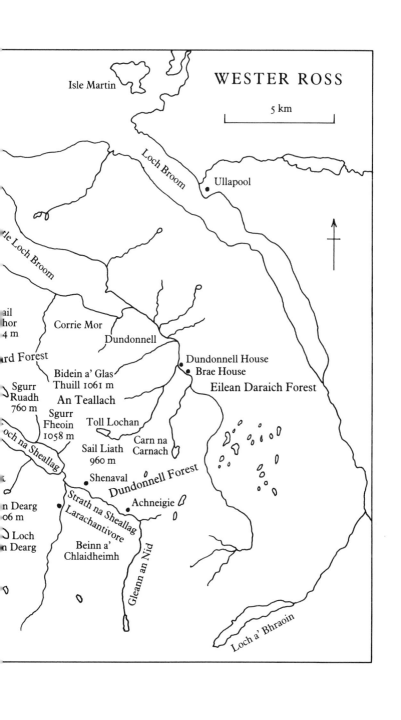

Plate 2.1. Loch Toll an Lochan corrie of An Teallach,
Dundonnell Forest, in the heart of Frank's study-area
for red deer in Wester Ross. (photo Tom Weir)

less profound, in the totality of An Teallach (The Forge),
was all-important to Frank's ecological and imaginative turn
of mind. The way this massif caught the sunshine, reacted to
the weather, fed and sheltered its deer, fostered its wildlife
and affected the minds of men who lived within its ken, all

registered with Frank. In the world of music he might easily have written a symphony after the fashion of Sibelius or Mahler. In the world of painting he might easily have created masterpieces in the vein of Landseer, whose work he admired greatly, Millais or Raeburn; his contribution was to literature in one of the finest essays on wild Scottish mountain country in *A Herd of Red Deer*.

In the Glas Thuill springs of water rise from the hill face, and their track is green till they join in a sandy-floored burn of crystal clearness, unsullied as yet by the acid of the peat. The grazing faces of the Glas Thuill and Toll Lochan corries are the summer haunts of deer and a few feral goats, but in winter, when the snow lies above the 1,700 feet [518 m] contour and sometimes below it, the corries seem empty of animal life. But they are not empty, for as I stand on the shores of the deep Toll Lochan below the buttress cliffs of Sail Liath on a cheerless February day of scudding mist and wet snow, a skirling flock of fieldfares may pass overhead, and on the sand at the lochan's edge a dipper sings his small sweet song – and the day is changed . . .

South of An Teallach is Strath na Sheallag, the wide confluence of two glens and their rivers at the head of Loch na Sheallag. The strath is an impressive place, flanked by the shapely peaks of Beinn Dearg, Beinn a' Chlaidhemh, and An Teallach. It is integral in the lives of the deer that roam again over a glen that has a long human history now almost lost. Strath na Sheallag – Strath na Sealga, 'the glen of the hunter'; Shenavall – Seana bhaile, 'the old town'; Larachantivore – Larach an Tigh Mhor, 'the foundations of the big house'; the names stand for a past age, with a few old men's stories. I am not the only man whose imagination has been raised to a state of sensibility by a first glimpse of Strath na Sheallag, coming over the unmarked track from Carn na Carnach. Men and animals love this remote strath, the deer linger on the bog between the rivers till late in June, the snipe drums high above the bog in the early mornings then, Highland cattle come up from Gruinard, and Highland ponies will gather there in May from a range of twelve or fifteen miles if the chance occurs. What are the reasons for the charm some places have for beasts and men? Shelter and a fresh bite are not a sufficient explanation . . .

When the snow is down, an east wind blowing hard, the sky leaden, and the tops partly hidden, Beinn Dearg and An

45

Teallach roar to one another from the unapproachable country of their summits. I do not know what causes this deep song in the high hills during the weather I have outlined. It cannot be explained away purely on the basis of wind and rock surfaces, for the roaring should be heard then under other sets of conditions which included high wind. I am inclined to place this roaring in the same category of sounds as the phenomenon of the singing sands . . .

In June the glen is fragrant with wild thyme. The hills rise so steeply from the shores of Loch Beinn Dearg that two men, one on either side, can talk to each other without great effort on a still night. One evening in early May I was fishing for my breakfast here after the sun had fallen. The country was still. A pair of black-throated divers were resting on the water a hundred yards away, unafraid of me. Then they rose to go back to their nesting loch, and the acoustic quality of the place enabled me to hear the sound of their movements, amplified but clean-cut. The wings beat on the water sharply for seventy yards until they were in the air. Their streamlined shapes circled the loch three times, making height, and their wings whistled loud in short staccato rhythm. The silence followed. When a hind barks here, the deer of two hills are alert . . .

Individual hills and glens have their own characters, and rivers achieve almost a personality in the imagination. I think the area of the gneiss in its aloofness and lack of outstanding landmarks has made the deepest impression. Nowhere have I felt more the ephemeral nature of individual man than after spending some days alone in this grey, broken country. I have lain sometimes on the western slopes of Beinn a' Chaisgein Beag, 'the hill of cheese', which are rich and pleasant and where, doubtless, man's animals have grazed in past times. The burns fall to the water of the Fionn Loch, gleaming as white as its name in the June sun, and there are traces of the dwellings of men. I have heard the singing of women's voices and the laughter of little children in this place. Perhaps the play of wind and falling water made these sounds – I neither know nor care – I was content to listen in the beauty of the moment.

These strange qualities of this part of the country, inviting or repelling, are real to men. Under Beinn a' Chaisgein Beag on the shores of the Fionn Loch they are happy, but at the head of Uisge Toll a' Mhadaidh the scene has changed. The cliffs fall steep to the loch and the ground about is as rough as could be with fallen rocks, deep peat hags, and heaped moraines. I have found it a strange place, and the same thought has been murmured to me by some of the few men of the country who have been there. These sensations may be caused through the eye by the dispositions of masses and planes and their relation to the course of the sun, as well as by the huge rock surfaces devoid of vegetation. There are many such places in the Scottish Highlands where seasoned men – myself too – have had to move out at nightfall. The sensation is not fear, for intimate knowledge of the place disposes of that; but there is discomfort sufficient to make a man move. These problems of the character of individual places must remain.

The country as a whole has a joyful quality, and the constant change of lights and shades to which I have referred are stimulating to the seeing eye. I have not fought the country these two years but have let it be my foster-mother. Her discipline has been stern but her smile is never far away.[40]

Frank's physical and spiritual experience following the deer in their mountain fastness was accompanied by the breaking of an intellectual trauma which had been moving through his life ever since he moved to Edinburgh to study under Crewe. Frank now found himself having to stand on his own feet both in the world of hardy, practical men such as the deerstalkers and in the academic world at a high level with a bee's nest of fundamental concepts. He began to rationalise his own physical and psychological relationship with his environment and to compare this with red deer as he observed their behaviour in response to environmental stimulae. He adopted an 'organismal' view of biology, meaning that he saw the driving force for life residing with the organism as a whole and not within any of its constituent parts and that the organism in its entirety reacts to environmental factors and genetical change.

At this time he was influenced greatly by the writings of E. S. Russell and H. E. Howard, and this continued into his studies of sea-birds on Eilean a' Chleirich. The adoption of organismal biology as his creed sprang from the fact that he was a student of the whole animal and not a cell-biologist, biochemist or anatomist and also from his passions for ecology, genetics and animal behaviour. It is not surprising, therefore – though it was probably disappointing and frustrating to himself – that Frank found the unifying principle binding these disciplines as elusive. He dwelt upon Russsell's words: 'Organismal biology therefore appears to fit comfortably in between the psychological sciences on the one hand and the physical on the other . . . We cannot claim for organismal biology anything like complete adequacy, or a close approach to full understanding of the living thing. The full secret of life will always elude a purely scientific treatment; it may be experienced, imagined and felt, but never completely pinned down and explained.'

He was motivated greatly by the fact that in the thirties much of the research on animal behaviour had been done with laboratory animals and little under natural conditions, especially with large mammals. The laboratory work of Professor W. C. Allee of Chicago in *Animal Aggregations* (1931) impressed Frank. Experimental work with tadpoles, small fish and the fruit fly *Drosophila melanogaster* supplemented by clinical observations of his own on sheep blow-fly *Lucilia sericata* and the buff-tip moth *Phalera bucephala* illuminated the fact 'that the two great natural principles of struggle for existence and of co-operation are not wholly in opposition, but that each may have reacted upon the other in determining the trend of animal evolution.' Frank saw this as 'a clear and beautiful concept' and had a tremendous urge to see it in the lives of large mammals and birds; what Allee had done in laboratory cultures he aspired to do on hill and island. He saw that Konrad Lorenz's greatness lay in his 'insinuating himself' into the ecology and communication of wild animals and that laboratory animals were in a 'false economy'. In watching the deer he applied the axiom that through their behaviour, mainly expressed in a complex pattern of movements, they were adjusting continuously their lives to maintain the 'ecological norm'.

Frank's thesis, whatever its philosophical frame, was based on counts and other observations of deer in time and space relative to known facts about seasonal distribution and behaviour of individuals and groups of both sexes. Stags and hinds differ greatly in appearance, body function and behaviour. Stags are larger, grow antlers and differ in metabolic rate and lifespan from hinds; for most of the year stags occupy different ground from hinds and thus have a different social order, food preferences and diet. It stands to reason,

48

Plate 2.2. A 'royal' (twelve-pointer) red deer stag in the
Glen Feshie Forest, Grampians, studied by Frank and his
stalkers in the Red Deer Survey. (photo David Gowans)

therefore, that the response of stags and hinds to the same set
of environmental conditions is very different. The myth of
the stag as 'monarch of the glen' had long since been explo-
ded and the matriarchy of the hinds was well known as the
binding force of the herds. What was not known, however,
was how such differing groups of hinds and stags were

created, maintained and ultimately dissolved and of how the unity and prosperity of the population was achieved in the presence of such a wide difference between the sexes.

In two years, working alone on foot in a vast and untractable land, Frank achieved his objective. He used the simple equipment of warm waterproof clothing, heavy shoes and thick hand-knitted woollen stockings, a small tent, telescope, binoculars, camera and notebook. Nowadays, a team would do the same with walkie-talkie radios, ear-tags and conspicuous collars, radio-tags, aerial photographs, new Ordnance Survey maps and the occasional use of a helicopter or tracked vehicle. However, nothing has changed in the techniques of stalking; the face-to-face experience of man and deer on the hill remains the same though the means of back-up are now more sophisticated and the methods of census far more advanced. Yet, one wonders if the criterion of success in this work rests only with more advanced technology when basic human qualities are involved and the timing of the senses is all important in working with wild animals.

> During the summer of 1935 I went barefoot, and after a fortnight of discomfort I had my reward. The whole threshold of awareness was raised, I was never fatigued, and stalking became very much easier. This ease in approaching animals was something more than what was gained by leaving off heavy and possibly noisy shoes. The whole organism worked in better co-ordination.[41]

The fruits of his work are contained in *A Herd of Red Deer* (1937), and although many of the ideas which flowed from his observations of the wild deer are now outdated, the work is still drawn upon today. This shows Frank as the pioneer he most surely was, noted for his acute powers of observation and philosophical turn of mind in his sensitive interpretation of the natural history of the deer, rather than a man of scientific breakthrough to which he in his greatest moments might have aspired. In looking back from old age to his heyday of scientific effort he saw himself as an ecologist of a 'raw kind' relying mostly on observation and of developing observation as a means for valid comparison, by finding datum lines and using 'scientific imagination'.

The frequent, detailed reference made by Mitchell, Staines and Welch in their *Ecology of Red Deer – A research review relevant to their management in Scotland* (1977) shows the enduring value and high quality of his observations; Clutton-Brock, Guinness and Albon in their fine treatise *Red Deer – Behavior and Ecology of Two Sexes* make eleven references to Frank including quotes in chapter headings on social groups and social interactions of stags and hinds which were at the core of his original thinking.

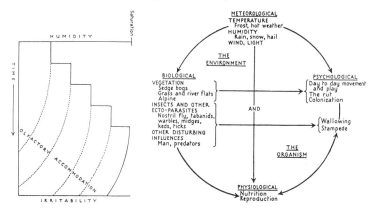

Figure 2.1. Two diagrams from *A Herd of Red Deer*: *left*, 'to show irritability to movement by disturbance in relation to humidity of the atmosphere'; *right*, 'movement in red deer' (by permission of Oxford University Press).

As was his plan, he witnessed the turn of the seasons in the North West Highlands and the up-turns which occurred among the deer as winter poverty and privation gave way to summer plenty, and as summer quiescence turned to the rut in autumn with stags breaking out from their corries with much roaring in the mountains. Calving in June is followed by the movements to high pastures out of reach of biting flies. Winter snows drive the herds together on low ground with scant, wind-cleared pastures and birchwoods to break the wind. The relationships between the weather and the deer fascinated Frank; the physiology taught to him by Henry Dryerre at the Royal Dick Veterinary College in 1928 had left its mark. Even small changes of air he noted resulted in corresponding changes in the movements and attitudes of the animals. The effects of sunshine, wind, rain and snow are

51

more obvious than those of temperature and humidity, yet the latter are of great importance since they influence the sense of smell upon which the deer rely for communication.

Suppose the relative humidity is varying from 20 to 40 per cent at intervals of from 2 to 3 hours, the wind is light south-easterly and the air is dry, as might occur in the Highlands in February, the deer are settled and fairly easy to approach. However, by the following day the wind veers to the south-west with an increase in temperature and relative humidity to between 60 to 100 per cent at similar intervals, the same deer are on different ground and altogether irritable and difficult to approach. The veer of wind continues to the north-west, the temperature drops, the relative humidity is steady and moderate and the deer are again settled and an easier quarry for the stalker.

> Many years ago I asked myself why, given more or less equal conditions of wind and skill, it is much easier to approach deer on some days than others; or, put in other words, why chances could be taken one day which would spoil the stalk on another. I think I might say that from that question grew the desire to do the work of which this book [*A Herd of Deer*] is a record. The question was one of the first to receive an answer, though maybe not the whole one, after the work was begun . . .

> . . . between noon on Friday, October 18th, 1935 and 4.0 p.m. on Sunday, October 20th . . . we have minute by minute variation of humidity between 60 per cent and saturation point until midnight of Saturday, October 19th. Three inches of rain fell during the three-day period and there was a high west wind. The deer were excessively irritable, and the slightest scent of a human being sent them galloping away. The rutting season was in progress, but the deer were in such a state of irritability and discomfort that the harems broke up. After midnight the temperature began to fall, the wind was round to the north, and the oscillations of the hydrograph became much less frequent. By 4 p.m. on Sunday there was a dusting of snow everywhere, the deer had come down a few hundred feet, they were less irritable, and before the light went on Sunday the 20th I was able to see the stags herding their harems again, and by the following day they were active and the harems discrete.[42]

V. C. Wynne-Edwards found Frank's correlation between humidity and irritability unconvincing (see p.224). Certainly the idea was based on first-hand observations and supported by an elementary knowledge of the scent-bearing properties of wet and dry air. However, the observations were also very subjective in as much as Frank was himself part of the subject under study, namely the reaction of the deer to his own behaviour and reaction to changing weather conditions. His keen eye for detail and descriptive powers were a great asset to him in his work. He has left some of the finest word-pictures of red deer ever written.

Here is an incident I watched high on the southern face of Sgurr Ruadh about noon early in July 1934. I was 400 yards away and saw all this through binoculars. A prime stag of ten points showing through his velvet was lying down, his legs under him, head forward and eyes closed. A small staggie was lying 10 yards away, chewing his cud and turning his head every minute or so to look about him. He sees me. Cudding stops. Five seconds pass and he does not move. Then he is on his feet and trotting to the big stag. The staggie lowers his muzzle towards the big fellow, coming within a yard of him. They both lift their heads together and look intently in my direction. Why does the big stag look so certainly towards me, for the staggie is behind him? Five minutes pass; I do not move; they do not. The sun is crosswise to us, if anything in my favour. The big stag lowers his head again, the staggie lowers his and walks away a few yards, not quite to the same place as before. He looks towards me, lies down again and in another minute goes on chewing his cud. The big stag has his eyes closed again and the heat dances over everything. After ten minutes I move to my knees. The staggie sees me and runs to his big friend. The stag gets on his feet this time and looks unerringly in my direction. But the air is dancing, the wind is in my favour, and the sun a little more so than it was the last time he looked, and I am very still. Five minutes more of intent gazing; they lower their heads together, graze perfunctorily for a few yards, and lie down again. I creep away and leave them in peace.[43]

Over thirty years later in August 1966 Frank took his son James from Milton in his landrover to see deer in the hills south-west of Drumnadrochit. Frank said, 'You don't follow the deer, you let them come to you.' Using the same 'glass' he had used at Dundonnell in the thirties, he had noticed twenty-six stags on high ground several miles away. He explained to James how the hinds should be on the lower ground with the calves. He chose a small glen with a stream, beside which was some herbage on which the heather could not encroach saying that this would be an ideal grazing run for red deer. They lay down on the hillside, blending with the heather, motionless for about twenty minutes, and then over the hill and through the glen came a herd of over two hundred hinds and calves. They came to about two hundred yards from the hidden pair at the nearest point and never knew they were there. James remembers it as a majestic sight. His father pointed out the behaviour of the leading hind, how alert she was, how the whole herd was aware of the turn of the head, the angle of her nose and ears. James was in awe of Frank's ability, during a short afternoon of his school holidays, almost to usher the animals to him and give the boy one of the sights of a lifetime. Though it was knowledge of the deer and their habitat which worked the magic, this knowledge sprang from something more than curiosity, rather from a deep reverence for the skein of life and its manifestations.

After his two years' work with the deer in Wester Ross, Frank had given the plain tale of the animal's life, but the study had left him with more problems than he knew of at the outset. It is surprising, therefore, that he did not hold to the red deer and continue the work for many more years. His liking for the animals, great attachments to the country and the obvious intellectual challenge which the work gave might have been enough to make him seek further financial support to break further into the field of social biology, using the groups of stags and hinds which he knew well. Only by staying with them and tagging them to ease observation could he have hoped to follow the life history of individuals and the groups to which they belonged. The record of his work is contained in *A Herd of Red Deer* (1937) which, together with his *Bird Flocks and the Breeding Cycle* (1938), was submitted as a thesis entitled 'Studies in Animal Sociality' for which he was awarded a Doctorate of Science at Edinburgh University and is of undoubted academic worth; yet it possesses an anecdotal quality and a lack of numerical back-up which would have made the continuation of the study the more compelling – there is nothing more annoying to the scientist than to have a promising run of data without the means of continuing the run to a satisfactory conclusion.

54

However, the Leverhulme money ran out and Frank did not elect to continue the deer study – perhaps he saw also the truth that a man working alone could not physically take it further. It was not until the fifties that he returned to deer work, then only part-time and restricted to general census work throughout Scotland as a whole. Then as Director of the Nature Conservancy's Red Deer Survey, Frank and his stalkers were breaking new ground in counting deer as an independent body in the Scottish Highlands. The aim was to see if such counts were feasible and to compare them with estimates provided by estates. Deer-forest without sheep, mixed deer-forest and sheep-walk and sheep-walk not regarded as deer-forest were the three categories of land counted. Though the small size of the team, changes in the weather and the seasonal movement of deer all caused difficulties in counting, the Survey showed that deer numbers had almost always been played down by owners and stalkers. The data up till 1957 were lodged with the Nature Conservancy but little use was made of it. However, Louis Stewart tells me that the counting methods developed during the Survey have been refined and extended to become standard in the work of the Red Deer Commission.

The ground of detailed biology of red deer in Scotland lay fallow until the late fifties when the Nature Conservancy commenced their research, to be followed by university workers in Edinburgh and Cambridge. The age and social structures of the hind and stag groups which so excited Frank were not followed until the seventies, when, over ten years continuous work at Kilmory on Rum, Tim Clutton-Brock and Fiona Guinness with their many collaborators, greatly extended the work. His own modest opinion of his deer work in Wester Ross is contained in two sentences, but these underestimate greatly the stimulus which the work gave to others.

> I suppose the most important outcome of my red deer work was to gain credence for an extended study of a group of wild animals to research. Also it established social behaviour as a significant ecological factor.[44]

Frank, Bobbie and Alasdair lived at the Brae House. Family life for them resembled closely that of stalker or shepherd with the man of the house away on the hill for most of the working day and sometimes days on end, and the wife and

Plate 2.3. Present-day view of the Brae House, Dundonnell, where Frank and Bobbie lived in 1933-40: 'The gateway to our island life'. (photo J. Morton Boyd)

child left to keep house and attend to schooling. They drove to Dingwall once a month for supplies; Frank was a very good, fast driver but a little impatient at times. Though together as a family, Frank's work, by its need for solitude among wild animals, imposed separation which may have been intellectual as well as physical; seldom does he make reference to any views which Bobbie had of his work or its results. He relished life at the Brae House 'set in no garden but is almost part of the hillside' and frequented by most of the wildlife of the North-West Highlands; yet he was candid enough about Bobbie's lot.

> The burn is forty yards away and dries out sometimes in summer. Not only must water be carried into the house but it has to be thrown out as well! And once inside, you will see that the walls are so permeated with damp that wall-paper will not retain its original colour for more than a week or two, and only with periodic help will it stick to the wall at all. The floor-boards are warped and lie open, and when we first went there it took us nearly two years to get top-side of the fleas. The boarding ceiling flakes whitewash into your soup if someone should tread incautiously overhead. Our fireplace is

56

a natural gem, just an open hearth with two stone hobs, so impossible to keep clean that we never try – so why grumble, says the masculine element.[45]

Bobbie recalls over fifty years later being happy enough at Dundonnell but was always anxious about future family finances. To Alasdair, the Brae House is still home: 'I never go to Dundonnell without feeling a certain thrill at seeing the house and walking up the brae towards it with a nostalgic look back at my childhood days there.' But where was the island life for which they yearned and when would they reach their island farm which was the ideal combination of their interests? In the times when they were together on the heights of An Teallach they looked westward to the Hebrides and dreamt of island days to come – and soon they did. Frank's sojourn at Dundonnell always distinguished him as an authority on red deer with a wider understanding of ungulates in America and Africa. In fact, it was only a brief interlude in his life and a stepping-stone to his island farm and beyond.

3

Eilean a' Chleirich

> Then came the island years, a curious mix-up of personal
> predilection and honest scientific inquiry. The one depended
> on the other inextricably. There are several kinds of fool the
> one who cannot learn sense at all, the one who can learn only
> by experience, and the romantic. Being a romantic is the only
> kind of wisdom for me, but have pity on the suffering roman-
> tic. I am also the kind that has preferably to experience
> something to know what it is about. So I, a seasick type afraid
> of the sea, chose to inhabit islands empty of other human
> beings. I wanted the cleanness of islands and to learn some-
> thing about boats.[46]

The Summer Isles lie between Rubha Coigach and Green-
stone Point across that wide bight of the coast which spans
the entrances to Loch Broom, Little Loch Broom and Gruinard Bay in Wester Ross. There are about twenty-five islands
and reefs named on the Ordnance Survey 1:25,000 map, ten
of which may be used for grazing sheep and only one of
which, Tanera Mor, 320 hectares, is inhabited. We shall
return to Tanera in chapter 8, for it was there that Frank and
Bobbie had their little farm. The outermost is Eilean a'
Chleirich or Priest Island (hereafter called Chleirich – pronounced 'hlayrach) which is 120 hectares and to which the
Fraser Darlings went to live from mid-April to late August
1936 and from 3 March to 30 July 1937. While living at
Dundonnell studying the deer they had visited Chleirich on
odd days and had been charmed by its beauty and opportunity to work on the social relationship of birds. When the
income from the Leverhulme grant expired they began to
look for pastures new and settled on the idea which had been
in their hearts for some time – an expedition to Chleirich.

The islands are the emergent hilltops of a drowned land-

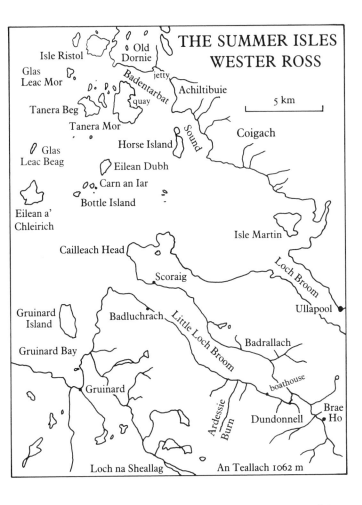

THE SUMMER ISLES
WESTER ROSS

Isle Ristol
Old Dornie
jetty
Glas Leac Mor
Badentarbat
Achiltibuie
5 km
quay
Tanera Beg
Coigach
Tanera Mor
Sound
Glas Leac Beag
Horse Island
Eilean Dubh
Carn an Iar
Bottle Island
Eilean a' Chleirich
Isle Martin
Cailleach Head
Loch Broom
Scoraig
Gruinard Island
Badluchrach
Little Loch Broom
Ullapool
Gruinard Bay
Badrallach
Gruinard
boathouse
Ardessie Burn
Dundonnell
Brae Ho
Loch na Sheallag
An Teallach 1062 m

scape of Torridonian sandstone graven by the glaciers of the last ice-age and since fretted by the sea and the atmosphere. They are of most irregular shape, low, lumpy and abrupt in aspect but have one feature in common with each other and with the mainland of Rubha Coigach; imprinted by the strike of the sandstone from south-west to north-east, the axis of the islands lies roughly along this line as do the little

59

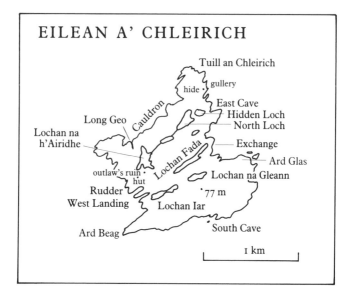

EILEAN A' CHLEIRICH

Tuill an Chleirich

hide •

gullery

East Cave

Hidden Loch

North Loch

Long Geo

Cauldron

Lochan na
h'Airidhe

Exchange

Lochan Fada

Ard Glas

Lochan na Gleann

outlaw's ruin •
hut

Rudder

• 77 m

West Landing

Lochan Iar

South Cave

Ard Beag

1 km

ridges, valleys and lochans. Chleirich is a particularly good example of a Torridonian tabletop over-run by the ice at about right angles to the strike of the rock. The result is a wrinkled landscape in miniature with lochans in the little steep-sided valleys completely unsighted from the sea. It was this broken yet ordered landscape which so appealed to Frank and Bobbie; the island had an 'interior' not possessed by high islands of similar size, giving heightened senses of privacy and solitude.

Sandy Macleod was the manager of the fish farm at Tanera Mor and the son of James Macleod who owned the major part of Tanera when the Fraser Darlings lived on Chleirich and later on Tanera itself. On 17 August 1982 he took me and three of my colleagues from the Nature Conservancy Council to Chleirich from Badentarbat Pier. The passage was bumpy with much spray from which we sheltered behind the wheelhouse of his powerful launch. The fresh south-wester sent white seas upon Sgeir nam Mult and the windward coasts of Eilean Dubh, Carn Iar and Bottle Island as we butted our way to the lee of Chleirich. The landing was in the quietness

60

Plate 3.1. East Bay (Acairseid) landing, Eilein a' Chleirich, looking to Bottle Island, Carn Iar and Eilein Dubh with Ben Mor Ciogach behind. (photo J. Morton Boyd)

of the east bay which Frank and Bobbie used regularly as the exchange rock for mails and supplies from Achiltibuie.

This was something of an achievement for me. I suppose that the first time I ever knew of Chleirich was when still at school in the early forties on reading *Island Years*. It was the spark of interest created then that resulted in my world-wide interest in island ecology; yet it had taken me about forty years to set foot on Chleirich, the island which started it all!

I was delighted at the thought and set out to make the most of the four hours which Sandy allowed us ashore. It was, of course, too late in the season for flowers and breeding birds but all the summer enchantment of the island was still there in great measure. I made a circular tour ascending to the highest point on the island at 78 m (256 feet). I obtained the fine panorama enjoyed by Frank and Bobbie on good days. On an arc of 180° to the east there was the clouded, mountainous seaboard, the long receding fingers of sea and the scatter of islands; on the opposite arc to the west was the Minch, the distant hilltops of Lewis and a sky of broken sunshine, dark

61

Plate 3.2. The campsite used by Frank and Bobbie on Chleirich in 1936-37 as it is today. The turf dyke and the pitch of their hut are bracken-covered; Frank's ditches (*right*) and the 'outlaw's house (*top left*) still survive. (photo J. Morton Boyd)

clouds and slanting showers. I descended by Lochan Iar to the west landing and pondered the scene of their landing among the dark rocks and wild seas in the growing darkness of 3 March 1937. From there I walked the portage to the site of the hut beside the outlaw's ruin at Lochan na h'Airidhe and saw in my mind's eye the huts and the bell-tent behind the fail dyke. There were the ditches they had dug and the little patch which they had cultivated over too short a period to have enduring green effect. On a dry flat between the ditches by the burn a compass-rose has been constructed with flat slabs. It had lain buried until Frank drained that little area when, much to their surprise, it appeared in the moss. I parted the brackens which now grow behind the fail dyke and found there the remains of the circular ditch which was dug around the bell-tent forty-six years previously. I was surprised at the close proximity of the outlaw's ruin to their camp because, I suppose, it does not appear in any of their published photographs or maps in *Island Years*.

My walk then took me by the Cauldron which was the name given by Frank to the exposed north-west coast of Chleirich. Even on this comparatively quiet day the seas

Plate 3.3. A compass rose in stone between two ditches in front of the campsite on Chleirich; it was exposed when the place was drained and the foggage cleared.
(photo J. Morton Boyd)

there were heavy, rising some six metres on the sandstone bastions and wonderfully exhilarating with a blowhole, flung spray and darting shags flying to young still on the nests. Nesting fulmars glided effortlessly in the up-rush of wind at the cliff-edges. After rounding the north point, I was in Frank's gull colonies, now at this late date almost deserted. Small flocks of thirty herring gulls and lesser black-blacks were still present with young of the year hatched and fledged. The remains of Frank's two hides over the largest herring gull colony were still there; one, that to which he moved for a better overview, still possessed some spars of wood and gave a pulpit-like vantage point of the rock platform beneath upon which the gulls nested immediately above the sea. I climbed into the hide and appreciated how cramped Frank must have been in it for long periods – and how cold and numb he must have been afterwards. The dark red sandstone of the gullery was whitened by gull droppings indicating a colony of somewhat similar size to that studied by Frank (65 pairs), yellow with saffron lichen and green with chickweed, scurvy grass, sea marguerites, thrift and fescue. Far below was the blue-green water marled with foam – mesmeric in its

63

motion – the red rock with a cream-coloured band of barnacles and in the midst a diving shag.

The island did not appear to have been grazed through the summer and the vegetation was ankle-deep in places. It is predominantly heath covered with green margins caused by the effects of the sea, sea-birds and grazing stock. The bell heather was still in bloom and the ling in full bloom with many patches of white among the purple. The heath community is interesting for its greater than usual amount of bearberry with abundant crowberry, creeping juniper and creeping willow. The devil's bit scabious pushed its tall stem above the heath as did the lanceolated plantain in grassy areas and the eyebright was growing higher and bigger than I have ever seen it. Mats of silverweed were spread across the sandy flats beside the old stoneworks on the west beach. Lochan an Gleann had a small phragmites marsh with a moorhen and with a small salt-marsh at Lochan Iar at the lower end near the sea; this little glen has a fine range of fresh to brackish water conditions in miniature. The visit had been made more interesting by the sight of buzzard, heron and wood pigeon. Wind-blasted rowans in sheltered nooks were already in fruit – not attractive to the wood pigeon which seemed well out of its way – but the heron knew that there were sticklebacks for the taking.

I have provided this personal portrait of Chleirich to confirm that the beauty which Frank and Bobbie saw in it was neither overstated nor of their own invention. No-one with a feeling for islands could fail to be impressed by Chleirich. I would have enthused even more, I am sure, if I could have seen the place in May or June, or could have stayed overnight bothying in the outlaw's ruin to hear the storm petrels come to their nests in the stone crevices. Little wonder therefore that the island has been designated by the Nature Conservancy Council as a Site of Special Scientific Interest and it is now owned by the Royal Society for the Protection of Birds.

But, I had seen my fill for the day, my time was up and I had to be getting back to the waiting boat. I would be unfair to Sandy Macleod, his boy assistant and my three companions if I did not say that I kept them waiting for an hour in a downpour while I went in a vain search for a valuable knife I had dropped on the way. I am most grateful to them for their patience and commiseration at my bodily condition when I returned soaked to the boat.

The island-going life has a set pattern which is well described in Frank's books and diaries of the thirties. Weeks of preparation carry an increasing tension about items being ready or available on time. There are also the chances of accident or misfortune which might prevent the expedition, even up to the last moment. But first of all there must be a good reason for going and this objective has a great influence on the preparations, since it determines duration of time, type of work, lifestyle and equipment to serve more than just basic needs. An eye is also needed to foresee eventualities such as storm damage, beleaguerment, a broken leg or the loss of an essential tool.

The island years followed hot on the heels of the red deer study which had imbued Frank with a desire to extend his studies in animal behaviour from deer to sea-birds and seals, both of which groups seemed to him ripe for study. The reason for going to islands was therefore an amalgam of work and personal desire.

> It [Chleirich] seemed heaven on earth to us when we first landed there, and each year we would say – if only we could live there. The quietness, the number of birds and the beauty of the little freshwater lochans hidden away from the wild ocean, all pulled at our heart strings. Was it the job of work or our own desires which drew us there to live in 1936? Call it fifty-fifty and let us not give way to introspection. The scheme of work on social behaviour of birds and the inter-relations of the several kinds living there looked quite good on paper, and as we had at that moment no income from research fellowships we had only ourselves to satisfy.[47]

What the writings of E. S. Cameron had done to stimulate Frank's thoughts and actions on the red deer, F. H. A. Marshall's Cronian Lecture of 1936 did for his work on gulls. Marshall had reviewed sexual periodicity and the causes which determine it, and Frank was fired by the original idea that in gregariously breeding birds the size of the colony is a factor in the synchronisation of reproductive condition in the birds. He felt that he could demonstrate this with the breeding colonies of herring gulls and lesser black-backed gulls on Chleirich and also observe the effects which these two closely similar species had on each other's behaviour and breeding success.

In making preparations for Chleirich in 1936 Frank extolled the virtues of the bell tent which was so much a feature
of camping before the war and has now completely disappeared. The design, dimensions, improvisations and management of the bell tent in winds of up to storm force were
among the logistics meticulously dealt with, together with
beds, mattresses, sleeping bags, food in tea chests, stoves for
cooking and heating, oven, rugs, deck-chairs, books, pens,
paper, cutlery, crockery, cloths and cooking utensils . . . all
in boxes. 'We also wrote on all the boxes with a blue pencil a
complete list of what was inside them. Even with all this care
it was a fortnight before we could find the Primus prickers!'

Preparations complete, a spell of calm weather is awaited
– a time which I have found over many expeditions to be a
great test of patience and commonsense and which I describe
from my own days at St Kilda and North Rona in *A Mosaic
of Islands*, which I wrote with my great island-going friend,
the late Kenneth Williamson in 1963. There is a point when
patience breaks and commonsense is replaced by an irra-
tional desire to get there.

The first passage to Chleirich by the Fraser Darlings on 8
April 1936 had all the signs of overworn patience, and a
struggle of minds; they and the boatman from Scoraig separately assessing the wind and sea, the temperamental engine
in the boat which, in breakdown, could put them in great
danger and the surf running white upon Chleirich six miles
away across the broken sea. 'Should we go?' That is the
question which gnaws at the mind and the boatman's wife in
the kitchen, who is normally shy, speaks boldly that 'It's no'
a day for Chleirich today!' But they went.

> We tried the south landing by the cave, just for the sake of
> trying, and we were becoming hopeful when a big wave
> nearly put us up the beach. We pushed off as hard as we
> could and made for home – after another quarter of an hour's
> prostration before the engine . . . It was a miserable task
> unloading the boat at Scoraig's pier and as I came home to
> Dundonnell I wondered if we should ever go to Eilean a'
> Chleirich . . .[48]

They did, on 17 April 1936, but not without some further
doubts in Frank's mind.

> I began to feel my responsibility heavy upon me. There were
> those who thought I was wrong to take a wife and child to an

uninhabited island at this time of year, and to live in a tent at that. Were they right and I wrong? I looked at these two (Bobbie and Alasdair) and these animals (goats and hens) under my care and all looked so unhappy. I asked Scoraig to turn back and try later. Scoraig said he was not wishing to turn the boat just now and would rather keep her nose into it . . . We were soon under the south-east point of Eilean a' Chleirich and Bobbie and I will not easily forget the relief of being on a comparatively calm sea . . .

'I don't care if we live here for ever now,' said Bobbie. Morag the little brown goat was very heavy in kid. It would have been cruel to walk her that mile (from the landing place) to the tent, so I made her comfortable . . . and as I came over the ridge in the darkness I was cheered by the triangular shape of light which was the tent. Bobbie's shadow moved to and fro as she busied herself making comfort for all of us.[49]

The Fraser Darlings again held themselves in readiness to go to Chleirich on 1 February 1937, this time with their friend Kenneth (Dougal) McDougal. They had left the island on the previous October and had spent the winter writing at Dundonnell, visiting in the south and preparing for their next visit to Chleirich and then in quick succession to the Treshnish Isles in the autumn. The Chleirich expedition was to finish the work on the gulls and that to Treshnish to start work on the grey seals. Day by day dragged on through February with a few breaks in the weather during which they awaited in vain a 'phone call from the boatman. On 2 March the wind slackened and their hopes rose. Next day was flat calm but noon came and with still no word of the boat, they consoled themselves in preparing a hearty lunch.

It was then that the 'phone message came from Achiltibuie saying that the boat was on the way. Now we were to go, the going was a nuisance; hot stew on the table for lunch and Bobbie's birthday plum pudding. We had indigestion for the rest of the day. Goats, hens, geese, canary, bedding and a thousand and one things had to be taken to the boathouse and it took us four journeys, two of which were made before the boat came. There were Jimmy Macleod, Donald Fraser, and Donald Macleod aboard, all in a most cheerful frame of mind. It was half-past four when we got away, by which time the wind had freshened from the east and was following us down the loch (Little Loch Broom). Dougal was forrard, Bobbie and Alasdair aft where it was warm. Donnie Macleod

67

took the tiller and Jimmy, Donald and I sprawled on the engine deck amidships . . . It was not long before Priest Island was nearer than anywhere else. The darkness was coming down and we could make out no details. We went round to the West Landing and anchored off. I didn't count how many dinghy loads came away from the launch for I was busy getting stuff above the tide mark on the rock. It was rather a nightmare pulling heavy boxes out of the dinghy and dragging them up seaweed-covered rocks in the dark. Jimmy and the crew went away as soon as the last dinghy was emptied. Alasdair should have gone back with them to Achiltibuie to start school, but we did not like the idea of his going off to new surroundings at that time of night, so we said no. When the boat had gone we laid Alasdair on the lee of the rock, put some rugs over him and a cushion under his head and told him to lie quiet (like a deercalf!). Dougal, Bobbie, and I set about sorting the perishable things from the non-perishables and making a neat heap of the former, over which we could place a tarpaulin. There was no moon, but it wasn't a very dark night because Venus was very bright, throwing a golden path along the sea, and before she had set in the west, Sirius was high to the south.

It was long past nine o'clock when we had finished. Then we came up to the hut, which we were relieved to find in the same position in which we had left it in October. It had withstood the stormiest winter in years. I was very tired, but thrilled, nevertheless, when our little friend the snipe rose from the bog before the hut and returned there within a few minutes. Two curlew rose also from the bog at the north end. What lovely sounds these were after these interminable weeks of waiting!

Bobbie made us plenty of tea and we drank much with slices of bread and marmalade. Then we put Alasdair to bed and put up the bell tent in its old place alongside the hut for Dougal and I to sleep in. We let the goats run loose, put the geese in the gulley (outlaw's sheiling) and the hens in the big goose box. It was eleven o'clock before we were in bed.[50]

Frank's Priest Island Diary 1937 shows how much variety there is in the simple island life against the daily time-machine of rising, walking the circuit of the island, making meals, keeping the refuge tidy and weather-tight, taking pleasure in minor comforts and getting off to a dry bed with a quiet mind, relishing the qualities of the wild and outlandish habitat. The weather is both a scourge and a delight and even slight changes in the direction of the wind, or in the

68

intensity of the rain, or the sun coming from behind a cloud, cause a quite disproportionate change in the island scene and the human spirit. Chleirich is situated where changes in the weather can cause dramatic uncoverings of mountains, coasts, islands and wide expanses of sea. The same can be said of the camp site which they were to use later that year on Lunga in the western bight of Mull.

The weather changes also cause changes in the habitat of the island itself. For a naturalist like Frank no two circuits of the island were the same; there was always something new which had not been there before and which had significance in the interpretation of the island ecosystem. This is particularly so with migrant birds. There is a breed of ornithologist whose greatest joy is to get to a small island like Chleirich, Isle of May or Fair Isle and do nothing but go round and round the island spotting and hopefully trapping and ringing song birds in passage. Frank, however, was not 'a ringer'; he did not rake through the island day by day to drive traps and nets and build-up the bird list, yet there was probably not much that passed him by.

Alasdair left the island for school in Achiltibuie on 8 March, five days after landing, leaving Frank, Bobbie and Dougal to face the stormy blast and the on-coming spring. By mid-March they had settled to camp life and were enjoying its variety, as the following week from Frank's journal shows.

> *Tuesday March 16th.* A magnificent morning. Cloudless sky and light south-east wind. The weather forecast says a gale and cloudy skies so we prepare for it. The hoodie crows have been messing about that cliff all day and I saw them there just on dark when on my evening round. Indeed, the S.E. gale has come, an absolute snorter. The herring gulls were not at the gullery tonight. I wonder if the weather has put them elsewhere? I saw a cormorant flying low over the waves at the north end. The waves were so big that he kept disappearing behind them from time to time as he made his way towards Glas Leac Bheag.
>
> This is the test for the 'Dome' tent, St Paul's Cathedral as Alasdair calls it. At nine o'clock two poles have come away from the screw head and have slewed round to a concave position. The guys and boulders are holding, of course, and she won't go down easily. Dougal and I sat inside her in this present crippled state of the tent and it was quite snug. We

lit a match and watched it burn steadily despite the gale outside. We should have liked to do something with this tent but were afraid it might get out of hand in this hurricane.

Today I dug another drain through the bog and Dougal completed the turf dike in front of the hut. It gives us good ground protection in a s.e. wind. The little Bresse hen has become truly tame for she keeps by us as we work and finds grubs. It is not that she is just cheeky like the others. Even when I was letting fly with the edge of the spade at a tough bit of turf she stood perilously close and quite unperturbed. Sometimes she lets us stoke her. How bonny she is with her black eyes, turquoise lobes and blue legs! The snipes are in the bog near the hut every night and we think kindly of these shy little birds which trust us well. I refuse to drain the stagnant dub in the bog which the snipes fly to in the evenings. It is only a few yards from the hut. Dougal thinks I am mad to leave a perfect midge breeding ground when a few strokes of the spade would remove it. But think, are there not innumerable other midge breeding places. What effect on the numbers of midges would draining this one small dub make? The snipe loves it and was on the island before I was. Last year we appreciated the company of these birds on those bad nights of wind in the bell tent. They came down at five minutes to ten always with a merry little 'chick-chack, chick-chack'. It would be an unforgivable thing to drain their little dub.

There were 40 or 50 shags on the west social rock this morning; no cormorants.

The big Chinese geese are growing much tamer and Bobbie is becoming very fond of them. They make a great noise of welcome whenever they see her. The gander is such a perfect gentleman to the goose. All the animals seem much more intimate with us here and we learn more of their personalities. Lily acts in a superior way towards everything as personal goose to Dr Fraser Darling! She sat on my coat this mid-day while I was ditching and gnawed at the buttons just like a puppy. Bobbie did some burning of the foggage this afternoon and Lily followed up closely picking at the tiny green shoots of new grass which were laid bare. I find it hard to realise sometimes that Lily is a wild grey-lag goose who has never been pinioned. She is as free as the air and if she wished to fly away and leave us, she could do so. The relation of Mother Kumpfan between her and me is too strong though.

There has been a good deal of hill burning going on this last week or two on the mainland; a sign of March in this countryside.

Wednesday March 17th. Well we got our dose of wind last night. How it screamed and buffeted! There was no hope of sleep. I went out at one o'clock to the bell tent. It was still up but every guy had slackened completely. A dry gale means that the guys won't bind. A gale with heavy rain means that the ground gets sodden and the pegs tend to pull out easily. If there was a gale I like a few drops of rain periodically to keep fabric and ropes tight. This gale, as I have said, was a very dry one from the east. I had to go out to the tent again at two o'clock to tighten once more. Then the rain began and I knew she would hold. Knowing Dougal's capacity for sleeping, I went to the 'Dome' tent to see what was happening. It was nearly down and two poles were sticking through a rent in the roof. It was also tearing round the foot where the stones keep it down. I thought it best to let her down altogether and put more stones over the whole thing. It took me a long time to wake Dougal. I dared not open the door of the tent, which was on the windward side but thought it best to crawl underneath from the lee. Through here we evacuated Dougal's bed and such things as might tear the tent. Then we let down the poles still standing and put boulders over her. If we had done anything more spectacular than that I fancy she would have taken charge. Dougal came down to the hut and we were in bed again by just after three o'clock. But not for much sleep. The wind continued a gale until the light came and all today as well. Even now it is more than a strong wind.

The gulls have left the gullery altogether and there are but a few odd ones about the coast today. The sea is terrific but the black guillemots appear to enjoy it. There must have been 30 of them in the Cauldron today playing in the water. I am not sure whether this play is courtship or not, or just play which leads up to actual courtship which I have observed to take place much later in the season than this. There is no doubt, however, that this play is a highly social phenomenon. They seem such happy creatures, diving and standing up in the water and flapping their wings.

The hoodie crows were around Ard Bheag most of the day. The wind and rain became unpleasant in the evening and I did not stay out long on my evening round.

Thursday March 18th. Hard labour today. East wind still very strong. I went to the South Cave after breakfast for a load of guano and brought back about a hundredweight on my back. In working through the deposit, which is really a kitchen midden of prehistoric days, I found a point of a stag's antler and many seal bones.

Dougal took the turf off the patch we are to make into a garden and I finished off the turf dike with the turves. Later I forked over the new garden and a stiff job it was. Then I spread the guano and fetched some shell sand from the little patch of it at the West Landing. I did some scratching with the fork at the grass patches between the drains I have dug. I should like to get these back to the green state they were in sixty years ago. It isn't a very hard job really – draining, burning off the old foggage, scratching out the moss and treading it well. I noticed clover in the bog last year. It only wants a chance. The herring gulls have increased in numbers at the gullery today. There are about 50 and they are roosting at the gullery tonight. The barnacle [goose], which had been ailing is now with the hens so often that I shall not mention it again until something outstanding happens.

Friday March 19th. Still the east wind, now with rain. I spent most of the morning indoors typing. Walked out for an hour or two before lunch, making for the north-west, but there were so many barnacle geese about that I changed my direction rather than put them up. I was interested to see the flocks of 14, 8 and 4 at the same moment for the observation confirms my opinion that these flocks are definite entities and not changing aggregations. I see that the larger flocks are in better condition than the smaller groups of 4 and the odd ones. It is harder to approach the larger flocks and the ones and twos are most easily approached. When I say approach, I do not mean stalk, for it is obvious that a larger flock would be more difficult to stalk than an individual bird. It seems to be largely a matter of condition. I remember from my deer work that if I found individuals going about alone for any considerable period, they were sure to be in poor condition.

After lunch Bobbie came with me to the south-west where I wanted to see if the hoodie crows were making any progress with nesting. I did see some fresh dried grass put in a nest-like way in a place in the cliff where I thought they might be. A little farther along, however, on top of the cliff under a peat hag, I found a dead sheep which I had not noted before. This, I am afraid, is the attraction which has brought the hoodies to this place and I am now doubtful whether they will stay here to nest. We went on as far as the cormorantry to find nothing of particular interest.

Came back to listen to the commentary on the Grand National. To that extent I have not yet become Hebridean. That race continues to thrill me.

We went down to the West Landing to carry up loads of shell sand and seaweed for the garden and thus we carried on until teatime, which is one of the best times of day. The herring gulls were at the gullery again tonight. I forgot to say that I went eastwards this morning and at one fall of rocks below a sea cliff I saw an otter playing in a little pool left by the sea. I crept down to within a few yards of him and watched him come out, lie on the rock for a little while licking himself and slowly disappear in a rickle of boulders. He was unaware of my presence.

Saturday March 20th. It was almost unbelievable to wake up to a morning of no wind today. The sea had calmed down although there was considerable swell. I made up a cast of a rubber lob worm on piano wire and decided to go out in the kayak. Bobbie was nervous and derisive. But Dougal and I went and caught two fair-sized lythe (pollack). Good stuff that piano wire. There was ample fish for the three of us for lunch and Bobbie took back all she had said. The swell was nearly enough to turn me up. I, however, was in charge of the boat and the responsibility of keeping her moving helped to keep my breakfast down. I have observed before that porridge is not a good type of filling to go to sea upon. I was always better after tea which, with us, is a solid and ample meal. While on the sea we paddled very close to a small flock of black guillemots. 'Will they fly or will they dive?' I asked Dougal. Nine flew and one dived and when he came up he looked most surprised not to see his fellows.

Before we got up this morning I heard the wrens singing and what the rock pipit thinks is singing. The glass has been rising steadily and although it is a dull damp morning today, the day has gradually improved and the sky is clear tonight. Dougal has put up a gate to our enclosure. At breakfast time the peregrine falcons were crying noisily round their hereditary nesting rock, but they disappeared during the day.

The herring gulls are roosting at the gullery tonight, two of them very close to my hide. Good.

Sunday March 21st. The first day of Spring. It would take much to persuade us of that today. It has been very cold all day with a strong north wind. The sea was rough and coming into the Cauldron in fine romping style; great waves and swells which broke early on the reefs and came the rest of the way white and scintillating in the sun. There were many hard showers of hail and snow through the day which made the animals scurry for shelter.

We seemed to spend most of the morning doing little jobs and I went for a short run round before lunch. Nothing much to report. I went a longer round of the north end in the afternoon. There were curlews and barnacle geese in plenty

73

and I saw one cormorant. Dougal went to the south side and saw five cormorants in the sea opposite their nesting rocks. They are trickling back evidently. Dougal made a rake of wood and six-inch nails which is a most effective tool for scratching the foggage and moss off the strips between the drains in front of the hut. That little field will come green again yet. Morag, the little brown goat, isn't too happy today. Very near kidding I should say and, as last year, she seems very stiff. I gave her half a gallon of oatmeal gruel in the evening and she mopped up every drop.

Monday March 22nd. It was pretty wild in the night and we woke to a great gale from the north. Fortunately we are well sheltered from that airt. As we lay in bed before getting up we could hear the waves booming in the Cauldron. It was very cold and snow showers were frequent as they were yesterday. Dougal and I went to the Cauldron after breakfast to watch the sea. Some of the waves almost reached the top of the cliffs of the main gullery which are approximately 50 or 60 feet high and the surf from the breaking of these waves went twice the height of the cliffs sometimes. There was a continuous wall of spray blowing over the top into Lochan na h'Airidh (our drinking water). We went on to the top of the north cliff, over a hundred feet high, where it was difficult to stand. We crept forward on our bellies and keeked over the edge. The updraught nearly took away our breath. It was pleasant lying there, not troubled by the gale because we offered so little surface to it. The sun came out on this expanse of green and white sea and we felt it good to be alive. So did the gulls which soared and dipped on the up-draught. There were two fulmar petrels among them and when we moved farther along in order to see the face of the north cliff it was to find four more esconced in niches on the rock face. This is their first appearance this season but I do not think they will stay long just yet. The bad weather will have brought them for a spell. On our way home past the North Loch, we saw a barnacle goose on the shore of the little tiny bay. It was obviously exhausted. Dougal went to pick it up and it just flapped on to the water. It made for the neck of the bay and I waded in to intercept it. When it reached me it dived to go between my legs, but I had hold of it. I took it back to camp and later in the day gave it food. The poor bird is indescribably lousy and full of bird keds as well. We took off a good many but there must be thousands left. Unfortunately we have no keatings or other fine powder which would do to suffocate the wretched parasites. It is always the same: even the healthiest animals have lice but health keeps down

74

the numbers. When an animal begins to go weak or get out of condition, the lice increase prodigiously and may be a serious contributing cause of death. The lice can't help it either. It is better for them that their host should live. When it dies, they do. The poor little goose has not much to say for itself; it feels too much knocked about. I should dearly like to tame it and keep it with Lily and the Chinese geese, but I have doubts whether we shall be able to bring it back to health and strength. These geese have a very beautiful black eye. This one shows no fear of us; too far gone I think. There are two or three more barnacles about the place today that look less happy than they did two days ago. Northerly gales are the devil.

We all went to the south cave in the afternoon for guano. We saw four cormorants at their nesting rock and two of them had started putting a bit of bracken in their old nests. They must be watched carefully henceforth. I saw a Leach's fork-tailed petrel fly by. The evening set in sleety and miserable, what we should call 'coarse'.[51]

And so passed a whole week spent mostly in keeping warm, dry and well fed but with a keen eye on what was going on around them, and all woven into a total experience of small-islands expeditioning in one of the stormiest areas of Europe. If an index were made of all the items of various kinds recorded in that week it would probably extend to several hundred! Yet the life was simplicity itself, a routine of sleep, toil, food, leisure (when spared) and back to sleep. In such circumstances a hot drink can take on a completely new dimension of pleasure and a dry, warm sleeping bag is heaven after day-long exposure to the storm, the cold and the wet.

4

Bird Flocks

I return to the reasons for Frank and Bobbie being on Chleirich: the amalgam of work and desire. The work was not of
course the physical grind of keeping body and soul together,
but the research on gulls and other seabirds. The desire was
the longing to be cut-off from the rest of the world to savour
the solitude and quiet beauty of a small world of their own.
The work and desire did of course combine in Frank's mind
since solitude and lack of disturbance were two criteria of his
observations on the behaviour of gull flocks in a natural
setting, as they had been for the deer on An Teallach.
Though there is little actual mention of frustration in the
studies of birds he made on Chleirich, Frank never found
them anything like such good 'material' for study and writing
as the red deer. He went to the Island in 1936 conscious of
the fact that if he sat quietly, out of sight beside a colony of
seabirds, that he would discover something new. This discovery he conceived as being achieved by two processes:
first, the direct observation of the birds; second, the interpretation of the observations against the existing body of
knowledge, particularly as presented at that time by Marshall
on sexual periodicity, by H. E. Howard on bird behaviour
and his own hypothesis on synchrony of breeding related to
size of colony.

My overall impression from *Island Years* and the Priest
Island diary of 1937 is that there was nothing like the physical
and intellectual drive in his work on seabirds that marked his
work on red deer. In later life he wrote to Francesca: 'bird-
watching satisfies one artistically much more than scientifically'. Judging from this and from experience of island
studies by myself and others when everything was completely subordinated to achieving the research goals, Frank's

76

work on the gulls seems relatively low-powered. He found the subject difficult to handle. Also, gulls and seals, as he was to discover later, spend a great amount of time sleeping or wakefully doing nothing whereas deer are generally on the move, grazing or lying cudding. When they did come to life in distinctive courtship rituals he was limited in his description of them by being unable to sketch spontaneously in the hide the postures of the birds, to record stage by stage as the postures of male and female changed; he resorted to verbal description only. Unlike deer, in gulls the sexes are similar in appearance and young breeding birds cannot be distinguished from their elders.

> Many types of birds when displaying show an individual posture which they maintain for as long as several seconds; they are, as it were, momentarily suspended in time. Two shags will become excited by billing and preening each other's neck; then their heads and necks will stretch upwards to their fullest extent. The birds maintain the position for two or three seconds. A photograph of it would give a relatively true idea of this type of display: but the postures of gulls are a changing pattern throughout the few seconds of time which they occupy and I have seen none of these moments of ecstatic immobility among them. The display could be shown adequately only by a cinematograph record or a long series of drawings.[52]

The following is one of Frank's verbal appreciations of display without drawings or photographs.

> A third type of display, in which both birds take part, usually occurs in strict relation to the square foot of ground which will become the nest, and it appears when the birds have taken up their own stances in the gullery. It is not generally thought that birds have a preformed mental image of the nest and an early conception of its purpose. And yet in the first week of April, a month before eggs appear, some pairs of herring gulls are already treating the immediate nesting site in a manner different from that of the surrounding ground. The birds may be pattering round the few square yards in the vicinity of the standing-place and nesting-site in an apparently fortuitous manner to the observer; but such an interpretation may not be correct. They converge on the depression of the nesting-site and on that place their legs flex, the whole body is tilted forward and each bird makes movements suggestive of the action of gobbling up some soft food

near the ground. The head moves up and down rapidly, involving to some extent the whole body. This is a ritual display normally occurring only over the nesting-site.[53]

This text is crying out for graphic illustration which he was unable to give. There is no doubt that he desired to illustrate *Bird Flocks* himself but after some encouraging efforts at Dundonnell while awaiting passage to Chleirich in 1937, he made a last attempt while on the Island.

> *Monday May 31st.* S.W. gale blowing and it continued all day . . . Spent a large part of this afternoon trying to draw herring gulls in various postures of courtship display and was *most* unsuccessful. I was so tired as a result of these fruitless labours that I lay down on my bed and slept for an hour.[54]

Frank clearly saw then that his work lacked a very necessary dimension. This was not an occasion in which a professional artist could be employed; the drawing had to be done by the student from the live subject *in situ* as was done later, for example, by Niko Tinbergen in *The World of the Herring Gull* or by Gavin Maxwell with otters in *A Ring of Bright Water*. He occasionally remarked how he envied me my own quite modest facility in drawing and painting, since he was acutely aware of a unity which existed in art and science and enjoyed greatly indulging his lyrical prose in communicating his science. Had he drawn and painted well, his books would have lent themselves as extravaganzas of nature awaiting the spontaneity of his pencil and brush; he did not and his books depend the more on his photography which, though exciting enough and good even today, was not of a standard equal to the text.

The work on Chleirich in 1936–37 is distilled in *Bird Flocks* and contains some original information collected in the gull colonies through painstaking observation from hides and from general observation of other species – cormorants, fulmars, storm petrels, eiders, crows, geese and other birds which caught his eye from time to time. He described ten different displays of gull behaviour and made counts of birds, nests, eggs, hatchlings and fledglings in four colonies of herring gulls and two of lesser black-backed gulls in 1936 and in two and two respectively in 1937.

The attention of reproductive biologists was mainly focused on captive animals and concerned their glandular condition and sexual behaviour, linking the function of the

78

Plate 4.1. A mixed flock of herring gulls and lesser black-backed gulls, which were the species studied by Frank on Chleirich. (photo J. Morton Boyd)

pituitary body with length of day. The function of the gonads was then linked to the activity of the pituitary and the stimulus created by breeding sites and displays. Frank read all this with deep interest and it occurred to him that the more intense the interaction of birds in a breeding colony, the quicker will each pair come to egg-laying and rearing of young. Logically, the larger the colony, the longer should be the time-span between first and last egg-laying, but Frank thought that the opposite might be the case.

He suggested that gulls in large colonies were subject to greater measures of sight and sound stimulae, resulting in faster glandular action with birds brought to egg-laying earlier than otherwise. Earlier breeding would in turn result in an abundance of young over a short period rather than moderate or small numbers over a long period; the former creates a prey–predator relationship which favours gulls while the latter favours the force of predators – a group comprising greater black-backed gulls, hoodie crows, ravens and pere-

79

grine. The hypothesis is capped by natural selection favouring birds of a highly gregarious habit, enhancing synchrony and maintaining the herring gull and lesser black-backed gull as flocking species. This linkage of factors is known as the Darling effect.

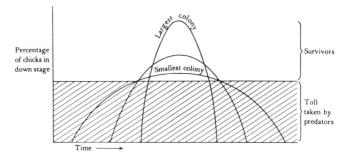

Figure 4.1. A diagram from *Bird Flocks*, 'illustrating how the survival rate is influenced by the "spread" of time in which the eggs of a colony of herring gulls are laid' (by permission of Cambridge University Press)

There was little scope on Chleirich for testing this hypothesis. The colonies were too few and too small to provide the necessary variation of the measure of synchronous breeding between colonies; at least one of the herring gull colonies was invaded by lesser black-backs and the nests could not be distinguished, and bad weather disrupted the count of one of the lesser black-back colonies. It was while he was writing his results in 1937 that Frank received on Chleirich a 119-page monograph published earlier that year by a German, F. Goethe, who, seemingly unknown to him, was working in a breeding assembly of herring gulls of over 6,000 pairs. Goethe found that the egg-laying period in his large assembly was well over a month but that different parts started laying at different times. This was opposite to Frank's theory but he interpreted Goethe's results as being consistent with his, if the different colonies within the large assembly resembled in size his study-colonies of 6 to 65 pairs on Chleirich. Later workers have suggested that the Darling effect holds good for colonies of up to about 200 pairs but not beyond that number. He did not take into consideration that the preda-

Plate 4.2. A breeding pair of herring gulls. (photo R. Goodier)

tory force often varies with the abundance of food, namely the more young gulls there are the more predators there will be in attendance. To complicate matters, it has since been established that young birds breed late and are less successful in rearing young than old birds. This fact clouds further Frank's interpretation of what he saw, since the relationship between age-structure and time-span of egg-laying did not occur to him.

There is little wonder, therefore, that the validity of Frank's theory and the data from Chleirich which he published in support of it was called in question or ignored. Tinbergen in *The World of the Herring Gull* (1953) did not mention it and only a passing mention of it was made by Lack in 1968 in *Ecological adaptations for breeding in birds*. 'It

81

[correlation of density of nests and the period of laying] recalls the effect claimed by Darling that in *Larus* gulls laying occurs earlier and is more synchronised in larger than in smaller breeding colonies owing to the effect of social stimulation. As shown for the kittiwake, however, though laying occurred earlier in the denser colonies, the spread of laying was greater in the denser than in the less dense colonies, which is contrary to Darling's claim.' Yet the Darling effect has not been forgotten as a hypothesis which, though somewhat beyond proof, still stimulates young minds, as much because of the person who first thought of it and of the place he sought to demonstrate it as for the mechanism of life which it seeks to describe. In 1980 Michael Gofhfeld of Columbia University, New York, stated that in his view 'the phenomenon of greatest interest in Darling's hypothesis is the role that social facilitation plays in synchronising their (birds') reproductive physiology'. Frank's appreciation of his gull study was modest.

> I do not wish to overestimate the significance of the social factor in the breeding cycle but to point out its existence. It is reasonable to imagine that when other environmental conditions are of an optimum character, the social factor would play a lesser part and when they are bad, it may become crucially important[55] . . . let us realise that a very small part of the whole problem of social behaviour in higher animals has been the thesis of this essay. A few observations have been given leading to a new concept which must be tried in the fire of future research and thought.[56]

The two summers which Frank, Bobbie, Dougal and Alasdair (when not at school) spent on Chleirich produced a great number of observations in the natural history of Coigach now enshrined in *Bird Flocks* and the first half of *Island Years*. You will not find the natural history organised in lists of species, tables of data, diagrams and appendices, but interlaced with all the other elements of the island story. The magic of island life and the desire to make the most of every minute of it radiates from Frank's journal of mid-summer when life was good.

> *Sunday June 13th.* This morning was dull and hazy but very calm and warm. I packed a tent and some stores and paddled off to the Glas Leac Bheag a mile or two north of us. Clouds of birds rose, calling loudly as I approached the islands, for

82

no one has landed there this year. Twenty-two greylag geese went away northwards – a hundred or more shags flew out to sea and rested on the water half a mile away. An enormous number of greater black-backed gulls flew overhead, nearly 200 of them I estimated. Flocks of 10–20 razorbills hurried to and fro and I saw six puffins flying to and from the island so I imagine they are nesting there. Black guillemots were numerous, so were eider ducks. Well, although the sea was so calm I could not get ashore for the swell. There is no beach or inlet of any kind on Glas Leac, only the rocks and cliffs. This was a great disappointment, but I had to be content with paddling round. A grey seal came up and looked at me with surprise and I met an eider duck with four ducklings. There is no heather on the island and the herbage seems to be mostly sheep sorrel and silverweed. The journey back seemed an awful drag. I saw a whale or two on the way home and two porpoises. This afternoon I took Bobbie out at low tide to see the underwater life of our shores – the sea urchins, the sponges, the orange sea anemones and the tropical forests of tangle and other weeds below us. Then we went further out into a shoal of mackerel. That sound is a good one to me now, the rapid crescendo-diminuendo as thousands of fish break the water for a moment or two and descend again with a very sharp twist and flick of their tails. Action in such close unison by very large numbers of animals is still an unsolved problem of animal behaviour . . .

Today has been extraordinarily dull and still and it is the kind of day when we see swallows here. Two were round the house for a long time just after tea and we were delighted when they perched side by side on the roof. There can be little hope of their ever nesting here, for they can find no mud to build with. I wonder if swallows and martins, martins particularly because they use much more mud in nest building, ever change their habits to overcome this difficulty. This would be good swallow and martin country as far as food insects are concerned, but mud is just non-existent and they would have to develop the habit of using cracks in the rocks. The bird is curiously bound by instinct and it is quite possible that the mud-building habit, now become an instinct, would limit geographical distribution. We have never seen a swallow at Dundonnell and they are considered rarities in this far north-west.

I went a quiet walk round later in the evening, listening to the storm petrels churring and purring in the stones and watching the mirror-like surface of the lochans. A common sandpiper ran up to within seven feet of me by Lochan Iar.

83

He stood on a stone and piped at me for a long time. As I was under Druim Mor and the night so still, the echoes filled the island with this one bird's notes. I like sandpipers. They are brave, fairy-like and graceful, running now, standing on a stone and flirping their tails continually, and then making a rapid run to pick up some small insect larva or crustacean from where bank and water meet.

I intended staying up till one o'clock to go outside to watch the night flight of the storm petrels, but at half past twelve there came a downpour of rain so I tumbled into bed.[57]

In the record of one day, mention is made of a mini-expedition, twenty-one kinds of animal and two of plants and some *ad hoc* theorising on the nesting behaviour and geographical distribution of swallows and house martins. The interplay of scientific fact through on-the-spot, first-hand observation with a spontaneous philosophy is laced through the hour-by-hour record of the island-life experience. The whole effect is charming and an impressive vindication of the *raison d'être* of the expedition, of the sacrifices they had made and the discomforts they had endured. As a comparison with the hard week quoted earlier, I have selected a week in June which contains all the qualities and rewards which the Fraser Darlings so fervently sought through their life and work on Chleirich; there are the ups and downs of family life mixed with adventure, the ever-changing panorama of nature, some thoughts on the history of the island, the drive of industry and pleasure of relaxation, the sunshine of midsummer's day, the rejoicings of a birthday celebration and a note of triumph in the award of a grant.

> *Saturday June 19th*. Mails all ready before lunch and I felt pleased with myself. A gentle rain fell most of the day. I went up the hill to look for the boat about three o'clock and I saw one come round the southern end of Bottle Island. It was a great disappointment to see that it was the Achiltibuie Hotel launch fishing. So I came down again and went fishing round the south side. There were six basking sharks about and some of them came quite near the boat but took no notice of me. The sea was very choppy with the north wind as I came round Ard Ghlas into the east bay, but the boat kept me too busy to feel sick. Anyway, it is the long swell that upsets me, not the short stuff. There was a shoal of mackerel playing in the east bay and I went round and round them with the white flies. They don't bite readily when they are playing and I

84

caught only one. Another got on and got off and left one of his eyes on the hook, poor thing.

This is typical of Frank's spontaneous concern for animals, an intuitive cherishing which was at the root of his research. Once he thought it necessary to collect a specimen of a puffin. On being seized in its burrow to wring its neck the destined specimen protested loudly and Frank thought, 'You should protest, poor thing, for why of all the puffins on this island should you have been selected?' Whereupon he returned the puffin to its burrow and went without his specimen.

After tea Bobbie was to come fishing with me as the sea had calmed somewhat, but we saw the launch rounding Ard Bheag. We ran down to the landing rock as pleased as could be. Alasdair was there with his hair cropped. Awful. But we got over it. First we have seen of him for six weeks and he has obviously grown in that time. Jimmy Macleod and his Mistress had brought their brother-in-law, a Mr Baird from Ayrshire, a hard-bitten but kindly-looking man who said when he was sitting in the hut with a cup of tea in his hand, 'I could live here and be happy for the rest of my life.' There is that feel about the inside of this island. It repels you by its coasts when you are on the sea but inside are the lochans and green places and the little hollow where we live. The best informed story of this island and the least sensational is that early Celtic Christian priests came into retreat here. If they did they lived in this hollow; on the very place where our little house stands are the foundations of an ancient building. These foundations have only become visible through our draining of the ground and by our pattering round the hut. You can see the shape of the building now in the grass. The door was at one end (strange for a house if it was one) and there do not seem to have been rooms in the building. It was about 20' long, east and west, and about 10' wide. Was it once a little chapel? Who knows? The building must have been of great age because the remains of eighteenth-century shealings still stand and one of them is the sheep fank. Nobody would have troubled to take down the building over which is our hut, to the foundation level just for tidiness. Rather should I think the outlaw built his little house (now the fank) from the stones of our building. The distance is but a few yards. The first reference to this island in history is that of Dean Monro of the Isles and it was called Na Clerach, the Priests' Isle, then – 1520 time.

85

Well, the outstanding item in the mail, apart from my birthday parcels which I must not open till Wednesday, is the grant of £50 from the Royal Society towards my work on animal sociality. It must be spent on expenses and not on personal affairs, but as we are already drawing on the personal allowance of the Carnegie for expenses that doesn't matter a hoot. I begin to think of North Rona. But no, let us get Treshnish through first.

After the launch had left and we had cleared up the letters and papers, Bobbie and I went to our fishing, and as we felt so at peace with everything we stayed out until midnight, by which time the phosphorescence was showing at each dip of our paddle and the fish were jumping out of the water all round us. It was a glorious night and I don't know what decided us to come in – perhaps the fact that we had fish enough for ourselves for two days, for the hens and for David the raven. It is so easy to go on fishing after you have enough and that is inexcusable. We saw two black-headed gulls in the west bay – a new record for this island, 64 species now.

Sunday June 20th. A good day but I was taken up most of the time with the proof-reading of my book; the last batch thank goodness. At my hide in the evening and slept out at the lesser black-back gullery.

Monday June 21st. The longest day and I have never seen a better. The sun was shining on me when I woke soon after four o'clock and it did not stop till I don't know what time at night, 16¾ hours bright sunshine. Bobbie and I spent the morning at the peats and built the stack. In the evening we took the boat round to the south cave and brought back a good load of drift wood. As it was so calm I climbed on to the island stack just off the south side of the island. There is a grassy hollow on the top. The only nest on the stack was a tystie's (black guillemot's) in a crack. Last year and earlier there were shags' nests on the face and cormorants used to build on the top of it. We saw blue butterflies today for the first time this year. Spent the night by the north loch.

Tuesday June 22nd. The longest day has gone and the good weather with it. Cold north-east wind, rain and a grey sky. By night time there was a huge sea running and the spray was breaking over the gullery. Spent some time at my hide until I was too cold to stay any longer and the rest of the day I was indoors indexing my book.

Wednesday June 23rd. 34 today. The pleasure of opening parcels grows no less. Bobbie sprang a great surprise on me with a copy of Cherry-Garrard's *Worst Journey in the World*, a book I have wanted for years. The weather was bad, the wind

86

having backed to north and increased to gale force; very cold. Worked hard at my index and last thing before turning in at midnight I sat in the lee of the old shealing and listened to the great purring and churring of the stormy petrels, and then to see them come out and fly about like fairies in the dimness of the northern light. A good occupation this of mine on a Midsummer's Eve. We had a birthday feast of chicken, strawberries (canned) and other good things which Bobbie brought from her store. The birthday cake was lovely.

Thursday June 24th. Wind very strong; backed to west with some rain and rose to gale force. Not long at the hide today, parents and chicks are lying doggo. Typed the index.

Friday June 25th. Wind still very high and not a moment without it. Bobbie and I were round the north loch and the lesser black-backed gullery and spent some time watching a chick hatching. Rest and activity, rest and activity, until with a final effort it was out of the shell to lie quiet for a very long time while the down dried. Common gull chicks hatched at north loch. Began the unpleasant task of polishing my book on bird flocks and the breeding cycle.[58]

Frank wished 'to serve, to give, to see and interpret'. However, he wished also to do all these and yet enjoy personal freedom which, when defined, meant his separation from those presumably he was set to benefit. Crowds he associated with filth and ugliness; solitude with cleanliness and beauty.

I find truth in wilderness, though another man may find it in the press of humanity. In my view humanity spoils when it packs, and I find myself moving to the fringe. Natural scenery is spoiled as well, water becomes unfit to drink without treatment, animals which give pleasure disappear or are exploited for profit, and everything takes on a soiled, second-hand character, all of which is unpleasant.[59]

The archetypal individual of the world he wished to avoid was the faceless, bowler-hatted bureaucrat; the man of the ever-fresh world of nature was himself. He would occasionally converse, often acrimoniously, with the bowler-hatted man, and would have been delighted to welcome him to his island fastness, ply him with tea and argue the day away on such subjects as personal integrity and self-respect. He found the island life a test of his temper and egotism. In his island isolation he found some difficulty in persuading himself, and

87

Plate 4.3. The ruins of Frank's hide as it was in August 1982, above the gull colony on the north-east coast of Chleirich. Wooden spars still survive amongst the rocks, and the gulls are still breeding. (photo J. Morton Boyd)

presumably Bobbie, that his particular form of service, giving, seeking and interpreting made more sense in contemporary society, than the same for Mr Bowler-Hat. The service was that of a working scientist using his calling to seek out the secrets of nature away from the effects of mankind and, through writing, enhancing the quality of life for countless people who might never reach an uninhabited island. Frank's sense of personal destiny as a leader of contemporary thought on the awareness and care of nature was born before he went to the islands. It was while he was on the islands that he became quite convinced that he had not made a mistake. This inner strength had its roots in the great wood of his boyhood, was fostered in his farm service with the Old Cock, was increased by his privileged years of contact with Blackface sheep, the red deer, the seabirds and the seals; the more time he spent in the field, the more he saw and the more authoritative he became not only in the factual sense of the naturalist but also in the emotional sense of possessing a special insight into the behaviour of men against the background of observed animal behaviour and natural processes.

Frank is shown in his diaries as an even-tempered man though this was not altogether true. Like his mother, he was slow to rouse but when roused was fearsome. He was well aware of the dangers of excesses of temper in the close living-quarters of Chleirich and seemed especially careful of his reactions. The events of the following two days show how the blindness to blessings which accompanies bad temper is unmasked by his spontaneous sense of wonder in his surroundings which quickened his mind to beauty, peace and pressing on with life regardless of frustrations.

Saturday July 3rd. It was a beautiful calm afternoon but the launch did not come and I chafed and grumbled because I had corrected proofs and indexed my book within a few days of last mail and it has all been lying idle since then. Bobbie and I took the boat round to the east bay in the afternoon and we thought to fish round from there in the late evening. We had tea outside and the broken-winged gull which can now fly came down to us for food. Freedom has made her tame. We went through the island to the boat just after 9.00 p.m. myself not feeling in too good a temper; and this was not improved by the fact that a fresh north wind had sprung up. I could see a bad bit of chop off Ard Ghlas but I thought we could get round it into straight water. Not so. The north wind catching us broadside drove us nearer the cliff, where the peregrines were screaming wildly, and into the choppy water which was of that unmanageable type where the sea comes up in pyramids and a plume of white shoots off the top. There is no rhyme or reason in this kind of sea and as we were getting too much breaking over us for safety I headed north into it and came back into the landing under the lee of the north shore of the bay. The episode added further to my sense of frustration for I had nearly gone forward in anger. We carried the boat through to Dead Stirk Bay on Lochan Fada and paddled about under the aspens and royal ferns which grow on the shores of this beautiful lochan. How calm was this water, sheltered as it is from the north, after the sea we had just been in. The bit of wind in the leaves of the trees was a loved sound and from the water these little aspects looked bigger than they are and very comforting. The honey-suckle tumbled over the rocks to the water's edge and scented

89

the air so that I was momentarily intoxicated by its sweetness. How lush this bank on a bare island! To hear the wind on these bits of trees, to smell the honeysuckle and to see the noble fronds of the great royal fern, and to feel the water lapping against my leg through the skin of the kayak, all this after the stark red cliffs and angry sea, assailed me with a sudden wave of nostalgia for the kinder country where big trees grow and undergrowth and a wealth of foliage. But is not this nostalgia part of the very joy this life gives? It is part of that succession of contrasts, physical and intellectual, which is the salt of life. On the north-western fringe of an old world I reach internal peace and occasionally experience these sweet yearnings for trees and lush foliage. If I go south the trees take on a heightened beauty and have a new fascination for me, but within a day or two comes the longing for the bare islands and indomitable sea coasts of this country; and this is no sweet nostalgia but a painful yearning which does not pass. There is certainly some asceticism in living here, though I am not sure whether it is not Epicurean. If it is, my Stoic philosophy isn't quite good enough.

However, the man who pulled the boat through the yellow flags at the western end of Lochan Fada tonight was in a very different frame of mind from that in which he had taken to the sea an hour earlier. I give you this as a little study of environmental impacts on one man's mind.

Sunday July 4th. Another beautiful day. We typed hard at the book and then went over the gulleries. Some of the gulls which lost their chicks in the great storm are now showing a recrudescence of courting behaviour. I doubt if they will reach the stage of nest building and egg laying again for July is upon us.

The wild thyme is wonderful this year; whole patches of ground are purple with it except for the golden heads of horseshoe vetch. The asphodel is flowering in the bogs now, brilliant spikelets of golden flowers, each one like a star. The ling heather is in flower too and some of the bell heather. Sometimes we wonder if we have ever seen the tormentil flowers so profuse and the golden suns of the hawksbit are also very abundant this year. The purple orchis is still flowering well and the sea pink has not yet gone from the cliffs. We have often remarked how these flowers of the west are either golden yellow or purple. The milkwort is blue and the stone-crop now flowering on many a rock face is pink; the bladder campion is white, also the chickweed, the Scottish lovage, the white clover and the heath bedstraw. The ragged robin, a darling flower, is about the island now and one or two stems of *Hypericum* [St John's Wort] are showing. Some day I must make a count of the island flowers, but I get a bit lost among the saxifrages, which are a study in themselves.[60]

Frank liked to use the word 'darling' as an adjective in its original unsentimental sense, meaning young or small and noble. He was impressed by the phrase in C. M. Doughty's *Arabia Deserta*, which described a mare followed by 'its darling foal'.

> We had tea outside again in company with the gull and the raven. David [raven] is bringing his relations about the camp much more now and it would seem that he, as our corvine ambassador, is helping to break down the tradition of hatred and persecution which is in the hearts of other ravens. I was reading today that in Iceland almost every isolated farm has its pair of ravens resident about the place. Here he is driven to the wild sea coast to eke out a precarious existence. And yet Britain fancies herself as being a nation kind to animals. Two of the young peregrine falcons are safe and we see them flying about the island with their parents and joining in the interminable feud with the ravens. Even these birds trust us nearer to them than would the falcons of the mainland. There the stalkers shoot them on sight. 'Why?' I asked one of them, one day, being sure of my ground. 'Well, they will be terrible hard on grouse,' he said. 'Sure enough,' I agreed, 'but grouse are a nuisance in a deer forest and are not welcomed so why do you kill the bird that is helping you?' 'Oh well (awkward shuffle) they're vermin whatever.'[61]

Before returning to Chleirich in 1937, it was planned to leave the island after the work was done on seabirds and go to the Treshnish Isles to study the grey Atlantic seal which bred there in the autumn. With luck, therefore, the family could have a field season starting on 3 March (they hoped 1 February) on Chleirich and finishing on Lunga on 24 February 1937, with two weeks in August for a flitting and the pick-up of Kenneth McDougall at Oban on the way to Treshnish.

Frank and Bobbie were clearly loath to leave Chleirich but they had their minds and their hearts set on a journey on which Chleirich was only a resting place. They had come to look at seabirds in the quietness and seclusion of the seabirds' world and had been rewarded in many ways for their efforts. By the time the gulls in the study colonies were fledging their young in early July, however, thoughts were drawn towards Treshnish and the seals: the final staging to their *ultima thule*, the greatest stronghold of the Atlantic seal on North Rona.

They left Chleirich on 30 July 1937 and returned often again for day-visits during their years on Tanera, but never again to stay as a family. The Chleirich experience cannot be purely distilled with all its ingredients but . . .

> The first day of May will long remain in my memory, for to begin with it was gloriously calm and mild. When you have had a long period of wind and wild weather and it is followed by a perfect day, activity seems to be frozen and all you can do is to lie about and heal your battered self in the quiet of it all. This morning had brought the welcome sound of common sandpipers to the lochans, that long-continued piping which is as moving to me as any music Pan himself might make. The sun shone through the canvas of the tent in the early hours, and I lay basking in it and listening to the sandpipers before I rose. This, I thought, was spring at last, and I let my imagination play with the picture of that active little mite standing on a stone at the edge of the sunlit water, his head and beak nodding and tail flirping, and then the ecstatic, vibrant flight over the lochan with a paean of his piping.[62]

5

Treshnish Isles

When Professor R. J. 'Sam' Berry and I arrived at Calgary
Bay in Mull at 9 o'clock on the grey morning of Saturday, 1
September 1977 there was no-one to be seen. A few small
boats bobbed on the tide but no boatman was waiting as
planned to take us to the Treshnish Isles. Sam enquired and
found the young fisherman at his breakfast with the effects of
the Friday night dance still heavy upon him. Killing time,
we strode around the sand dunes looking at the erosion and
the snails and then went to the jetty. The door of the cottage
opened and out came our skipper in thigh boots, hauling on
his jacket; we were on our way.

We sailed close to the shore to Treshnish Point under the
treeless sloping ground around Treshnish House with its
engaging pattern of hay-fields, stands of oats and rough
overgrown meanders of ungrazed pasture. Ahead was the
open sea with the low undulating profile of Coll and Tiree
stretched across the horizon. We awaited the surge of the
Atlantic swell as we rounded the point and were encouraged
to find that the little boat rode it well and, with its forward
weather screen, shed the spray. We were able to keep dry
and observe the passing scene with fulmars and Manx shearwaters gracefully skimming the sea's chaos. Guillemots and
razorbills were flying like salvos of missiles across our crazy
path. The Treshnish Isles were now appearing and disappearing over our bows and drawing nearer every minute.
Our reasons for going were to see these magnificent islands as
naturalists, visit Lunga where Fraser Darling had his camp
in 1937, and take off a research student who had been landed
on Lunga a few days earlier to catch mice for Sam's use in his
genetical research.

The Treshnish Isles are the summits of a submarine plat-

93

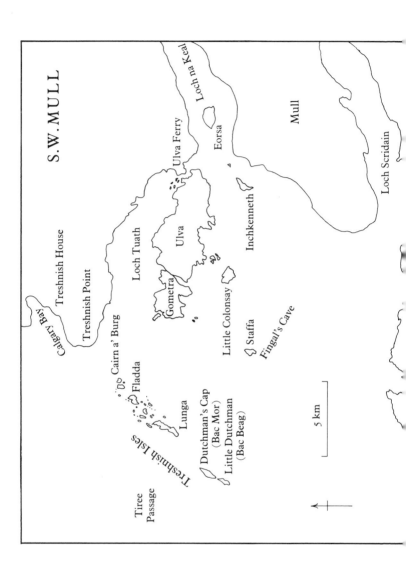

S.W. MULL

Calgary Bay
Treshnish House
Treshnish Point
Cairn a' Burg
Fladda
Lunga
Treshnish Isles
Tiree Passage
Dutchman's Cap (Bac Mor)
Little Dutchman (Bac Beag)
Staffa
Fingal's Cave
Little Colonsay
Gometra
Ulva
Loch Tuath
Ulva Ferry
Eorsa
Inchkenneth
Loch na Keal
Mull
Loch Scridain

5 km

94

2 km

Cairn a' Burg

ruins

Sgeir na h' Iolaire

Fladda

Sgeir nan Erionnach

Creag a' Chaisteal

Sgeir na Giusach

ruins

Dun Cruit

camp

Sgeiran Mor

Lunga

Cruachan 103 m

Dutchman's Cap

TRESHNISH ISLES
ARGYLL

Little Dutchman

eau at about 20 fathoms which extends south-westward from Treshnish Point on Mull. There is an 11-km chain of islands in two clusters: to the north containing Lunga (69 ha), Fladda, the Cairns with ruins of Maclean's castle and many smaller rocks; to the south lie Bac Mor (Dutchman's Cap) and Bac Beag. The lava flows and ash beds of Tertiary basalt have been eroded by ice, sea and weather to form a line of islands resembling a battle fleet; from the north west as viewed from the Tiree Passage, Lunga appears like a battle cruiser, Bac Mor a dreadnought and Bac Beag an aircraft carrier, all steaming in line. They have fine stepped landscapes with wave-cut platforms almost unbroken shore-cliffs of columnar basalt and possess spacious flat terraces and tablelands. Between Lunga and Fladda there is a maze of reefs and tidal channels which at high tide dissolve into well-

95

separated rocks and at low tide is a heavy carpet of wrack and tangle cut through by dark streams of clear water.

We entered the archipelago through the very narrow but deep channel between the Cairns, with shags showering off the rock across our bows. The water was alive with them diving in panic for fear of being run down by the boat. Large flotillas of eiders took wing as we emerged under the old castle; the slaps of their wings on the water came back to our ears from the perpendicular wall of Burgh More. As we passed Fladda we scanned in vain the hollow at the haven for the remains of the fishermen's hut mentioned by Harvie-Brown in 1892 and by Frank in 1937, but we were now in the midst of the skerries, weaving our course through tangle-fringed lanes of olive-green water with grey seals peering at us from many directions. A sudden snort and thrash of the water close-by was followed by the streaking spindle-shaped form of the seal under the boat. Every moment was full of the wonders of nature, though we were much too late in the year for the nesting seabirds and the flowers; the glories of puffins and sea-pinks were not ours to enjoy but this was made good in part by the seals, the bird flocks and autumn colours russet upon the shoulders of Lunga. We were also sailing backwards in time into Frank's *Island Years*. As we approached the tombolo on the north point of Lunga we could see Sam's student in the throes of packing-up. Our landfall was on Creag a' Chasteil where I stepped ashore at the same place as the Fraser Darlings on 25 August 1935.

For a few moments I stood among the deserted puffin burrows on the crown of the rock and in my mind's eye reconstructed the scene. There off-shore was the little fishery cruiser *Minna* (which took my own expedition to North Rona in 1960), the flit boat in the weedy channels and the party on the shore with the paraphernalia of the expedition. I had again the mixed feelings of arrival on the uninhabited shore: relief, expectancy and exhilaration. It was on Creag a' Chasteil (Castle Rock) that Frank was to meet Old Tawny the large bull seal who became a centrepiece in his seal studies on Lunga and was the analogue of Old Switch, the worthy stag of the deer study in Wester Ross. Even now as I looked down I saw the descendants of Old Tawny looking up at me with their enquiring, wide-awake faces; their dark eyes and penetrating stare said 'I know you; I know all about you;

96

Plate 5.1. Lunga from Creag a' Chaisteal at low tide, showing the weed-covered shore on which the Fraser Darlings landed and where Frank met 'Old Tawny'. They camped on the broad terrace high above the shore. (photo J. Morton Boyd)

there is nothing about you I don't know. You are man, my enemy. Go away to your own place and harm me not!' Yet Frank with his great patience and his 'way' with animals became their friend, as recorded in his Treshnish journal of 1937.

Sunday, September 5th. This is the twelfth anniversary of our marriage and it has been one of the days of my life. After breakfast we heard the seals calling loudly and we went to the cliff edge to see 12 of them out on the edge of the Castle Rock. Soon there were 16, and several more swimming in the pond. Old Tawny for once was not out of the water and all the seals ashore were cows. They squabbled and wailed a great deal whenever another came out of the water or when they shuf-fled about on the wrack-covered rocks. There was a distinct tendency for the seals to edge nearer the water as the tide ebbed, and so there was a constant slight movement in the whole group. We ourselves were waiting for the full ebb of the spring tide so that we could walk over to the Castle Rock to explore there. At noon we could cross and by this time Old Tawny was out and lying alongside the cows. We crept down

97

to the sea's edge at the east of the pit and got a good way over before we had to cross the open stretch in sight of the seals. Dougal, Alasdair and I crawled over the mass of wet tangle and wrack on our bellies, myself encumbered with £50 of camera and lenses, as well as my binoculars and telescope. It was agonising but exciting. Once over, I could not resist an attempt to stalk the seals and so left Dougal and Alasdair to explore the rest of the Castle Rock for themselves. There was a big stalk before me all on the seaweed. I got over one stretch and then to get in the lee of a rock it was necessary to cross some water rather than go round the edge of it. I left my boots and stockings on a rock and waded in nearly to my middle. One seal came near to me in the water and was most interested in my slow and laboured progression. She was not frightened. In mid water I changed the lens in my camera to the 13.5 cm, snapped my friend in the water and went on again. How slippery was the bottom! At last I was over and crawled up the sunken rock and along the top to get one or two fairish pictures of the seals at 45 yards. By this time I was sweating and very excited. I took off my coat, telescope, binoculars, and other oddments, and with my camera I slid down the side of the rock into some shallow water, crawled across and got still closer to the seals – about 20 yards in fact. But they were lying so flat to the rock that I could see I should not get a good picture. I whistled a tune to them and one or two looked up and called and then lay down again. I was bold now and felt I must get closer. On over the seaweed towards the great belly of Old Tawny which seemed to hide everything else. At last I was up to them and I could have touched Old Tawny. The desire to tickle that great expanse was great, but I wanted a photgraph, not a bit of fun. For a time I did nothing but contemplate this great seal who has got hold of my imagination. He is immense. His coat is the colour of seaweed and every breath he took was like a great snort. Once when the cows were quarrelling he seemed annoyed and he raised his head and gave a deep roar. The very rock seemed to shake and I felt about the size of a periwinkle there beside him. I looked at his mouth and the big yellow teeth and I looked at the black toenails in his front flippers. I looked at his long hind flippers and the little tail. Then again at that big belly and the mane of almost sandy hair. Old Tawny is the Ron Mor of Treshnish, and for me he is the symbol of life in the sea. At last I pulled myself together and focused on him for a head study. He raised his head and looked calmly at me. I pressed the shutter release and the unusual small sound alarmed the seals. Old Tawny slid down

98

into the sea. Here was a tragedy – I had used my last exposure in the spool. They were not seriously alarmed, and though they slid silently and slowly to the water, one cow remained by me and was a minute or two before she followed the others. And there was I with no film left. The seals in the water came up to look at me and because I was still and moved carefully they did not go away into deep water but stayed in the sound. I went back to my two lots of gear slowly and carefully and still the seals swam about on the surface of the water. I was so glad I had not seriously frightened them. I met Dougal and Alasdair coming back from the north-eastern corner of the Castle Rock, where they had been fairly close to another big bull seal but, said Dougal, he was not anything like the size and personality of Old Tawny. We got back to an immense and special lunch which Bobbie had made for the day. We needed a sleep after lunch for that we did not get last night. Bobbie and I walked to the south end of the island and back home to tea, after which I smoked a cigar and felt that life was good and very full. If only I have got Old Tawny's portrait I shall be satisfied. His portrait means more than his skin and perhaps in the future I shall be able to look at that portrait and think that Old Tawny is still ploughing the wild waste of sea and reef about these remote little islands.[63]

A day-old grey seal pup will react aggressively to the human touch and although some old cows and bulls will hold their ground, most go into the sea at the sight or smell of a human. Young will often move into the water at the slightest suggestion of danger such as the drift of scent from an unsighted party several hundred yards away. However, it was obvious to Frank that, if he employed the stalking techniques which he had used in the red deer study, it should be possible to approach the seals much more closely than anyone had done before in the wild. By prostrating himself in their sight and taking advantage of cover and wind in his approach the results could be quite sensational.

The tide was flooding and I could see that if I did not cross the weedy tombolo to Lunga I might be cut off just as were the Fraser Darlings when they landed. The slippery boulders made the going difficult and painful but soon I was ascending the path to the ruined cottages and, beyond, the site of the Fraser Darlings' camp. Sam was in discussion with his student who had succeeded in catching live mice and had them carefully prepared for the long journey to Sam's laboratory

Plate 5.2. The ruined houses on the broad northern terrace of
Lunga, to the south (right) of which was the campsite. In the
background is Creag a' Chaisteal (high tide, *left*), Fladda
(*centre*) and Mull. (photo J. Morton Boyd)

in the Royal Free Hospital Medical School in London where
they would be used in breeding experiments. This was the
fulfilment of a desire which both Sam and I had for many
years, to find out whether or not the *house mice* which infested
the Fraser Darlings' camp still survived in the *field mouse*
habitat on Lunga. The former, having been introduced acci-
dentally by man in the absence of the latter, had extended its
range into the field after the human community departed in
1859. This is the opposite of St Kilda; there both species
were present at the evacuation in 1930 but by 1932 the house
mouse was extinct because, it is thought, the field mouse
invaded the deserted houses and ousted the other.

> The mice must have lived a truly rural existence for eighty
> years, for when we came to the island they greeted us with
> open mouths. They threw off their field habits immediately
> and became house – or rather tent – mice once more. They
> inspected everything and found it good, and the trodden
> earth floor of a bell tent made an excellent sports stadium for
> them at night-time. The bolder spirits would climb on to the

sugar-box table and make it a sounding-board on which to slap their tails in bravado. Oh, it was great fun, but we had to curb their hospitality in self-defence and do something about them.

This was another emergency in which Dougal's ability as a handyman came to the fore. With immense patience he fashioned water traps which would lead the mice to suicide. He rounded the ends of a piece of wood so that it would rock when set across a bucket, and across this piece he set another, on the end of which he stuck oatmeal with the help of black treacle. The unsuspecting mouse climbed on to the mainstay, ran along to the cross-piece, turned at right angles to the oatmeal and – plomp, he was in the water at the bottom of the bucket; the devilish engine which had been his ruin came back into position again to entice the next victim to his doom. The mice never got wise to this device. For myself I am very fond of mice and I feel it hard to bring myself to catch them, for they are sprightly and diminutive, and tame ones have given me such pleasure all my life. But here on this island where we had no protection of bins and so on; and where, when there was a calm night, we were anxious to enjoy it, we were compelled to be drastic and put sentiment on one side. It was horrid letting the little things drown in a smooth-sided bucket, even more horrid and callous when we ourselves lived so often in some danger from the sea, and, lastly, we had butted in on their island, so to speak. Nevertheless, if we had not caught any of those seventy-five mice which we killed during our stay on Lunga, I fancy our stores would have been in an indescribable state. There are plenty of mice left there yet.[64]

While the life of the red deer was already well known by tradition and natural history rather than by science before Frank went to Dundonnell in 1933, much less was known about the grey seal. On the hill with the deer he knew a great deal more about his animal than he did on the shore with the seal and though there was much in common in the approach to both studies, the seals contained many features and unknowns not possessed by the deer. Evolution had not simply made them very different variants of the mammalian form in their anatomy, it had also moulded them differently in less obvious ways. For example, the rutting stag does not defend a territory; he accompanies a group of hinds in their territory and fends off other stags in challenges. The grey seal bull, however, does defend a territory precisely imprinted in his senses and possesses the cows which gather therein. Again, the deer have mating and calving seasons four months apart; grey seals mate only three weeks after the pup is born. All the inter-related factors of anatomy, physiology and behaviour which Frank described so sensitively in the thirties have since been greatly elucidated by two generations of scientists among whom I and my second son Ian are numbered. Ian's PhD thesis in 1982 at Cambridge was entitled 'Reproduction in grey seals with reference to factors influencing fertility'.

Frank arrived on Lunga with no previous field experience of seals other than observing them in passing during his years on the north-west seaboard. However, his reading and personal contacts both in local lore and in academic circles provided for him a most attractive field of enquiry, centred on an animal with distinct human appeal, based partly on fact and partly on legend. The distinctions between the common seal and the grey were already well known. The common or harbour seal is smaller than the grey; gives birth to its young in June on tidal rocks, unlike the grey which breeds in autumn above high tide mark; has the young in the sea with the dam from birth, unlike the grey which suckles on land with the young deserted by the dam before entering the sea. The unerring point of identification of the two species is the shape of their nostrils; the common has them in V shape while the grey has them well parted. However, Frank was not troubled by common seals obscuring his data on greys on Treshnish though there are colonies of commons today not far away in the sea-lochs of Mull and on Tiree.

In the late thirties many of the facts concerning the breeding behaviour of the grey were already described by Harrison Matthews and his colleagues working on the Pembrokeshire colonies. In the Hebrides the traditions of seal hunting in North Uist, Harris and Lewis had been documented in legislation, yet the grey seal remained a beautifully mysterious creature, here one day and gone the next. Frank's logic was similar to that with the deer and the gulls; if he had the perseverance and patience to reach a seal nursery, and lie quietly unnoticed by the seals, he could not fail to bring back a bookful of new information supported by some startling photographs. This, of course, was also well recognised by his publishers of both articles and books and earned him some much needed cash.

His plan was basically similar to the gull study but without any deep hypothesis; he simply wished to plot the build-up and decline of the breeding assembly and make comparisons with other animals. In the grey seal, the arrival of adults of different sexes is followed by the development of territories on and above the shore by bulls, the invasion of these territories by pregnant cows fresh from the sea, the birth of pups, the nursing period of pups, mating of cows as they come on heat, departure to sea of 'spent' bulls and mated cows, and finally the departure of the last fully developed pups. The whole sequence of events was already programmed by nature; it could simply be a matter of getting to the breeding site and getting the study under way. However, there are limits to what a single worker can do, both on account of physical endurance and having only one pair of eyes and hands to measure and record all that is going on.

Tuesday, October 5th. The study of animal behaviour, at least of wild animals in their natural habitat, is the kind of amusement which might cause grave doubts in the mind of your pukka scientist. Here is no set of experiments you can devise or timetable to work to. In short, the animal and its life cannot be hurried and if you are not getting on fast enough, well, there isn't anything you can do about it. One thing is certain, if you can be patient and watch long enough you will get your story and perhaps there is such a thing as having a flair for being at the right place at the right time. This flair might bear analysis and turn out to be the reaction of the mind working with long familiarity with animals, but to all intents and purposes it is intuitive and you have it or you haven't.

Today was the sort of day when I could do nothing positive in my seal-watching . . .[65]

Even in the days of active research with Ph D, D Sc, F R S E after his name, Frank had an inner doubt about his science. His lack of application at school and the specialisation of his tutor in English literature resulted in a poor grounding in mathematics; his conception of algebra was vague and he never learned calculus. He did not come through the forge of University honours, but ascended into the field of academic research in ecology and animal behaviour from a diploma in agriculture. That in itself is not necessarily a drawback but it may have been within the context of Frank's work in the

103

thirties when he aspired to academic excellence in a field which lacked the discipline of exact science and in the fifties when he was appointed as a reader in ecology at Edinburgh University. In the latter he inspired many students with his lectures, but the second-year course tended to be a repeat of the first year. He did not fit the world of the academic and found himself at odds with academic colleagues and the work of the Department.

I only once heard Frank out-pointed in debate; it was at the Jubilee Symposium of the British Ecological Society in March 1963. As I recall, L. B. Slobodkin, an experimental ecologist from Ann Arbor, Michigan, working on populations of micro-crustacea in laboratory conditions – the opposite type of biologist to Frank – challenged Frank's concept of energy flow in the ecosystem and exposed his ignorance of elementary physics to the distinguished audience.

The deer study had been substantial and satisfying but the gull study had been rather short in results, and lacking in recognition and fulfilment. In later years he mentioned his disappointment at not being elected to the Royal Society of London. He saw himself then as an explorer in the middle ground between animal behaviour and ecology and felt that he possessed something special in the philosophy of science which most of his academically distinguished contemporaries did not have.

> My own work is on the borderland of ecology and the study of animal behaviour. What do we know of how wild creatures spend their lives? The literature of natural history is full of anecdotes, but there are comparatively few books giving a consecutive story of an animal's life. I am trying to find out what animals do and what are the factors influencing them on what they do. If we are sufficiently inquisitive, we can find out much of the effects of environment on behaviour and such knowledge is of direct application to wildlife conservation.[66]

One of the credibility gaps which Frank encountered concerned the intuitive way in which his mind linked the behaviour of animals with that of himself and with mankind generally. He believed that to interpret nature correctly, the observer has to be 'at one' with his surroundings and this led to adjustments in his own behaviour such that he was 'accepted' by the seals, not in the banal sense of Tarzan and the apes, but in the sense of being able to observe animal behaviour in a way closed to all but those who are so privileged or even gifted. A sense of élitism is introduced in which no amount of intellectual prowess in the framing and testing of hypotheses can alter the facts as they are observed in privacy with nature. In his mountain and island solitudes Frank was becoming as much of a mystic as he was a scientist.

Towards the end of his life during a family picnic on the shore near the Findhorn estuary, James asked his father whether the sound of the sea was mind-altering in an hypnotic sense. He replied that he had found this so when on the islands. 'The sea subtly detaches one from immediate, practical reality and casts one into a kind of mystic reverie linking one's life and nature, fusing visual stimuli with meditation – as opposed to the monastic mystic who attempts to cut off visual stimuli.' Perhaps living near the sea during his years of intellectual endeavour helped create this mystical habit of mind in him which alarmed conventional scientists.

Frank's anthropomorphic interpretation of seal behaviour could not bring him credit among scientists nowadays, though it might have done so in the thirties; nevertheless, his writings have had a great effect on the public mind and probably contributed significantly to the now widespread public awareness of and sensitivity to the killing of seals in Britain and elsewhere. They are as fresh now as on the day they were written:

> *Thursday September 2nd.* It was delightful to watch the expressive movements of the flippers. The fore flippers can reach a long way and can be used very like our own hands. The seal may scratch his belly gently or he may waft a fly from his face, now and then half close his hand and draw it down over his face and nose just as we often do. The hind flippers are sometimes stretched out just as we do our arms and then they are folded one inside the other, as we do our hands often enough in moments of repose.

> *Friday September 3rd.* Between four and five o'clock I was on the cliffs above the Leac over the low westerly reefs on which terrific seas were breaking. There were several seals in these breakers in complete command of the elements. The seas would break over them and they would come up in the trough looking as if they were thoroughly enjoying it. I recognised Old Tawny there. When I went down in the evening a few were popping their heads out of the water in

the sound and I heard one or two calling while they were still in the water. When I was whistling to the seals this morning one of them called back.

Saturday September 4th. At dead low tide I went down to the sea's edge at the sound and began to whistle to the seals. First there was one and soon there were four seals interested in me and my whistling. Old Tawny passed through the sound farther over to Creag a' Chaisteal but he took no notice of me. What an immense seal he is, and with what calm dignity and indifference he goes by! There is no doubt at all that this seal has dignity and an outstanding personality. As the tide was rising in the afternoon we saw the seals playing again to the west of the sound in the breakers. Old Tawny was just below us fishing round a sunken rock. I say he was fishing because he was not just playing on the surface and diving for short periods but was down for a good five minutes each time and came up only to get a fresh draught of air. We could see his shape and movements in the water perfectly and the markings and scars on his back . . .

Thursday September 9th. This is a red letter day because the first pup or calf was born this morning on Castle Rock . . . I could hear close to me the baby talk of the little seal. The sound is like that of so many young mammals, the human included. My heart warmed to it and I wormed over to the little thing. Its head and colouring reminded me so much of my great bitch hound Grainne. I remember we used to call her the grey seal sometimes. Well, I took some photos of this little calf snuffling beside me unafraid and then I crawled away from the seals and got back to the channel as it was filling up knee deep. I couldn't hurry because I was in sight of the seals, but I was in a state of delight when I got back up our cliff to see all the seals where they were when I set out. I had been so near to them all without frightening any of them . . .

Friday September 10th. I was watching the first calf being suckled this morning. The mother has two teats on her belly set very close in the skin and there is no outward shape of udder. She goes up to the calf, the calf nuzzles her side and the mother thrutches over on to her side so that the calf can suck at either of the teats. It suckles at each several times and after 5 or 10 minutes the mother shuffles back to the sea. Suckling takes place every two hours or so. Dougal came back to tea to say that there were many seals on the south end of the island and six newly-born calves. We went down there immediately after tea and watched them. Some of the babies were crying. One mother came up to feed her baby, and after suckling the mother tickled the baby with her fore flipper from the lower part of its belly to near its head. Baby liked it, and waved his own flipper happily. Then the mother fondled baby's head with her flipper used as a hand and just as we might do. Baby lay on its back and waved its flippers at its mother . . .

Sunday September 12th. I went to the south end in the morning and found another calf born – 8 in all. The attentive mother of yesterday was acting the same today and her calf is a fat and active little fellow. The cows are very jealous of their young, though the general atmosphere is one of amity. The calves, left alone for long periods, lie on their backs and wave their front and hind flippers in the air just like human babies; or they go fast off to sleep, as even a human baby does occasionally. I am amazed at the likeness of these great seals to human beings in much of their behaviour. They are indeed the people of the sea . . .

Tuesday, September 14th. There was a bull seal on the tiny beach and he looked bad-tempered. He was running blood from new wounds in his neck and shoulders, and the cows were snarling at him as he edged his way down towards the water. He came near the calf of the Attentive Mother and took hold of it in his teeth and began to worry it. The mother went for him but he had given the little calf nasty bites on the hind flippers and on the back. The calf shuffled hurriedly to safety – a very frightened little man. Soon a great bull showed his head from the sea and he showed he was afraid because he snarled. The great bull came up two or three yards more with the wave and with the same never-wavering look on his enemy. But the frightened bull did not run away. Suddenly the big fellow from the sea launched himself forward at the other's neck and the fight was on. He got hold of a great mouthful and shook the other bull. They tore at each other and bellowed and the blood ran freely. The frightened one turned for the water and the big one turned with amazing quickness and grabbed his flippers. Both went into the water like this and time and again they came to the surface, always together fighting, and the sea was stained red round about. The fight lasted a good five minutes . . .

Monday September 20th. This afternoon I saw the big bull seal and the Attentive Mother copulate. This act is performed in shallow water, the seals lying on their side. They are united for ten minutes. Courtship is pretty rough. The female snaps at the male and then tickles him in the ribs with her fore-flippers. He grabs hold of her with one fore-flipper and I saw his claws draw blood. The two roll over and over in

107

the water at this stage. They copulated again after an hour's interval and the course of action was similar. This cow's baby was born on September 9th and this is eleven days later, so the gestation period must be almost a year [now known not to be so – about nine months with implantation of the blastocyst in January and February].

Wednesday September 22nd. I saw a calf born at the south end this afternoon. Delivery took less than a minute, and the seal cleansed within ten minutes. After the birth she flopped round to nuzzle it but she did not lick it. The calf just lay where it was dropped for a quarter of an hour, when the mother came up to it again and went over on her side to allow it to suckle. It did not do so. She went five or six yards away and lay quiet for another quarter of an hour, came back, offered herself again, and the calf sucked . . .

Friday September 24th. One cow did not go to the water with the rest as I counted the calves. She allowed me to 4 feet and I took a head study of her. I daren't go closer for fear she would jump and snap in fright for her baby was there too. I talked to her and asked her to hold her head up for me and she did, but only in a lazy sort of way. She looked at me with mild interest and lay down to sleep again. I stood up and walked away and still she didn't go, and on my way back I stopped again to speak to her. How I longed to scratch her and stroke her but I was not anxious to frighten such a nice trusting old thing. I left her in peace . . .[67]

Frank transcribed the seal story as recorded in his Treshnish journal into two chapters of *Island Years*. It is a popular mix of the life of himself and Kenneth MacDougall with Bobbie absent from 13 to 17 September taking Alasdair to school at Gordonstoun, and the life of the seals. The scientific information is not separated from the everyday story of island life and though this is as it should be for the popular reader, it is unsuitable for the scientist. The scientific side of the Treshnish expedition was continued into that of 1938 to North Rona when he wrote *A Naturalist on Rona*. This he described as 'a book of literary and scientific essays' and embodied within it a great deal of the information already published in *A Herd of Red Deer*, *Bird Flocks* and held unpublished in the Treshnish and North Rona journals.

There is little doubt that Frank's reputation as a scientist would have been enhanced if he had written separately for two distinctly different audiences: the general public (in the way he did) and the scientist through the specialised scien-

Plate 5.3. Grey seal cow with a few-days'-old pup. Frank first watched the birth, nursing and weaning of the pups on the beach platforms of Lunga. (photo J. Morton Boyd)

tific press in ecology and animal behaviour which were getting under way at that time. Had this been done, I and others would have made much greater use of his work. It is, for example, very difficult to extract from his charming and interesting writings on the grey seals, data which gives an accurate assessment of the numerical status of the breeding assemblies through the season; only by having these numerically stated can the dynamics and structure of the assembly be effectively described. Frank's works are not numerical in character; the exceptions were the PhD thesis on the Black-face fleece and the *West Highland Survey* with a professional statistician included in the survey team. They have the character of literary works in natural history and human affairs rather than scientific treatises; this is what makes them so widely interesting and readable, and though Frank would have grudged losing any of his popularity, he desired wider scientific recognition. In any case at that time he and Bobbie were living on his research grants and fees from writings. He wished the best of both worlds but on balance became more popular than academic in his scientific thinking. There was no choice but to write to make ends meet. The following sentence interjected into the seal observations conveys his anxiety:

> *Thursday October 7th.* . . . Mr Mackenzie came in the afternoon with some mail and I learned that the Cambridge University Press had accepted my bird book. What a relief and a blessing![68]

I climbed to Cruachan of Lunga to obtain the fine panoramic view of the islands so much enjoyed by the Fraser Darlings in their leisure moments and to obtain portents of weather and the arrival of the mail launch from Iona, their life-line with the outside world. At that moment I could see Tiree to the west become enveloped in a rain storm which was travelling upwind and would be with us within half an hour; just time to have a quick look round.

The Treshnish Isles are a fine refuge of wildlife. They are uninhabited, composed of volcanic rock giving rich soils enhanced by sea spray and the manurial effect of seabirds, wild geese and domestic stock. They possess a mantle of maritime vegetation rich in grasses, herbs, mosses, algae and lichens; a full complement of marine algae displayed on the shelving littoral and sub-littoral plateau; insular populations of terrestrial and marine invertebrates; fourteen species of breeding seabirds including puffins, Manx shearwaters and storm petrels, wintering flocks of barnacle and greylag geese; common seals and breeding grey seals and possibly also otters. The islands are designated as a site of Special Scientific Interest by the Nature Conservancy Council and have been a private nature reserve created by the late Colonel Niall Rankin and maintained as such since his death in 1965.

Frank and Bobbie never took to Lunga in the way they had done with Chleirich. Camping on the side of a pyramid did not appeal to them after having had the shelter and privacy of the little glens of Chleirich. Frank complained that he could not go *into* Lunga in the way he did on Chleirich; they were both islands rich in wildlife but of very different ecological character. Life on Treshnish in autumn lacked the touch of high summer, the harangue of breeding seabirds, the gaiety of flowers and the longish spells of calm weather. Treshnish also lacked the comfort of a hut and the work with the seals on the wet, slippery shore had probably more physical discomfort accompanied by a greater sense of achievement than with the gulls of Chleirich. While Ian MacKenzie serviced them well from Iona, and the Robertsons who lived on Fladda while fishing lobsters paid them a visit, Treshnish did not have the strong link with the local community as did Chleirich with Alasdair at school in Achiltibuie and their friends the Frasers and the Macleods keeping a weather eye on them. Some of the worst weather of all their island days occurred on Treshnish:

> *Thursday November 4th.* I wrote last night with the wind and rain beating hard against the tent. I slept for an hour as soon as I got into bed, but then no more at all for the weather became a hurricane. The rain stopped at 3 o'clock and I was sorry because I knew the tent would soon dry up and I should have trouble getting the guys thoroughly tight in such a gale. Trouble began at 4 o'clock when the eave ripped from part of the windward side of the tent. In half an hour another stretch of canvas had gone and the increased wind resistance which the tent now offered was causing us concern. At this moment I felt I should go to the boat and see she was all right, for with such a gale coming on her shore at a spring tide there was no knowing how far up the sea would come. It was just then approaching high tide. I went down to the boat, finding it difficult to keep my feet, and as I went down the cliff path a thrush came up from the ground and hit my electric lantern. I picked it up and placed it in a bieldy place under a rock but the poor little soul had not wits enough to stay there. It flew up into the night and I saw in the light of my lamp that the wind carried it towards the sound where the sea roared. I wished then I had kept the thrush in my pocket until morning and I can only hope it came down on land. The boat, which we had pulled up at the north end this time and not at the Dorlinn, was all right, though spray was reaching her. The tide was higher than it has ever been before in our time here. When I got back to the tent the whole of the eave had ripped off and the side had come in and was cracking about us like a cannon. Bobbie went over into the store tent and began making room there. Dougal, whom we had called, helped me get essentials from our poor tent and then we lifted the pole from the ground and let her down before she ripped to ribbons. We put boulders on the top of her and she was quiet. Both Dougal and I felt it keenly because this tent has been a good friend these two years. Even now, the guying system has worked perfectly and disaster has come through the canvas itself giving way and not by the tent blowing down.

III

By this time it was after six o'clock so we made breakfast – plenty of the best porridge and endless tea. The sunrise was the most wonderful I have ever seen and the most dangerous. The gale was still blowing as hard as ever and when I looked at this riot of green and gold, steel-grey patches of bright cobalt blue – a colour I have never seen before in the sky – I knew we could expect no cessation yet. And I was right. All through the day the gale blew, while we built a shelter of driftwood and tarpaulins for the stores in the ruins of one of the old houses. Bobbie arranged things in the little bell tent which must henceforth be our home. We were tired at the end of it all because apart from the labour there has been the continual difficulty of keeping upright. There has been no lull at all and now as I go to bed it is still going hard. I have no anxiety about this tent because it is smaller than the other, new for this trip and of the same specially heavy material, and I am so sleepy it is doubtful if even this wind can keep me awake much longer.

Friday November 5th. I fell asleep soon after 8 o'clock last night and knew no more till 1 o'clock, when it was still blowing. Asleep again and woke at 7.30 (6.30 your time) to a blessed calm . . .[69]

It was also on Treshnish that Bobbie fell sick. Strangely no mention is made of this in Frank's journal, which for the week concerned is devoted almost entirely to observations on seals:

Exactly two days after her return [17th September] Bobbie fell ill – really ill . . . she had brought back scarlet fever. This ran a flaming course for nearly a week during which she grew thin . . . The poor girl could eat little or nothing.

All this time the wind was blowing hard from the south-east and south, directly on the tents. These two winds are always unpleasant ones in this part of the world, and at this time they were more nerve-wearing than ever. Oh how I wished it to be calm to give Bobbie a bit of peace, but no, it just kept on blowing hard. I was very troubled. Ought I to put up a flare and get help, supposing a launch would come in these high seas. What was the good anyway? Looked at from the social point of view, Bobbie was at least in a natural isolation hospital, and as for her as an individual she was better where she was than being carried away. What does the treatment for this kind of disease boil down to in the end? Waiting till the fever has run its course and keeping the patient open and warm. So Bobbie endured her adversity and said she felt much better a week later; then she began the characteristic peeling of the skin, but she got none of the pumice-stoning of the soles of her feet which is my chief remembrance of convalescence in childhood. I was much relieved when she stood on her feet once more.

The danger of scarlet fever is in its sequelae: no sooner had Bobbie begun to feel a little better than I came in one morning to find her in great pain in her ear. This troubled me far more than the scarlet fever, because this might mean a complication we could not relieve. That afternoon I put her to bed again with nearly a quarter of a pint of rum inside her. She has told me since of the blessed feeling of disassociation it brought her and I crept about quieter than a mouse for the three hours she was asleep as a result of my dose. Then, of course, the pain came back when she awoke, but I did not wish to use more rum until last thing at night, because its effects would obviously lessen and a system full of alcohol is being handicapped in setting its house in order. But severe pain is also dangerous, so I immobilized poor Bobbie with rum for those dreadful hours of the early morning when pain is at its worst and hope its lowest . . . We gave Bobbie hot bottles to put to her head and these helped a little.

Then suddenly at ten o'clock the next night she felt a quick relief from pain and pus began to flow from her ear. It was as if pressure had been lifted from the whole camp . . .[70]

The pattern of life was as up and down as the weather. People who live cooped-up on a small island require to live as much for each other as for themselves. Trivialities become larger than life and an ability to retain a normal judgment of events is paramount in achieving that 'Even Tenor' which was so quickly achieved by Frank and Bobbie when they settled-in for the first time on Chleirich as a new experience. There is no record of sulks and silences which can mar an expedition, and little or nothing of the irrationalities and bad decisions which long periods of solitude can bring. By the end of the Treshnish expedition they had lived through twelve months of isolation both there and on Chleirich, and if there had been any doubts about the wisdom of going on to North Rona, they would have shown themselves long ago.

There was an air of triumph in Frank's description of their last hours on Treshnish. By mid-November the seal breeding was almost over and he had it all in his notebooks, on film and in his mind as the first witness. Of course man had for centuries visited the breeding grounds of the great seal, Ron Mor, in the Scottish islands mainly as a hunter, but none had stayed from beginning to end to see the entire saga of the seal's birth, courtship and mating on the wild sea's edge. In Frank's mind, Treshnish was but an outpost of Ron Mor's 'people'; the great seal of Norse mythology had his head-quarters in the wide solitudes of ocean, seen from other parts of Britain only on the fairest of days; inaccessible, as far removed from man as could be in the isle to which the seal has given its name, North Rona, described in the words of T. S. Muir:

> O these endless little isles! and of all little isles this Ronay!
> Yet, much as hath been seen, not to see thee, lying clad with soft verdure, and in thine awful solitude, afar off in the lap of wild ocean, – not to see with the carnal eye, will be to have seen nothing!

By November, Bobbie had fully recovered from her illness and all three were in great heart. There was lovely winter weather with time to enjoy life – washing, shaving and even going to the length of having a bath! It was at this time they climbed the Cruachan to view the winter sunsets to the west of the Dutchman's Cap. In describing these Frank's pen becomes a brush with a palette of glorious colours: mother-of-pearl cloud, tints from violet, vermilion to red, rose and yellow. To the east the snow-capped cone of Ben More, Mull was roseate. With their job well done, plenty of good food and calm weather they had a sense of well-being which made them rather disappointed to see the fishery cruiser appear to take them away two weeks ahead of schedule. Frank's last entry in the Treshnish journal is:

> *Tuesday November 23rd.* Tonight the starlight is wonderful and the air still. One or two seals are crying full and clear, and I know what a nostalgic sound this will be for me now. It will go along with that of the barnacle and greylag geese – noises that will stir me all my life now. Indeed, this music of living things is becoming symphonic in the halls of my mind and it moves me ever more deeply.[71]

Kenneth McDougall (Dougal) had turned up on Eilean a' Chleirich for a fortnight in June 1936, had returned to join Frank and Bobbie in Dundonnell in the following October and accompanied them throughout the expeditions of 1937 to Chleirich and Lunga. On 20 October Dougal and Frank sat awhile in warm sunshine on the top of a fortress-like rock above the Dorlinn talking lazily of the affairs of the world.

114

'It seems to me,' said Dougal, 'though it is one of those things you hesitate to say in a sophisticated society, that it is doubtful whether all that is meant by art and culture is the right thing by which to judge a civilisation, nor should it be considered one of the major ends to which a civilisation moves. Surely the true criterion of a civilisation and its aim should be the right behaviour of the people one to another. If a society exists in which behaviour has reached a state of justice, mercy and rightness, and the pitch of individual sensitiveness is high, can it achieve a much higher state of civilisation by technics? I doubt it. The art and culture part of it is a symptom of civilisation, a kind of creative froth coming out of the beer. If the beer is inert, you get no froth, in which case the people will lack the social and civic sense I am talking about.'[72]

Dougal's contribution to the life and work of 1937 must have been immense and his discreet presence in the Fraser Darlings' camp was a great reassurance to them. By rights it is he who should write this book. Sadly, I quote from Frank's dedication of what I think was his best book, *Natural History in the Highlands and Islands*:

Kenneth McDougall, M Sc, M R C V S
† Normandy, August 1944
who knew and loved the Highlands and Islands
and the wild life therein.

But on this September day as Sam Berry and I stood on the Cruachan the scene was grey, wet and cold. Soon we were shrouded in the rain from Tiree and had to hurry past the Darlings' old camp-site now overgrown with bracken but still running with rabbits, past the ruined cottages and down the track to the waiting boat. As we drove back across Mull to catch the last ferry from Craignure to Oban with our memories and precious cargo of live mice, we talked of having that day trodden hallowed ground.

6

North Rona and the Birds

On a clear morning in June 1934 at the summit of An Teallach, Frank saw North Rona for the first time as a small
hump breaking the northern horizon 'afar off in the lap of
wild ocean'; on looking down he could see also the Brae
House at Dundonnell and the Summer Isles with Chleirich
and Tanera scattered in the sea to westward. That was in the
early days of his red deer study and already the calling in his
heart for the islands was at work in his mind; little did he
know then, however, of the island-going life which was to
follow and the path which was to lead to North Rona as a
worthy goal.

The amalgam of desires for life in small uninhabited islands and for study in animal behaviour in the same setting
had provided motivation for going in the first place, and
sustained their enthusiasm, driving them on from one stage
to the next. The distant sight of Rona came at a time before
he had mapped out any such progress in his work from deer
to seabirds to seals; nevertheless it made him wish a wish that
he might one day go ashore on North Rona. Gradually,
throughout their years at Dundonnell, Chleirich, Lunga and
Tanera, North Rona became a lodestone in their family life:
the place where their work among the islands would find its
consummation.

Their journeys to Rona started as two of mine did later in
a fishery cruiser from Loch Broom and after a rough passage
they reached the shelter of the island and prepared to land on
12 July 1938.

> All the same, cold and rainy as it was that early morning, and
> wretched as I felt, that first close glimpse of Rona thrilled
> me. Here was the speck in the sea at last. A noble shape she
> was, of rounded hill and sheer cliff on the east, sloping away

116

to sea-level at the south-west; how green her mantle, and the band of white surf played along the black foot of her cliffs! I knew little more until I heard the engine bell ring for half speed, dead slow and then stop. We were in the east bay of Rona and my spirit rose above seasickness, for it is the wonder of that first view that has remained. My heart was full of sheer joy . . .

It was tremendous and awe-inspiring. The swarms of puffins, guillemots and razorbills circled like bees from the hive of the cliff; kittiwakes flashed white from every coign of the rock face which would hold a nest, and fulmar petrels glided silently on motionless wings like small monoplanes. Shags flew hither and thither, black and cumbrous compared with the grace of the smaller birds. The sound of it all was the most thrilling a bird watcher knows – the composite skirl of a million throats proclaiming that it is summer. All I could think in that moment of wonder was – and we are going to live here and know every bit of this place as if it were home. After all, it was home.[73]

Alasdair's first sight and memory of Rona, as described to me, was of Frank picking him out of his bunk where he had lain seasick all night and leading him up on deck: 'I was totally fascinated by that great west cliff and its teeming myriads of birds and the noise was like nothing I had ever heard before. My physical misery disappeared immediately.'

Of the eleven visits I made to North Rona between 1959 and 1967, one sticks out in my mind for its connection with Fraser Darling. The party embarked on HMS *Belton* (Lieut. I. P. Teesdale RN) at Ullapool. We found the ship's company licking their wounds from the night previous when they had made passage from the east coast through the Pentland Firth and round Cape Wrath. They had had a flirtation with the Maids o' Mey, the savage overfalls in the Pentland Firth caused by the tide running against the gale; the crockery had been smashed and most of the drawers emptied on to the deck. However, the 'citadel' was ship-shape again and the oncoming watch were refreshed and ready to go. *Belton* was a coastal minesweeper assigned to fishery protection duties and a fast if rather light vessel, capable of darting quickly the 100 miles to North Rona and back between the storms and manned by a young, daring crew. However, on this occasion for a reason which was to become known later, the Captain seemed particularly keen to meet the challenge and with all our gear securely stowed, we left Ullapool before dawn and made for Stornoway passing Chleirich on the way. On entering the harbour, Lieut. Teesdale drove the minesweeper into the middle of the basin in front of the Town Hall, turned her in her own length and backed her into a neat berth between a trawler and a coaster with inches to spare. Very nice 'longside, and there on the quayside was a tall, well-dressed man clutching a briefcase. He could have been mistaken for the archetypal bureaucrat, Mr Bowler Hat. In fact, he was Geordie Leslie, now Rear-Admiral (retired) and then Captain of the Fishery Protection Squadron, joining the *Belton* for the North Rona trip. As 'Captain Fish' he had to approve the use of one of his ships to take the Nature Conservancy expedition to the island and being himself available at the time made sure of fulfilling an ambition he had had since first visiting Frank and Bobbie on Tanera in 1941; later he made the drawing of Tigh an Quay which adorned the wall at Shefford Woodlands House and became the frontispiece of *Island Farm*.

The passage to Rona and the landing all went well until we assembled our radio. We did everything according to the book but the transmitter remained dead. While we were getting our camp established with the help of the sailors, and the ship did a local fishery patrol, Geordie visited the ruined village and chapel and had a good look at the seals. Finally he entered the sheep fank where the Fraser Darlings had their huts in 1938–39 to discover that we, as they, had radio trouble. Geordie sized up the situation. The ship was about five miles distant to the east and the sun was bright to the south. 'Have you a mirror? Let's try for the R E M on *Belton*,' he said. 'Er, no, at least I don't think, in fact, I'm pretty sure we haven't,' I replied in a bit of a quandary. He walked over to a pile of paraphernalia, lifted a biscuit tin lid and a hazel stick. 'What are the odds on my getting the R E M?' he said with an air of great certainty. He got no takers as he jammed the hazel stick in the east corner of the fank and stuck himself into the west corner with a good angle to the sun. The stick was the sight of the heliograph and before settling on it, the bright reflection from the tin lid danced merrily all round the fank walls. 'R E M – R E M – R E M' he signalled with us all agog. Almost immediately, the ship winked a brief but brilliant reply and within thirty minutes we walked down to

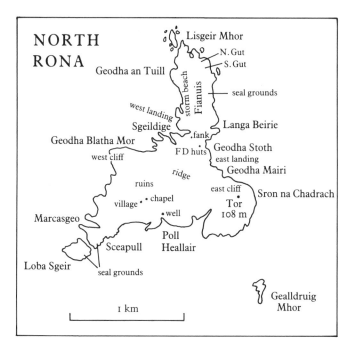

NORTH RONA

Lisgeir Mhor

N. Gut

S. Gut

Geodha an Tuill

storm beach

Fianuis

seal grounds

west landing

Sgeildige

Langa Beirie

Geodha Blatha Mor

.fank

west cliff

F D huts

Geodha Stoth

east landing

Geodha Mairi

ridge

ruins

east cliff

Sron na Chadrach

village • • chapel

Tor
108 m

• well

Marcasgeo

Poll
Heallair

Sceapull

Loba Sgeir

seal grounds

Gealldruig
Mhor

1 km

meet the incoming boat and who should be first off – the
Radio Electric Mechanic! Both sailors and landsmen alike
thought this a truly impressive performance and it was
capped by the REM having our transmitter sorted out and
working in no time.

North Rona lies 75 km north-west of Cape Wrath; it is 120
ha in extent and rises to a height of 116 m. It is approximately
triangular in shape and comprises a central ridge running
north-east to south-east with sheer terminal precipices and
two low promontories sloping off to the north and south-
west. The former is called Fianuis and the latter Sceapull and
these are the areas upon which the grey seals haul from the
sea in great numbers to breed. A steep, green north-facing
hill sweeps up from Fianuis to the central ridge and the
broad southern side of the island is a grassy slope upon which
is placed, towards the west end, the ruins of chapel and
village. In 1980–81 a lighthouse was built on the summit of

119

Plate 6.1. North Rona in summer, showing a meadow of thrift, the ruined bothy on Fianuis (these are seal grounds in autumn), the east bay and Toa Rona, 108 m (now the site of a lighthouse). (photo J. Morton Boyd)

the island in the south-east and although this is unmanned the sequestered, undisturbed quality of the island has been shattered – one of the costs of the oil boom in Shetland and Orkney with navigational aids for tankers.

Rona is rich in antiquities. Among the ruins stands St Ronan's cell built, it is thought, by a hermit monk who may have moved there from Eoropaidh in the north of Lewis in the eighth or ninth century and may have had a direct connection with a monastery on Iona. The cell is an oratory with an altar and may stand today unaltered from the time of its origins. Built on to it is a small church which is probably medieval and was used as a place of worship until the departure of the last family in 1844. The oratory opened into the chapel but it is possible that, over the centuries, the floors of both buildings had been raised by soil and straw so that to enter the oratory from the chapel, a man had to crawl on hands and knees. Alasdair remembers being let down into the oratory, from a hole in the roof before the entrance was cleared, to ring young fulmars, being covered with their oily regurgitate and reeking of it for days afterwards. Frank spent many happy hours excavating the oratory and also rebuilding the wall and door to the chapel. When uncovering the altar, he discovered a shaped piece of serpentine which he believed must have been brought there from Iona (by St Ronan himself?). In his pocket Frank carried some pebbles from Iona to Rona and before he took the stone he placed these pebbles on the altar in its place. This stone was presented by him to the Nature Conservancy Council and is now on display in the NCC's office in Inverness. Surrounding the church ruins there is a burial ground with rude headstones. One modern imported stone commemorates the death of two Lewismen, Malcolm McDonald and M. McKay, on 18 February 1895. Some of the stones are roughly shaped crosses and have been moved from time to time since they appear in different positions in different photographs in books; one cross had three holes in it and is shown well in Harvie Brown and Buckley *A Vertebrate Fauna of the Outer Hebrides* but had disappeared by the Fraser Darlings' time.

> *Friday, July 29th.* . . . I regret to say that North Rona has not escaped from vandalism and petty pilfering. In 1885, in Harvie Brown's photograph, there was a cross with three holes in it in position west of the chapel. As far as I can make out it was still there in 1932 . . . Now it has gone.[74]

Tradition has it that 'The Rona Stone' was taken to Eoropaidh chapel in Lewis, probably in the mid-1930s and from there it has been lost – Cleopatra's Needle has at least been cared for!

Immediately to the south of the graveyard there is a cluster of roofless dwellings, faired to the hillside with thick walls of turf over stone and tunnel entrances. One, probably rebuilt by the unfortunate Lewismen in 1884, has a gable with fireplace and chimney, door and window spaces. The largest house has a group of four chambers, one large and rectangular and three small and rounded, with two tunnel entrances and some of the chambers connected with low passages. The building probably contained dwelling house, barn and byre within the same mound of stones and turf. Another small building at the extreme western edge of the village was most certainly a granary; it contains a fine corn kiln.

These ruins are set in some 12 ha of *feannagan* or lazy-beds which provided the families with their grain harvest. These are cultivation ridges in which systems of parallel ridges of soil with intervening ditches are created to improve drainage and tilth, and result in a corrugated landscape. It would be possible for only a part of the area to be tilled by the men using the *cas-chrom* each year and the crops were very exposed to both weather and sea spray. That part not in grain would produce hay, and both oats and hay were probably stacked in little yards in the lea of the houses. The whole cultivated area is enclosed within a head dyke which was probably maintained in a sufficiently good state to exclude hill stock. There is a well below the chapel which goes dry in summer, when that at the cliff edge above Poll Heallair still gives issue, tasting of peat with a touch of the sea. A bothy on Fianuis is of different construction to the village house and may have been built by the unfortunate Lewismen or seal hunters in the second half of last century. Low walls on Fianuis may not be related to grazings but to turf cuttings for fuel since this area has been substantially skinned of its turf.

Frank's diary of the first days on Rona in July 1938 confirm it as the place they expected it to be; the anticipated climax of the hard journey through the islands had arrived.

> *Thursday, July 14th.* I woke at 5 o'clock to brilliant sunlight and to the sound of the thousands of seabirds. In fact there is always the sound of birds here; few people can have lived in such close proximity to an immense population of birds like this one. Nearest to us, only twenty yards away, is the bank above the tunnel cave of Sgeildige, inhabited by many puffins and a few fulmar petrels. These birds are quite tame and do not attempt to fly away as we walk by them. How solemn and important these puffins look with their great bibulous noses, grey cheeks, black mantles and white waistcoats. They stand upright in large companies, like a lot of longshoremen on a harbour front. Some toddle up and down and others take a short fly over the sea and back again. If the weather is very bad they go down their burrows, and if they have young down there, they are often busy flying out to sea to catch numbers of tiny, silvery fish which they bring back in their big beaks, all tails lying out and down one way. You would think when they came back the birds would make straight for the youngster, to deliver the fish as it were, but no, they often stand about the mouth of the burrow for a few minutes with

122

Plate 6.2. Puffins nested close to the Fraser Darlings on North Rona: 'the puffins would come down about us looking solemn and important with their bibulous noses, grey cheeks, black coats and white waistcoats.' (photo J. Morton Boyd)

their catch in their beaks. What *are* puffins thinking about all the time?

There is a storm beach of boulders, shingle and little pockets of white sand, lying on top of the cliffs and stretching northwards from us for more than half the length of Fianuis, the northern peninsula of Rona, and Fianuis means 'witness' or 'lookout'. This storm beach holds an important place in the ecology of North Rona because it provides habitats for two species of birds which are not found breeding elsewhere on the island, and were it not for the storm beach, would probably not be here at all. These are the Arctic tern and the black guillemot or tystie. The terns, of which there are a hundred to a hundred and fifty, breed as a colony on the south end of the storm beach, i.e., at the place nearest us and only 50 to 100 yards away. They keep up a perpetual chittering scream and if we go near they swoop at us and occasionally actually strike with their feet. Although I know they are not likely to hurt me seriously, these birds make me duck sharply as they swoop at me. I have tried to take photographs of them in flight and I find they are much faster in movement than the herring gulls which I was taking in flight last year. The terns lay their spotted eggs on the bare ground and they are extremely difficult to find on this broken ground which holds so many speckled pebbles of hornblende gneiss. The

123

black guillemots nest underneath the boulders a little further north on the storm beach and there will be fifty to seventy of them, quiet douce folk and great friends of mine. And to complete this natural orchestra which is constantly playing there is the great concourse of guillemots and kittiwakes to the south-east of us. They are never quiet.

Friday, July 15th. Another brilliant morning which got me out of bed in fine fettle soon after six o'clock. We had some tea and then went out to take some photographs of the guillemot and kittiwake colonies which are in the geo a hundred yards or more to the south-east of us. Then breakfast and out again with a colour film to see what we could do, both at the birds and the scenery. The surf was as big as ever though the sea had now calmed and the view of Fianuis from the hill was magnificent. We finished off the colour film on the Chapel and ruins and views of the south-west corner – Loba Sgeir – which looked well with the sun on it from behind us and the surf breaking on the low rocks there.

The three of us went down to explore that south-west corner this afternoon after we had dug some garden among the ruins and planted cabbage plants and sprouted potatoes. It must be one of the barest places in Scotland, this low, serrated expanse of rock. It gets at you in the same way as does that great face of quartzite which slopes down into Gleann an Nid at the head of Strath na Sheallag. For the first time I felt the remoteness of Rona and the wild strength of the place. As I sat on this bare rock I felt very acutely what a frail hold a single human family has, living alone on a small island. Times before I have realized the physical limitations of one family containing only one man – there are so many things you just cannot do – but here I saw the elemental strength of wind and water, and I was awed. Bobbie was wanting away from the place, but I felt it good to sit around for a while and dwell on my own insignificance. I have noticed it before, on the top of a mountain in mist, and I thought of it here, a whole lot of stuffing goes out of you when the ground beneath your feet becomes devoid of any vegetation. That thin green carpet of more simple life which clothes the earth is a thing of untold comfort. Our place is above it, and when we are on a great place of bare rock, we also are naked and of little consequence.

Tuesday, July 19th. A week on Rona today. It has been a full and happy one. Tonight I climbed over the hill to the water hole, the sea and island wrapped in mist as it has been all day long. It was almost a silent world at the top of the hill for the mist blankets the sound of all below. A few terns were screaming overhead and the blackbacks hovered about, crying raucously. The chapel and the low ruins appeared out of the mist as I went down the other side and the sheep leapt over the lazy-beds. These ruins of Rona, quiet in the sea mist, how poignant they are. The world has forgotten Rona and her Chapel raised to Christ. The ancient race starved to death and their history is lost. But the sea mist and the birds maintain the greenness of Rona and the world would be poorer without this little isle, remote as it is. The breath of Iona is in it.

Then I turned back from the water hole to the thicker mist at the top again and as I came down the northern slope the black rocks of the west side of Fianuis and the white surf playing on them came dimly into view. The shape of the peninsula became plainer as I came down and the sea rumbled louder. This is Rona weather and beauty is in it . . .

Wednesday, July 20th. . . . I saw another very wonderful thing this afternoon. There was a flock of about two thousand kittiwakes closely massed on the island skerry at the north end of Fianuis; a pretty enough sight as they were like that, but when all of them suddenly took to the air and of necessity fanned out to give themselves flying room, it was a vision prodigal in its loveliness. It was like a gigantic unfolding of resting life into brilliant animation. Perhaps two seconds after the birds took to the air, they began calling. Even a single kittiwake can make a lot of noise with the cry which gives the bird its name, but when two thousand throats cry out together, I stand in wonder. The sound is like a paean of praise. Our bare northern islands often produce these moments of spontaneous exuberance and, in the right sense of the word, magnificence.[75]

These early days on Rona were full of magic for the Fraser Darlings. They were intoxicated with the sheer beauty of the island; nothing in it seemed to jar and no amount of wind, rain or discomfort took the edge off their enjoyment. To be bemisted was a state of exhilaration and not of melancholy. Every moment was different in the mood of the island of which they quickly became a part by adjusting almost intuitively to storm and sunshine, feeling themselves as carefree as the seabirds. Frank clearly let himself go in his conversations with the birds and seals he met on his rounds of the island even more so than on Chleirich and Lunga. His mind was gripped tight by a sense of history by which, remembering the descriptions of Monro and Martin, he could put roofs back on the clachan amid a haze of turf smoke and see the place alive with short, dark people. Beyond that he had a vision of the Iona connection, of which there is no record other than the stones of St Ronan's ancient cell into which he read the connection. It is a haunted place. I have stood alone in the tiny oratory in a great gale; the air inside was still but outside the wind tore at the rough, lichen-covered stones like a demon, such that I heard many whispering voices in the walls. It was as if all who had worshipped there over the centuries of its being, had returned and were seeking entrance.

Through July and August, day followed day, with a rapture of physical and spiritual well-being. Their interest and energies were first applied to the seabirds for they had arrived at the height of the nesting and there was hardly a direction in which they could turn without coming across birds sitting on eggs, brooding chicks or flying close-by with a swish of wings. Their main aim was not to continue the detailed study of synchrony of breeding with colony size as had been the aim on Chleirich with the gulls but to measure the size of the breeding assemblies, make general observations of the natural history of all species, especially the storm and Leach's petrels, take photographs of them and observe the passage of migratory birds through the island.

The counting of the seabirds took them into every corner of the island to which it was safe to go without mountaineering tackle, and this meant that they quickly got to know the island in detail and enriched their knowledge of the birds and their habitat. Frank estimated that there were at least 100,000 puffins, about 25,000 guillemots of which 13 per cent were 'bridled' (possessing eye-ring and stripe), 1,500 razorbills, at least 600 pairs of fulmars, 500 pairs of greater black-backed gulls, 100 to 150 pairs of Arctic terns and 50 to 70 pairs of black guillemots. They were unable to count kittiwakes and small petrels or even to provide an informed guess as to how many of those were present.

The expeditions to Chleirich and Lunga had brought the family in contact with the night-flying petrels, which nest in rock crevices and burrows and remain there silent and motionless in daylight hours. After dark the partner birds arrive from sea, perform their nuptials or brood exchanges and depart back to sea in darkness. The benighted island is in

126

Plate 6.3. Bridled guillemot on North Rona. Frank found
that about 13% of the island's guillemots were bridled.
(photo F. Fraser Darling)

bedlam. Chleirich had storm petrels; Lunga stormies and Manx shearwaters and North Rona, stormies and Leach's fork-tailed petrels. It was the Leach's which Frank was keen to meet following the discoveries of two young naturalists, Ainslie and Atkinson, who had hitch-hiked to Rona on a drifter in 1936 and spent four weeks on the island. He wished above all to obtain flash photographs of flying petrel and succeeded (see Plate Xa in *Island Farm*).

> *Saturday, 23rd July.* A rather subdued party of three [Fraser Darlings] set out about midnight for the village, wrapped up extraordinarily and carrying cameras, lenses, electric flashlight gear and so on. The wind was moderate from the s.w., and it was good to get into the shelter of the main house. By half past twelve several petrels had come and were flitting about. Then more came in rapid succession and those already in the burrows in the drystone walls began to sing in an ascending trill which was most pleasant to hear. It seemed to me that more petrels gathered about the place immediately after these trillings. Soon the birds in the air began to scream, but this was no unpleasant sound. It was a succession of ten or a dozen notes in a definite cadence and of varying pitch. I let go two flashlight bulbs in an attempt to get a picture of the birds in flight. This is an expensive business, but one good photo of this rare, nocturnal bird in flight would pay for the apparatus I have bought for this job.
>
> We came outside the ruins and the village was full of these silent-flying but otherwise noisy birds. Their speed of flight is amazing and the nature of it, erratic. Here, there and everywhere, the dark shapes flitted, and sound came from the air and the ground all about us. How exciting it was for the three of us! We flashed the torch into one hole from which the trilling sound was coming and we saw the black eye of the petrel, its lovely, darkly-shaded grey face and the shiny black bill with the nostrils in a tube above it.
>
> The three of us stood silent a while longer, watching this beautiful and little-known phenomenon of the northern summer night. St Kilda, the Flannans and Rona; after these you must go to Iceland or Greenland, the Labrador coast and the Aleutian Islands in the northern Pacific Ocean.
>
> We reached home again by a quarter to two. Alasdair went to bed with a warm drink and, while Bobbie was making a cup of tea for us, I went over to the little drystone hut on Fianus where I thought I saw the petrels flying. The fork-tailed petrels were there too and in the eastern side of the storm beach . . .

128

Sunday, 24th July. So good was the night and light with it that I ought not to miss going over to the petrels again at the village. Bobbie insisted on coming with me. We set out at 12.30 a.m. not having lain down for a rest beforehand and we didn't feel so dead as the night before. Alasdair did not go with us tonight, either. There seemed even more petrels flying tonight but there was not the same amount of trilling from the birds in the burrows. Was it fancy made both Bobbie and I think that the birds flew lower and more silently when the big black-backs flew overhead? There is no doubt that those brigands do get some of the petrels, both stormies and fork-tailed. We heard one or two stormies purring in the ruins as well tonight.

As I was going about trying to take photographs of the birds in flight, with the electric flash apparatus on my camera, it seemed to me that the birds had their own routes of flight. I cannot say definitely that this is so, but at intervals of seven to ten seconds a bird came over the same place with a similar pattern of flight. Sometimes the birds' paths would cross and we saw several collisions in mid-air. One of them brushed my cheek with its wing and often I felt the wind of their flight in my hair. I used six large size flash bulbs, having set the focus of the camera to 7 feet for three and 12 feet for the other three – stop f.8 and speed 1/200th second. I am literally working in the dark this time, with this tackle, and I shan't know the results I have got until Christmas or later. This is the hardest thing in photography I have tried so far. One good picture will repay me well for a dozen flash bulbs and the electric apparatus. But more than repayment, I shall be pleased as I have rarely been pleased.

We came back to the hut soon after two o'clock and the storm petrels in the dykes round us were making more noise than I have ever heard from them before. As we lay in bed before going to sleep it was absolutely grand to listen to this most comfortable of sounds and to the occasional staccato cries of fork-tailed petrels as they flew round the hut from the storm beach . . .[76]

Every day brought its migrant birds as a surprise and delight. They added twenty-four new species to the bird list for the Island which now stands at some 120 species. White wagtails, wheatears, turtle doves, ringed plovers, golden plovers, a green sandpiper, little stints, greenshanks, redshanks, dunlin, swallows, and a hen harrier brought peace and enjoyment to the family in isolation.

129

7

North Rona and the Seals

If the huts in the fank in Fianuis were home to the family, they regarded the ruined village as a holy place to which they came back again and again to ponder. These circuits of the island in the bird study took them through the ruins which were eye-catching and an endless source of mystery and wonder. As often as not they would tarry in contemplation. The ruined chapel with its collapsed doorway was crying out for rebuilding, which aroused Frank's flair for drystane dyking. It is natural, therefore, that if anything might heighten further the enjoyment of life on Rona, it would be a bit of needful drystane masonry and thus they set their hearts on the rebuilding of the fallen southern wall of the chapel which contained the door and the only window – the results of which are well illustrated in *A Naturalist on Rona*, Plate 9.

> Wednesday 27th July . . . It has struck me that as there is this photograph extant, showing the place in better state of preservation than at present, I should be justified in clearing away the pile of fallen stone and with the utmost care rebuilding the fallen portion which can be seen in its original state in Harvie-Brown's photograph. Today, therefore, I went forth on this delicate task. First I had to clear the stone from the work and I had to shift a lot of loose earth before I could get the true line of the foundations. I was puzzled to find that the portion of the wall of the south side which was east of the doorway was much thicker than that west of the door. If I built up on that it would make a great bulge. Fortunately, I had taken Harvie-Brown's book with me and on referring to the picture I found that the bulge had actually been part of the Chapel . . .
>
> The main wall went up as far as the lintel at the doorway. I had found a great, broad stone under the door when clearing the work, and there was no doubt that it was the original

130

Plate 7.1. The erection of the huts in the sheep fank on the neck of Fianuis in 1938. (photo Fraser Darling Collection)

lintel. It was too heavy for me to lift into position, so I lifted each end in turn and Alasdair put stones underneath. Thus I got it to the height, just above my middle, and then, by putting all behind it, I lifted it bodily into position. It sat perfectly. This was a strange thing about the whole job – I hardly ever handled a stone twice and the wall went up at a surprisingly fast rate. Bobbie came in the afternoon and helped with the middle filling. We had built to a height of over 6′ by the time we stopped at half past five. Standing back and looking at the work, I was glad to see that it would not be easy to tell the difference between my walling and the original.[77]

By the end of July the seabird season was nearing its end and a transition was taking place in their interests from seabirds to seals. On 9 August came the first dramatic change with the departure *en masse* of the guillemots; the shoulder to shoulder throngs on the airy cliff ledges were suddenly gone. Next day, the puffins departed; no longer were their burrowed tenements full of stuffed white shirts, morning coats and expensive noses. Gradually thereafter the other species departed throughout August and as they did so Frank's atten-

131

Plate 7.2. Frank standing by the doorway of St Ronan's chapel, North Rona, after he and Bobbie had rebuilt the doorway; behind him is the wall they rebuilt and the roof of the cell. (photo Fraser Darling Collection)

tion became more and more fixed on the seals, since he knew that a rather dramatic sequence of events was likely in August which would signal the onset of seal breeding. This was the time for which he had waited ever since he started thinking about Ron Mor, and Rona would provide what Lunga lacked – a large assembly of many thousands and the invasion of the island (not just the shore) by the seals.

It is perhaps a perfectly natural tendency that when a human being with the sensitivities and intellectual gifts of Frank is placed in close contact with nature, his mind should react very positively to what he sees. The reaction of sympathy with fellow creatures is common among animal lovers and the feelings which Frank had for the seals might be no different from that of Robert Burns for the field-mouse; yet the extent to which Frank's mind – and heart – reacted was unusual. The blatant use which he makes of his observations on seal behaviour in comparing it with human behaviour is illustrated well by his description of young seals below his camp.

> *Tuesday, 9th August* . . . These young bulls are playful lads. Sometimes they are a bit rough to each other and even to the young cows which are along with them. It seems to me that bull seals outside the breeding season, and particularly a lot of young bull seals, prefer at times a monastic sort of existence and I suspect the psycho-biological foundation to be very much the same in seals and men or boys. I don't think even sociologists have realized the deep-lined biological foundation of uni-sexual associations within societies.
>
> When young females come into these male groups of seals, the normal courteous relations between bull and cow (on the bull's side only, I should emphasize) are suspended. The young bulls might not be quite so rough with them as with their own sex, but a young cow is likely to get snarled off a rock, prevented from getting out of the water or get a snap or a scratch. I have watched this kind of thing happening, and especially this morning, and sometimes the young cow loses her temper and flounces out of the way. This kind of behaviour can be very funny to watch. You get comparable conditions in human society; for example, in a set of mixed tennis there is a tacit agreement not to discriminate, and if a girl joins a climbing party, assuming she is worth her salt, she is apt to get cross if she is obviously given preferential treatment or is shielded from hardship. Occasionally, girls get cross at not receiving special treatment and when they

133

flounce away are very much like my little cow seal who couldn't get out on the rock because of those rough fellows who were treating her as one of themselves. I believe our human behaviour in such circumstances to be only a development and refinement of the primitive behaviour I see among the seals. Indeed, these seals are a parody of human nature.[78]

On 16 August Frank observed a large bull only one hundred yards from the hut and realised that this was the first bull taking up his territory further from the sea than any seal on Treshnish and that the invasion had begun. A month was to pass before the birth of the first pup on 14 September. In that time the life of the family was geared to causing as little disturbance as possible by careful movement about the island using stalking techniques when close to the seals and to observing the build-up in numbers of bulls and cows on the grounds.

During this time Frank wrote a diary and also a set of essays published as *A Naturalist on Rona*. The diary provides a bitty description of day-to-day dispositions of seals in the various parts of the grounds *with* numbers; the essay, 'Ron Mor: The Great Seal' gives a synopsis of the seal breeding at Rona *without* numbers. The following are contrasting treatments of diary and essay.

> *Monday 12th September* . . . Bobbie called my attention first thing to a big old bull lying up the hill little more than 50 yards from the huts. He was lying asleep with his head on a big cushion of sea pink. He did no more than turn over and sleep all day.
>
> I went north after breakfast and though I went full into the wind of the seals on Leac Mor, not one moved or raised its head. As I was crawling up the south gut I came near one of the brown pools from which two eyes were regarding me. Behind these large eyes was a round head. I moved on my way out of the gut over into the north gut and then looked back to see what was happening. The big bull continued to lie there, quietly looking up the way I had gone. When I got to the head of the north gut I skirted across the head of the south gut as well, thus giving the bull seal my wind 50 yards below. He remained quiet. It is evident that lying doggo is the reaction of these beasts when they come far up from the sea. I could never have learned this on the Treshnish Isles because the seals do not go far above high tide mark. These in the gut of Fianuis are 200 yards from the sea, and the one near the hut is quite 50 feet above the water . . .

134

Plate 7.3. A grey seal bull on North Rona, fresh from the sea.
(photo F. Fraser Darling)

Sunday, 18th September . . . Bobbie and I went northwards in
the morning and saw the bulls, cows and calves in the guts of
Fianuis. No new calves as far as we can see and all the cows
are in the north gut. There were one or two bulls lying about
on the green north of the guts and a bull was on the black,
peaty patch to the south. Things were pretty quiet. We went
to the north-west corner of Fianuis, between Geodha Thuill
and Lisgeir, and counted 170 seals lying out on the rocks – all
ages and sexes from yearlings upwards. They made a grand
sight and I took several photographs. I noticed one very light
grey adult bull; he was almost like a cow in colour. I also
noticed that several of the yearlings have those spotty rashes
on their chests and arms, and round the mouth. The spots
irritate and the little seals scratch them raw.

Down to Marcasgeo in the afternoon where I saw the hen
harrier again, and two herons flying about the south shore.
There was a bull seal lying at the top of the sheer 40 feet cliff
on the north side of Sceapull. It is evident that the seals do
breed there. The cows were out on their usual rock in Marcasgeo.

Northwards in the evening just before the darking. I am
struck here on Rona with the way the cows lie happy together
on the breeding grounds. That was never so on the Tresh-

135

nish. This evening, for example, I saw three cows actually touching each other as they lay, and a calf sucking one of them. There was a big bull in the cliff pool on the extreme west side of Fianuis, 50 feet above the sea. I shall call this the Kittiwake's pool because one young kittiwake stayed on it for several weeks.[79]

Frank wrote as a man inspired when he brought all of this experience together, within actual sight and calling of the seals. He believed that he possessed some means of communication with the seals which was neither supernatural nor superhuman, but which was rare and intuitive. In fact, those of us in seal research who came afterwards repeated much of what he did and obtained similar interactions which since have been described in scientific terms. Whether or not his communication with and interpretation of the seals was real or fanciful he knew that he was a pioneer, believed himself possessed of a gift of communication with wild creatures and expressed himself as he knew how, in a grand style!

But as I live longer in the lonely places of the islands there come moments of compensation. The great seals of Rona accept me as those of the Treshnish Isles never did. It has been grand and inspiring to go down to the sea's edge and see two or three hundred seals come racing through the water in joyful movements towards me. I have found ways to speak to them so that they are not afraid, but pleased. Those old bulls of great dignity remain on the outer ring of the group of faces, though one of the biggest of them will come close in. The cows are nearer to me, their expressions soft and inquisitive, but the yearling seals have the wondering faces of little children, and in their confidence they have come out of the water to my feet as I have sat there on the rock, using my voice in the way I have learned. That secret of the voice which will bring them is mine alone and will remain so, lest it should ever come to be misused. At these times I do not carry camera or binoculars for the seals do not like them; nor do other animals for that matter. One day I called a blind cow seal out of the sea and she came near until her muzzle was but a few inches from my face. She was unafraid and returned quietly to the sea. And now the mother seals are high on Rona near the door of our hut and our own child plays among them. They seem neither to resent nor fear, but to accept him as part of the indigenous fauna. The little calves themselves are more afraid than their mothers, and they will not play . . .

The seals which come ashore to breed in Geodha Stoth do

136

not make Leac Mhor their waiting-rock. They lie out on the ledges under the Tor and in Geodha Mairi. But an east or a north wind makes this impossible for them and they go over to the big skerry of Gealldruig Mhor, where they may stay until the wind gets round to its favourite airt of south-west. Then they come back again into the east bay of Rona, and I was once lucky in seeing the great joyful crowd return. They came back playfully, undulating through the surface-layer of the water in obvious enjoyment. A happy, romping people on the move, where the children could tease the old men with impunity; an ancient people in their ancient home, but not yet grown tired with civilization. The great seals are the people of the sea, and it is not to be wondered at that Gaeldom should have invested them with a half-veiled but occasionally irruptive humanity.[80]

The days were full of incidents of family life: the enjoyment of walking together on a day of great clarity to the top of the island; Bobbie's resourcefulness with meals and housekeeping; Alasdair's salon at which Frank played the harmonica, and Bobbie and Alasdair sang; making a boat for Alasdair; a game of rummy; visitors; nursing the wireless into life; fetching the water from the south side and a bag of wild mushrooms. The salon always ended with one or all of these three hymns: 'Lead Kindly Light', 'Now the Day is Over', and 'The Day Thou Gavest'. These were among Frank's favourites and were chosen for his Memorial Service at St Cuthbert's, Edinburgh. He liked particularly Cardinal Newman's 'Lead Kindly Light', his heart always responding to: 'O'er moor and fen, o'er crag and torrent . . . till the night is gone. One step enough for me'.

Frank had not long arrived on the island when he complained of bad dreams. These were portentous of a breakdown in the expedition. The first real jolt was the arrival of the fishery cruiser to take away Alasdair to school. They were clearly all very upset at this and their decision to keep him on the island did little to ease the stress. Frank was all for packing the boy off on the cruiser with no-one to meet him at Stornoway and see him safely to school in Moray; Bobbie refused to let him go in such circumstances, yet she could not go with him and leave Frank alone on Rona. The event showed how ill-prepared they were for this crucial event. They remained unhappy and silent all that day adjusting in their minds separately to the consequences of their decision.

However, they did not know then that within two weeks the whole family would be back at Dundonnell with Alasdair on his way to Gordonstoun. Courageously, they put the matter to the back of their minds and carried on with the work on the seals; Frank killed a young bull for dissection and they had a good meal of seal's liver and bacon. But on 29 September Frank's nightmare returned also as the 'second sight'. He dreamt that the cruiser would return to evacuate them and *was* relieved on awakening to realise it was only a bad dream; yet the 'Munich Crisis' was upon them though Chamberlain had not yet obtained that fateful piece of paper 'Peace in Our Time'!

My relief was short-lived, for we had not risen more than half an hour when the cruiser appeared off the east side of the island. I do not think I have ever felt my heart sink so completely as at that moment. We got the wireless receiver running and tuned in to our short wave-length. Cap'n M. was telling us to get ready to leave. All the same, there was a fresh south-easterly wind blowing and a deep swell coming in from the west, and I knew that he could never get us off just then. He said so himself the next minute, and we saw the ship move away. Splendid. With a bit of luck this normally wretched wind would hold and we should remain until the international situation cleared.

This again was false optimism, for Cap'n M. is a tenacious man. He was back again in an hour because the Atlantic swell was dropping a little – enough to let him lower a boat. On this occasion we held conversation with him in an effective manner, but one which reflects no credit on me, because I ought to have learned to transmit and receive signalling in Morse code with flags. I went on to the steep hill face with a pile of towels and my pyjamas. With these I spelt out letters and words on the green hillside, and the cruiser sounded a short blip on her siren after reading each letter. Bobbie was down at the hut receiving the spoken word from the cruiser on the wireless, and Alasdair was making liaison by running to and fro between us with the messages. No matter whether we wished to stay or not, we must go, and that quickly. Bobbie dropped a few necessities into two sleeping-bags while I tried to leave things shipshape about the camp. Our departure from Rona was that of destitute refugees. It was an almost hopeless task trying to catch our three hens in daylight on a bare island. One refused to be caught, and somebody dropped another going over to Langa Beirie where Cap'n M.

138

had brought the launch. The seals were disturbed and I was thoroughly unhappy.[81]

Of this unhappy time Alasdair writes to me: 'Frank was aware of his second sight particularly when working on the chapel, when he sensed that the Munich Crisis would pass. So certain was he of this that he nearly refused to leave Rona and it was only Captain M. saying that he could not promise to return if we refused to leave, that forced us to leave. I remember standing petrified against the wall of the hut at the thought that we might be stranded. In fact I was the first to see the *Vigilant* that morning, shouting to my parents in the next hut. What an awful feeling of let down.'

This was the worst possible luck, since, as I was to discover in my own expeditions to Rona in the sixties, Frank and Bobbie were compelled to leave the island about two weeks before the peak of the birth-rate of pups and, by the time they returned to the island on 23 November, the breeding season had largely run its course with numbers of seals declining as spent bulls and mated cows departed to sea and as the plump, sleak weaned pups also found their way offshore to disperse widely on the British coasts from Ireland to Shetland and Aberdeenshire and as far as the Faeroes, East Iceland and Norway. A Rona pup was found dead in East Iceland on 4 December 1960 about six weeks after it had been tagged on the island on 31 October.

What Frank did not know at that time, but what he feared, was the complete collapse of his plans for seal research – plans which had been drawn up patiently since he spied Rona that June day in 1934 from An Teallach. The false hope created by Chamberlain affected him as it did everyone in Britain who had any aspirations for a peaceful life and he returned with Bobbie to pick up the pieces and start where they had left off, hoping that the events of September 1938 were but a temporary setback. On 22 November the cruiser returned to Little Loch Broom and took them back to Rona in calm weather without Alasdair, then at Gordonstoun. They jumped ashore, ran up to the hut, found that all was well and waved-away the ship.

> We had not time to realize this new Rona to which we had come, but even as I was climbing up those slippery rocks I noticed a pair of long-tailed duck and the fact that hundreds of fulmar petrels were flying from the cliffs. We waded

139

through a sea of mud and grumbly seals, saw a couple of seals among our tinned stores under the upturned coble and another one on the doorstep. The seals had brought down the wireless masts and were romping through the wire entanglements which had once been the stays . . .

And now we came to consider the abomination of desolation. The place and mess were indescribable, but one thing pleased us – our two hens were alive and apparently well, uninterested in the food which we almost immediately offered them. No doubt this immense concourse of seals and the number of dead calves made a plentiful supply of food for birds . . .

Those acres of Fianuis which had been lush fields of chickweed in the summer were now a sea of mud. The place was black in the dull daylight of winter. The northern face of the hill was a vast black slide down which we could see several seals making their way at a great pace. We climbed up there with difficulty to fetch water from the well on the south side and had the surprise of seeing seals on the top of the ridge, three hundred feet above the sea. It was altogether amazing. There was another young seal at the extreme edge of the sheer west cliff, one which a few days later I saw fall the three hundred feet to its death. There were seals young and old round the edge of Geodha Leis, a terribly dangerous place, because if they take the hundred-foot jump into the sea they are liable to fall on rocks which are just covered down there. One day I saw a big bull seal go down when he was chased by another, and he just burst when he hit those rocks. I was thoroughly upset by this event, because I felt it need not have happened . . .

Bobbie and I covered the island that first day, and by the end of the second had counted 850 live seals and 150 dead ones. All the first lot which were calves when we left at the end of September were away to sea now. My Treshnish estimate of infant mortality was about 10 per cent, so I reckoned there must have been 1,500 calves born on Rona. That means a total population of seals about the place of roughly 5,000, a figure I also estimated by actual counting.[82]

After that first day back, the five weeks until they were taken off on 22 December 1938 were an unending struggle against the elements; it was as though they were living in a wind-tunnel. The storms followed each other in quick succession with ominous short spells of calm bright weather between, in which the island was swathed in raging seas and far-flung spume. The island was clad in wet withered grass.

Plate 7.4. Grey seals in heavy surf in Langa Beirie, North Rona, typical of scenes described by Frank after great storms. (photo M. E. Ball, NCC).

The surface of Fianuis was a bare expanse of rock and mud littered with remains of dead seals too large or too tough for the gulls to dismember. The cliffs were deserted by their great concourses of breeding seabirds, full of the gaiety of nesting, mating and the feeding of exuberant young. Gone also were the little churring petrels from their comfortable shadow seats in the crevices of the drystone works and storm beach. The floral charm of summer and the drama of the seals in autumn were but a memory. It was difficult to see it as the same place; yet, when the calm spell came with its sunshine, Rona was restored to its symphonic self – a place of superlative marriage of earth and sea and sky. Even at night in the starlight, the phantom play of the aurora borealis above the wide ocean brought a shiver to the spine.

Sadly this was to be Frank's last contact with the seals. Had he been able to live through the entire season with them as he had planned, then he would have had the full story; as it was this chance had been lost and the attachment to the seal work which he had before their compulsory evacuation was not there on their return. He sensed the loss, hoped that the opportunity would come again but realised that this could only be so by enduring all over again the storms and tribulations of isolation as well as the joys. It was, however, to a great extent the end of the island-going journey, the reaching of the *ultima thule* and it is disappointing that they should have failed to complete the pages of the natural history of the grey seal which they set out to write.

Frank's mind was not done with seals, far from it. Whether or not they would have had a re-run in 1939 of their arrangements for 1938 is uncertain, though they did return in June 1939 to retrieve equipment they had left behind at Christmas 1938. However, he now saw a greater opportunity which employed much of the knowledge he had gained in Treshnish and Rona, but extended it greatly. After all, the gap in his experience due to his absence from Rona in October 1938 did not invalidate the fact that Rona held the largest known breeding assembly of *Halichoerus grypus* in existence, that the island was inhabited by the seals for three to four months of the year and at other times they were dispersed, presumably to other parts of the British coasts. 'Where did the Rona seals go in spring and summer?' That is the question which dominated Frank's mind. Only by having a knowledge of this could a national plan for seal conservation be hatched. He noticed phenotypic differences between the seals of Treshnish and those of Rona, which he took to indicate different stocks in a large single biogeographical population living in Scottish waters. This led him to believe that the separate breeding assemblies among the Scottish Islands were isolated biologically at breeding time, but at other times the seals from different breeding stations probably shared the same coastal areas.

During these stormy December days of 1938 on North Rona Frank had in mind an itinerant survey of the grey seal in which he would follow the migration of the seals to and from the breeding grounds. He planned to obtain a grant to purchase a 40-foot Fifie and, with Kenneth MacDougal and Bobbie as his crew, sail the coastal seas in north-west Britain observing seals or the lack of them. How he intended to identify animals from North Rona among others from Orkney or Harris he never said, and since then adult grey seals have only recently been successfully marked with the use of tranquilising drugs. Many thousands of pups have been tagged and branded since Frank's time but, due to the tags disappearing before the seals became adult and the brand-marks becoming distorted in the growth of the animal, evidence of the movements which Frank aspired to research has been very hard to obtain over thirty years by successive teams of workers. Most pups seem to return to the assembly of birth, but a cow branded on Rona as a pup in the sixties was found nursing a pup on the Monach Isles, North Uist in the seventies. There was also the problem of Frank's sea-sickness; his journals of sea-going speak of consistent prostration and helplessness, not of a Fifie skipper sharing the north-western seas with seals. He went as far as visiting the boat builders in St Monance, admiring greatly both the craft and the craftsmen, but the project was abandoned at the outbreak of war and Frank's last contact with the seals as an original researcher was on 22 December 1938 when he and Bobbie left snow-covered North Rona.

> The snow settled the weather, and three days before Christmas we rose to a calm sea and a white, frozen Rona. It came light just after nine o'clock in the morning when we had climbed to the summit cairn on the Tor. Never had we seen the view so magnificent as on this which was to be our last morning. The sun was rising behind the far, clean line of the Sutherland hills and tinted the whole of our snowy world a rosy pink. The atmosphere was clear and still, and even as we watched I spied a dot thirty miles away between Cape Wrath and the Butt of Lewis. A ship undoubtedly, the first we had seen for a month. The dot was certainly coming nearer, and it must be the cruiser coming for *us*.
>
> The two gale-battered folk of twenty-four hours ago became two carefree children . . .[83]

8

Tanera Mor

Old Dornie is a sheltered little harbour on the south side of Rubha Mor Coigach. This was to be my take-off point for the Summer Isles where, in a day, I planned to visit Frank's haunts on Chleirich and Tanera. As I drove by Strathcanaird and Loch Lurgain to the sea in rain and wind, I was sure that conditions would prevent putting to sea and this was confirmed by the bleak prospect of the scatter of dark bemisted isles which awaited my arrival at Badentarbat. Across the bay I could just see Chleirich as a shadow through the rain and, much nearer, Tanera Mor with its sprinkling of houses and in the midst the old walls of Tigh an Quay, the site of Fraser Darling's island farm of the early forties.

At last the twisting road gave me the signpost to Old Dornie and soon I was confronted with a score of little boats safely tucked away from the stormy blast, that is, all but one of Orcadian breed, the *Peedie Lass*, which stood by the stump of a jetty. I was soon aboard and, somewhat to my surprise, on my way to Chleirich. The skipper, Lyon White, was a retired banker, but could have been mistaken for a man who had spent his whole life at sea. His little boat was trim with a beautifully tuned engine which throbbed at our feet. On being welcomed aboard a mug of hot coffee was thrust into my hand and sipping it pensively I chatted to my four fellow-travellers, all, for one reason or another, deeply interested in the Summer Isles and Fraser Darling.

When we emerged into the open sea from the narrows of Caolas Eilein Ristol it was obvious to me that wind and sea would indeed prevent us reaching Priest Island. Once among the cluster of the inner Summer Isles we would be protected but the six-mile passage of totally exposed water didn't look good for the *Peedie Lass*. I was not surprised therefore when,

Plate 8.1. Tigh an Quay at low tide in 1981, showing the quay which Frank and Bobbie rebuilt, the walls of the old fishing station and their hut still in position. Behind is the Irish park with trees and the land they cultivated.
(photo J. Morton Boyd)

with our boat bumping heavily and in drenching spray, Lyon came beside me. 'Doctor, she'll take us to Chleirich alright but we'll be in some state when we get there – and there's the gettin' back!'

Right enough, with no sign of any slackening in the storm and the anxieties of getting there and back, putting us ashore and retrieving us in trying conditions, it was a foolhardy ploy on such a day. We all knew it and stifled our disappointment. There was always a chance that conditions would be better tomorrow, and today we could visit Tanera. The heading then was for Tigh an Quay.

As always, disappointment took a bit of the heart out of us, leaving us with our own thoughts for a few moments. I turned over in my mind the sickness and disappointment in

145

previous expeditions when, after perhaps six months of active preparation in 1954, I failed to reach both North Rona and Gasker, in 1956 Shillay (Harris) and 1958 North Rona. This occasion was slight in comparison with these.

With the gale on her starboard quarter the *Peedie Lass* went bowling towards Tanera Mor, the conversation was rekindled and spying the broad band of wrack exposed on the on-coming shore, Lyon White began to have his doubts if he would be able to land us at Tigh an Quay. However, there was still three hours of ebb to go and we were just able to put the bows of the boat to the end of the quay; with the help of a rope we scaled the stonework which the Fraser Darlings had restored so laboriously during their stay. Suddenly, I had a deep sense of the presence of Frank. The times without number he had talked to me of Tigh an Quay made it natural that I should feel that I had been there before and that Frank himself was about the place. I could imagine exactly his tall dark figure coming through the arch just as he had done to welcome me on many occasions at Shefford Woodlands House or Lochyhill when, of course, he was much less physically fit.

I was delighted to see that a hut still stood on the site where Frank and Bobbie erected theirs in 1940 and was now occupied by the farm manager and his family. On this day of wind and rain they were all at home with what seemed to be both sets of in-laws and a few friends all on their summer holidays. Nevertheless, we were bade 'come in' in true Highland style, 'take off your wet things' and have mugs of steaming coffee and biscuits. The discussion centred on the Fraser Darlings and other occupants and occupations of Tanera. I was interested to learn that the hut was indeed the extended dwelling used by Frank, Bobbie and Alasdair and to see the interior in what must have been a very similar state to their home when they moved out of the old schoolhouse near the cliff-edge. They disliked the schoolhouse and relished the greater comfort of their hut at Tigh an Quay. Frank extolled the magnificence of the view from the windows.

> It was 20th February [1940], a day we were due to go to Eilean a' Chleirich with the crofters to gather the hoggs and ferry them back to the mainland. What a blessing then, at the end of that long day, to come ashore and for the first time step into the little house at the head of the quay instead of having

146

to stumble up the cliff path! We were too excited to sleep well that night. Next day as we sat at table we looked forth at a view which has never palled: the parapet to the Planestones appears just above the bottom of the window, the quay stretches away obliquely, then the two-mile band of sea, the patchwork quilt of the Achiltibuie crofts, the moor; and beyond this the three isolated groups of mountains, Quinag, Suilven and Canisp, Stac Polly and Cul Mor. It is a mountain view for the epicure, no tumble of mountain after mountain; just these three groups whose shapes are so beautiful that none can excel them in the length and breadth of Scotland.[84]

Frank lets himself go on this view over several pages of *Island Farm*, describing it through the change of seasons and the annual kaleidoscope of nature: great northern divers, Slavonian grebes, gulls, herons, Arctic terns, eiders, mergansers, curlews, purple sandpipers and ringed plovers. I am sure that this list could be much longer if rendered as a bare list but Frank also devotes time to their individual settings within the window pictures. He concludes:

To come down to that little wooden place on our own ground was in the nature of a fulfillment. We were happy and hopeful of the future. We not only owned a bit of derelict ground but were occupying it and felt a tremendous surge of energy rising within us to make that ground fruitful.[85]

The rain slackened and I went off on my own while the others went their way, pottering and continuing the *ceilidh* with the residents at Tigh an Quay. It was a very poor day for photography but I was determined to obtain a record of the place as it was now for comparison with former times. I was impressed at the way the quay had survived the years; though some further restorative work may have been done since the Fraser Darlings' time, its present condition seems to stem from that time and confound a few of the wise-acres who forecast its downfall at the hands of the easterly winds. How marvellous it would have been if the restoration could have included the full content of William Daniell's print 'Pier at Tanera', which depicts the golden years of the Loch Broom herring fishery when the fishing station at Tigh an Quay was in full production. This print conveys the spirit and effect of a Dutch painting and this, of course, is due in part to the Dutch fishing buses in the anchorage; such boats, though picturesque, are alien to the background at Achiltibuie, Stac

Polly and Cul Mor; instead they match windmills and Flemish farmhouses against a flat horizon. Perhaps Frank and Bobbie in their ideology of life saw in the rebuilding of the quay a purpose out and beyond the stonework or the daily task which put it there; a reaching out for the golden time of prosperity, contentment and happiness which emanates from the Daniell print.

There came to mind the visit which a mutual friend of my own, and quite independently, of Frank's, made to Tanera in August 1940: Russell Martin, who now lives in retirement in Edinburgh.

> A doctor of medicine rowed over to see us one morning: we had never seen him before, but by lunch-time we were good friends. He had worked with the Eskimos of the Coppermine River area and had sledged into the wild Thelon Sanctuary of North-West Canada where I have long wanted to go. It is not surprising that such a man proved a grand help at the quay in the afternoon when the tide was slow. We got the first stone to the final level at the inside end of the quay on that day – a huge Caithness blue mudstone which had lain buried below for perhaps sixty years. That stone has come to be called Blue Martin, in remembrance of this friend of a day who may yet return to find pleasure in the finished work.[86]

Dr Martin is rightly proud of his 'Blue Martin' stone in the quay at Tanera, the more so because of the person who named it after him not simply in gratitude for the physical help he gave on the day, but also in respect of a man who 'had sledged into the wild Thelon Sanctuary'. Later, they corresponded and the following undated letter, probably written by Frank from Tanera in 1941, is testimony to the harmony which was struck that day between kindred spirits.

Dear Martin

I was delighted to hear from you, but as I read through your letter it gradually dawned on me that you were not at the Sanatorium in your professional capacity but as a patient. Is that right, or may I hope that I am wrong? I do hope I am wrong, indeed.

Thank you for your kind words about the book and also for the loan of that book which was most useful to me. It seemed a very sound piece of work, though a little weak on agriculture (which wasn't his subject and is mine!). I ought to have written you long ago, and have many times repeated the address 45, Glen Urquhart Road, which I got from Mrs

148

Macrae with intent to write you. It really does seem a long time since you were here when I think of you helping us get that particular stone on the end of the pier. We associate it with you and call that stone Blue Martin (You will remember it is not Torridonian Sandstone but one of the blue 'mud-stones' which were brought here from Caithness in 1784). We finished the main fabric of the pier on 18th November that year, 1940, getting into position the biggest stone we handled in the whole job. It had to be tied to the block and tackle at low tide, have floats attached and be hauled up at high tide and slid into position. We cemented the top of the pier last year so that it looks pretty good now and makes a splendid harbour. It has always been our hope that you would blow in again some time.

We have done a lot of work since you were here. The garden is greatly extended, a good deal of land in the big park is ploughed, the hill is green and well fenced, we have built a byre, cleared that courtyard place, built a wall across it and made the far side into a farm in which there is a new barn filled to bursting with homegrown corn and hay. We shall be keeping 6 beasts this winter where three years ago there was only a bite of summer grazing. We have two new little huts in the garden, one being my study and the other the spare room. We really have found life a trifle easier this last year than when you saw us. No, I have no trouble at all with my leg. The lameness suddenly went after a year and I have to think which leg it was now. All the thickness round the Achilles tendon has gone and the only lumpiness is on the inner protuberance of the ankle, the part which hurt far more than the fibula ever did and for a much longer time.

Alasdair is at school at Fort Augustus still and very happy. It gives me quite a turn to think that in another three or four years he will be ready to go to Oxford and I shall have to raise the wind somehow. I can hear you say 'Why aren't you sending him to a Scottish University?' Well, I don't admire them very much, though when he has got his degree at Oxford I should much like him to do a bit of research in a Scottish University and afterwards to work in Scotland. Three of our universities are little else but technical schools and utterly fail to give that liberal quality of education which, with all their faults, Oxford and Cambridge do manage to dispense. We are too damn parochial here in Scotland, and suffering far too much from an inferiority complex. I left Scotland a month ago for the first time since the war and had nearly a fortnight in Oxford and London and in one university department the director of it said to me 'You know you are almost the only link we have with Scotland and you are the only Scotsman who ever comes down here to talk with us.' The world of learning should not be national or insular but culture certainly should be, and coming to your remarks on Scottish nationalism, I must say that we have ample room to develop a national culture before we go in for expensive political experiments in nationalism. I entirely agree that much more of Scotland's affairs could be managed from St Andrew's House, but we are getting on, e.g. the Ministry of Agriculture is not even under the same Minister but under the Secretary of State for Scotland.

Yes, I have hopes of Tom Johnston. He did me the honour of asking me down to Edinburgh in June to talk over West Highland agriculture. Just recently it has been suggested that I should spend about half my time establishing demonstration crofts on the West Coast, and doing advisory work among the crofters. This seems the logical outcome of our work here and I do hope it materializes, for I am as keen as ever, though suffering no delusions, and certainly not sentimentalizing the crofters. I shall record minutely and hope to gather data enough to feel able to compile the study of the West Highland problem which has been in my mind so long. When I was in Oxford, the Secretary of the Clarendon Press emphasized this very matter and said he thought the University would wish to publish it for me. If I do it, it must be done as well as I have power to do it, and be a scientific piece of work completely free from political bias and sentimental claptrap. It is very much in my mind, so don't think I have shelved it.

We have had no summer at all here and never two settled days together. There has been very little sun and no heat except for occasional mornings or afternoons, never whole days. Nevertheless, our marigold crop has done better than the swedes and we shall certainly grow them again. We have also got an excellent crop of field carrots. The fly hasn't got here yet. Neither, incidentally, has the warble fly of cattle, and I can't make out why because the mainland over the way is thick with it.

My wife joins me in kindest regards and hopes of seeing you here again before too long.

Your sincerely,

F. Fraser Darling.[87]

I walked through the 'walled garden' which was the name given by them to the compound surrounded by the walls of the old fishing station, which they cleared of fallen masonry,

Plate 8.2. Frank at one of his favourite jobs, drystane dyking. Here he is with hammer at work on the wall of the old fishing station, Tanera. (photo Fraser Darling Collection)

paved and baffled with a transverse wall against the easterly wind. The crazy paving, which they found after they dug out the courtyard, is well exposed in the enclosure, due to the vegetation having been grazed down by enclosed stocks which are penned there from time to time. The walls of the old buildings are in poor condition; they are built of rough hewn blocks of Torridonian sandstone which have weathered differentially and have lost much of their mortar, and their bonding is not good – not nearly so good as in the drystone walls built by Frank and Bobbie. The arch is a strong construction and on the outward face possesses the old harling which still clings to the east end of the ruins.

I passed out into the big park which they had reclaimed from rushes to grow oats and good grass. Wandering through the rush beds to the little wood at the top of the park planted by Geordie Leslie after the Fraser Darlings left Tanera, I was even more strongly possessed by the presence of Frank there beside me. In his later life he seldom talked to me about Tanera; perhaps when provoked he would talk with a sense of wonder about the beauty of the place, draw some examples from it of nature and human nature to illustrate a passing point in discussion, but never to expose the events which led to his parting from Bobbie and to the abandonment of the island farm. The magnificent little quay, the hut full to

151

Plate 8.3. Bobbie stane dyking at Tigh an Quay in the building of the 'walled garden'. (photo Fraser Darling Collection)

overflowing with life had served as a psychological palliative to me on arrival on Tanera; the old fishing station, still displaying some delightful signs of their labours, had not dispirited me even when seen through a drizzle; the sight of the rushes and the waterlogged park possibly looking just as it was before they worked it brought sadness, the more so since I knew it to be symptomatic of many crofting townships, including that of Achiltibuie in sight over the ruins. I could hear him repeating words which he uttered and was criticised for forty years past about the sense of defeatism in the West Highlands; perhaps his greatest fear of those lonely, wartime days was that he would himself be consumed by the same defeatism and this he fought against with all his might. His immutable conviction that man and nature were one creation led him to believe that the bending of the will and the conditioning of the mind can work miracles. Such miracles he also knew came through the practicalities of life and not by procrastination and arm-chair philosophy.

> The success of a croft as a home and a food-producing unit for the family depends on the ability of the ground to produce winter food as well as summer grazing. A full barn means the possibility of winter milk and a good stack of manure at the end of the winter. We cannot get winter eggs economically in the Highlands and Islands, but we can preserve them easily

152

in summer when they are plentiful. A supply of milk and eggs through the winter alters the whole outlook of a crofter's household. For myself, I should add vegetables as well.

The West Highlands may be cursed by a prevalence of high winds and a high rainfall, but they are blest with a mild, soft climate. We can certainly grow cow food and a plentiful, varied quantity of vegetables for the table if we get our arable land into good heart. If we have not as big an acreage as we should like, we must achieve results by intensifying our methods of cultivation to increase the yield. That has been my policy on the small island of Tanera in the Summer Isles, though I have a long way to go yet before I have brought the ground to its full capabilities . . .[88]

Alasdair remembers: 'On the islands we rarely had red meat, twice a year at most when we killed a sheep. In summer, fish was plentiful and I kept the house going with lobsters caught in my own creels. Lobster salad was regularly on the menu. In winter the diet was perforce vegetarian. My mother was adept at providing a variety of excellent dishes and milk was plentiful with butter and cream cheese. Eggs were pickled and we gathered Greater Black-Backed Gulls' eggs off Glasleac Bheag in the spring. They were strong but made superb omelettes.'

It is not every croft that can grow vegetables and soft fruit profitably, but there are many thousands that can. I reckon we were at about the limit on Isle Tanera, a treeless windswept island open to the Minch and to the east winds as well. High winds would tear winter vegetables out of the gound at times and kill the new growth on black-currant and gooseberry bushes. The problems of shelter were considerable but not insoluble. The crops we have grown on Tanera have been well worth the effort, and we have had a constant succession of fresh vegetables through the year; the soft fruit has kept us supplied with jam and bottled fruit, beside the amount eaten fresh.

This war has shown us that there are two kinds of capital, the one of money and the other of resources, and there can have been no doubt which was the most valuable, the £50 in the bank yielding 25s. a year, or the good cow and the place to keep her which that sum may have represented. The 25s. is a reduced interest facing increased prices and absence of the goods it might buy. The cow is constant and her produce will make healthy bodies today in a way money cannot do.

What we are seeking in the West Highlands and Islands

are not necessarily big cash profits, but the good life, a satisfaction and content of being in the land we love.[89]

The rushes of the big park Frank never returned to see; yet he saw them constantly in his mind's eye and with them the condition of the land in the Highlands and Islands generally. During the early days on Tanera they were naturally very proud of their 'ten acres Scots, or thereby' of derelict land and buildings, and responded to the challenge by having a vision of the future. Frank then never predicted that in four years the island farm would be no more and his vision of extending the action and influence of the Tanera work to the scale of a Highland estate evaporated. However, the fact that the ruins and the rushes remain does not mean that the island farm was a blind alley without sequel, for it was while Frank was on Tanera doing his reclamation work that his horizons were widening and he was given a timely opening which was to consume him for several years. The extension of the island farm was not to be fulfilled by extending the scale of demonstration from croft to farm to estate but through an advisory and educational service in crofting agriculture and a full-scale study of the socio-economic problems of the West Highlands and Islands. The island farm had become the primer of something much bigger. In 1943 he wrote:

> Perhaps we shall never finish Tigh an Quay and it will remain a road on which we have travelled hopefully. The place and our work on it have had their influence on the outside world, for good or ill. A wind-swept doom-ridden island property has begun to flower again and principles we have used can be applied elsewhere. My own life here is on the point of enlarging and changing, in that the Department of Agriculture for Scotland has asked me to devote some of my time to travel in crofting areas with a view to establishing crofts and advising crofters how to improve their holdings. For over three years Bobbie and I have worked alone, sometimes with doubts as to whether it was worth while unless the idea went further than Tigh an Quay, but usually with a deep enthusiasm.[90]

These words are indeed poignant. Within a year the island farm was finished; Frank and Bobbie were separated; a new person called Averil Morley had entered Frank's life and in June 1944 the West Highland Survey was established by the Development Commission 'to examine the Highland problem in the spirit of scientific inquiry, to gather a solid body of

154

facts for analysis and synthesis which would serve as a foundation for a future policy for the region', with Dr F. Fraser Darling as Director – the whole idea was his in the first place !

His raw-boned experience in harness with the Old Cock in the hill country of his youth and his diploma from Sutton Bonington equipped him far more for the role of an agriculturalist than a researcher in pure science. However, erudition and a hallowed sense of the practical met in Frank to ignite an evangelism in agriculture which sought improvement in the spiritual and technical standards in crofting agriculture, *by demonstration*. That was the moving force behind Tigh an Quay and of the campaign to which it gave rise. In *Crofting Agriculture*, published a year after he left Tanera, he distilled the substance of the campaign: an amalgam of the theoretical side drawn from diploma days and the application of such theory to crofting conditions as he had found them in the real world. In discussing what is 'good heart' in the soil he writes:

> The soil needs air to allow it to crumble to a good tilth and the germs need air to help them convert manure. We get air into the soil by ploughing and cultivating, but better still by digging. The deep thoroughness of the spade is one reason for the greater fertility of a garden compared with a field. There is no doubt that where the use of the *cas-chrom* still continues better crops are grown than by horse-ploughing. In the old days in the Highlands the crofter was doing in effect what I was suggesting . . . namely, treating his arable ground intensely. He did a bit of ground well and got a crop. Not only did he get a higher yield in one year, but he was building up his ground, making capital for the future.[91]

All this was in advance of a proper agricultural advisory service to the crofter. The eternal struggle of the crofter against the waterlogging, leaching and acidification of his soil is rather lost in Frank's exhortation to spades and *cas-chroms* and made somewhat unreal by his reference to the 'old days'. Today, the crofter has great difficulty in obtaining machines which are suited to his working conditions. For example, modern ploughs are unsuitable for traditional seed-bed preparation and the combine-harvester has put the smaller handier binder out of production. There is a moral in this which Frank would have been quick to draw, namely, that in this time of great unemployment the spade should once again come into its own, the advance of the rushes should be

155

checked, new soil capital should be recreated and smoke should again rise from the chimneys of reroofed townships.

The crofter's view of Frank, for those who knew him well as a person, was as a gifted man with a very odd sense of life, both in humour and all seriousness. Some of us who live outside the crofting scene and go there from time to time, tend to be wise-acres when coming to pass judgement upon crofting practice, often to be proved wrong. Frank was different in respect of his professional qualifications and his desire to stay and show them the way. Yet, even his closest crofter friends saw in Tigh an Quay an operation which they and their forebears had invented and lived by for several generations. He may have imbued it with the zest of a newcomer which had gone out of them through a century or more of routine drudgery, and put some finer textbook touches to jobs of cultivation and husbandry, but the crofting community was unlikely to be moved greatly by Frank's results. However, stay and toil he did, and 'outsider' though he was, no-one in 1944, when he travelled in the crofting areas gathering and disseminating knowledge, could but recognise his credentials with the spade as well as textbook. The spade, unlike the pen, was not the implement of a lifetime for Frank, but island days did roughen his hands and broaden his insight of himself as well as of nature. In making Tigh an Quay he muses:

> Let me tell you more of what this man of science is not doing according to the books and what his attitude is to the practical application of science to such a complex of natural history as agriculture is. I am wholly in favour of anyone engaging in farming having a scientific education in the principles of agriculture, but that education should not be designed to give him a set of ineluctable precepts on which, if he keeps them, he cannot go wrong . . . The man who goes so far towards recognising the value of science as to collect the practical results of research and experiment and apply them, without going to the trouble of acquiring training in science is in some danger, for he cannot rightly assess his own circumstances and once he is off the rails he does not know where he is. The man who knows no science nor seeks its results is still common in the farming world; he works by tradition, by intuition and by magic. There is some safety in tradition but no flexibility; a good man can do wonders by tradition, but he who resorts to magic is truly lost . . . This

156

man Fraser Darling with his unhygienic cow-byre and his wee bit of dairy of dry stone wall and corrugated iron roof is not renouncing science at all, nor are the health of his cattle and the good flavour of Bobbie's butter and soft cheese under such conditions any proof that science does not matter . . .[92]

I stood in the depths of the little wood at the head of the big park. It was the worst of days without sunlight in the canopy, birdsong and the hum of insects. The wood was a living monument to the experimental days of Tanera. A mixture of conifers and broad-leaved trees, it possessed a height and density which could not have been achieved by stands of a single species; nor would it have been so attractive to wild-life. Spruce grew side by side with sycamore, birch, rowan and willow; a concoction of trees without pedigree but with wholesomeness of purpose. Livestock enjoyed its shelter and browsed its rowans; even on this rain-soaked day it was busy with birds – blackbird, thrush, robin, chaffinch, wren and dunnock. On looking north from the pass above the wood to the Fraser Darling's 'ten acres Scots, or thereby' the place looked much less derelict. The rushes of the big park were screened by the wood, and the sycamores, hawthorns, elders and apples which surrounded their garden beside the ruined fishing station provided comfort in a stark land at the sea's edge.

The life-span of Frank's island farm did not last long enough to see his ideas about trees and crofting tested. He knew well why the seaboard was bereft of its natural wood-land and so lacking in plantations. Fragments of the old birch forest persist on the south shore of Loch Osgaig, at Eisg-brachaidh, and in the basin of Loch Sionascaig within a dozen miles to the north of Tanera, and as early as 1549 Dean Monro mentions woods on Gruinard Island (the 'forbidden' isle of biological warfare fame) and Isle of Ewe within a similar distance to the south. The Inverewe Garden is a clear demonstration of what can be achieved in the growth of a great range of both native and exotic species of tree on the north-west coast, and there are many plantations of exotic trees around big houses to provide shelter and amenity of which the nearest to Tanera is at Gruinard House. All of these are small woodlands, but they demonstrate a potential of a type which Frank was always quick to latch on to for its ecological worth without fully working out the economic issues involved; if the ecology was right the economics would be right in the long-term seemed to be the underlying reasoning which has never quite stood the test of time.

> But the provision of shelter to the crofting townships, with their plethora of gimcrack barbed-wire and bedstead fences which provide no windbreak, is a job for the State and the landlords together. It should be put plainly to the crofters that the loss of a small percentage of the nearest common grazing would be more than made up by the shelter which a ring of trees planted there could give to the township. A wide belt of trees would add much to the appearance of a township, though the plea of amenity would cut no ice with the average West Highlander . . . The wind is so strong on the coast that the choice of shelter timber is itself a problem . . . It is my belief that Sitka spruce will be the best tree for the first few rows, then Douglas firs, followed by Scots pine and larch.[93]

Research into the performance of all species of trees both native and exotic has moved on considerably since Frank wrote these lines in 1943 and there have been a number of demonstrations which reaffirm most of his views. However, the potential of the lodgepole pine as a good doer on deep peat and highly tolerant of high winds and salt had not been widely applied in the North West Highlands; now lodgepole pine has replaced Sitka spruce in many exposed, coastal moorlands. Demonstration plots set up by the Forestry Commission in Caithness and by the Nature Conservancy on Rum demonstrate these qualities of lodgepole pine, which can provide a fine 'nurse' for other more sensitive species, though it is very vulnerable to 'strike' by the pine-beauty moth.

> Once land has shelter in the West Highlands the culture of soft fruit and stone fruit becomes easy. Blackcurrants give an enormous crop if well mulched with seaweed. Stone fruit (perhaps even peaches in the more favoured shelter niches) do well against walls. It is our intention to bring fruit culture on cordons, as this method would tend to mass the trees and allow control of the wind factor.[94]

There was still two hours to go before the ebb would lift the *Peedie Lass* from the shore by the end of the quay. This gave me time to climb the hill above the wood to obtain a wider view still heavily beclouded and faded by drizzle. I was within sight of Chleirich across a wild sea full of skerries,

158

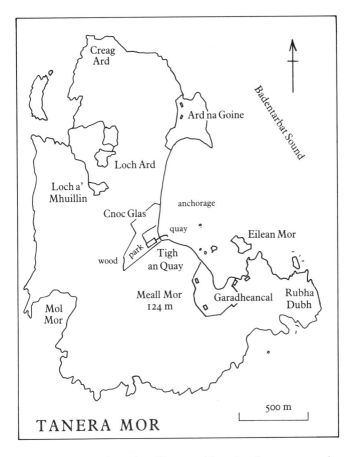

Creag
Ard

Ard na Goine

Loch Ard

Loch a'
Mhuillin

Cnoc Glas

anchorage

quay

park

wood

Tigh
an Quay

Eilean Mor

Meall Mor
124 m

Garadheancal

Rubha
Dubh

Mol
Mor

Badentarbat Sound

500 m

TANERA MOR

with the surges bursting like naval bombardment upon the
north headland. There was then no doubt in my mind that
we would have been in trouble had we gone to Chleirich that
day.

Through my binoculars I examined the island with great
care. The dark irregular shape dominated by the hill in the
south was broken by thin lenses of freshwater behind the east
bay: Lochan Fada, Lochan Beag and North Loch. All other
sides of the island were hidden from view and I could not set
eyes on their camp site in a hollow on the west side, nor could

I locate the sites of the gulleries which Frank studied. I felt downcast but, as I have related in Chapter 3, I was successful in reaching Chleirich in August 1982 and from the summit of the Island on that day looked north to the hill of Tanera with some feeling of triumph.

As I returned through the big park to the shore I remembered the photographs which Frank put in *Island Farm* showing the big park 'before' and 'after' the ruins were tidied. I thought of haymaking far removed from this derelict place, which had in its history a spark of the promise and prosperity with which Frank imbued his children's book written at Tigh an Quay in 1938–9 on *The Seasons and the Farmer*. About the hayfields and the mower he writes simply yet vividly of a bygone time.

> Hay is dried grass. Making hay is one of the ways in which the farmer makes provision for his animals against the winter, when grass grows only very slowly.
>
> Years ago, all the grass intended for hay was cut by men with scythes. One man would start, his scythe sweeping through the grass from right to left just above the ground, and the grass would be laid as a swathe at his left side. Another man would follow the first, cutting through the standing grass at the leader's right hand. You would see in those days several men strung one behind the other and six feet to the right of the man in front, and each with a swathe of grass to his left. Every three minutes the rhythmical 'swish-a, swish-a' of the sweeping scythes would stop and the men would sharpen their blades with a long round stone which they carried in a leather pocket on their hips.
>
> A fine rasping sound that was, of stone on steel, and when the sharpening was done you would have seen each man look into the sky and feel the edge of his scythe with his thumb, to feel if it was sharp enough. Then they would bend again to their work.
>
> It was very warm work mowing hay in June, so those men used to start their work as dawn lit the sky, and then at noon they would rest until five o'clock, to start again for the remaining hours of daylight. It was hard, hard work, and at the end of it all each man would have mown about one acre of grass.
>
> Now the scene is changed. Two horses draw a mowing machine upon which one man is sitting. A flat blade of many teeth moves quickly to and fro with a merry clatter in a slot which has as many teeth as the blade; and a swathe is laid to

160

one side as fast as the horses walk. Perhaps when you grow a little older and some sounds you hear bring memories back to your mind with a rush, there will be no sound which brings summer to your mind so clearly as the sound of a mowing machine at work early on a June morning. And there will be the heavy dew and the scent of the newly-mown grass. These are things which once you have known you will never forget. That busy, singing machine, the two horses and one man can mow ten acres in a day.

When the farmer is haymaking he hopes for fine sunny weather. The sun and dry air shrivel the grass and man helps this to be done as quickly as possible by turning the swathes when the upper side is partly dry. Then several swathes are drawn into one *windrow* by hand or with a horse-rake, and haycocks or *quoils* are made. The half-made hay is left in quoil from one to three days, after which it is *tedded* out in the sun with a hay fork. Once more it is put up into windrows when dry and the hay waggons come down between them to be loaded. If hay is not dry when it is stacked it becomes very hot, so hot that it may catch fire. In Scotland where the weather is often rainy at haymaking the farmers make very small stacks first, which will not get hot. The bigger stacks are made later when the hay is quite dry. Haymaking is an anxious time for the farmer; no food that man has made up of other things can take the place of good hay for his animals.[95]

It was lunch-time and, the rain having abated, the others were picnicking at the end of the quay. A new house has been built for the manager of the modern fish farm on Tanera, to the north of Tigh an Quay. The manager, Sandy Macleod, was brought up on Tanera and is the son of James Macleod, who owned the rest of Tanera during the Fraser Darlings' time. Indeed, it was the memory of James Macleod's cottage and garden during a visit (probably his first) which Frank made to Tanera by kayak from Chleirich in June 1937 which played a part in their deciding to buy Tigh an Quay.

James Macleod's cottage had a small garden in front of it bounded by young trees which he had planted for cover. My eyes feasted on that garden of flowers for several minutes, on the brightness and gaiety of colour in lupin, primula and many more blooms which are grouped in the mind as old English garden flowers.[96]

By the time I had finished my lunch-time *ceilidh* with the Macleods the *Peedie Lass* was again afloat and we made the return passage to Old Dornie in a bumpy sea with much flying spray. In the end we could not reach the jetty and Lyon White took the boat to the buoy and, in the gale, put us ashore on a heavy mattress of slippery wrack. The portents for Chleirich next morning were bad and when the morning came were indeed confirmed. I resolved to try again another day and before leaving Achiltibuie found shelter and tea in the houses of the Fraser Darlings' great friends, Mrs Abie Muir in her cottage near Badentarbat pier and her brother, Donnie Fraser, at Achnahaird. Alasdair stayed with Donnie during his schooldays in Achiltibuie and used to walk over to Achnahaird every Sunday for lunch and to play in the dunes with his life-long friends, William and Jimmy Muir. Mrs Muir, who was eighty-five years of age, had very clear recall as had Donnie, though he was absent for part of the time in Rhodesia. Both held Frank and Bobbie high in their hearts for different reasons and still regarded Alasdair to some extent as one of themselves. Mrs Muir speaks Gaelic as the first language of her whole long life and does so with a strong north-west coast dialect and accent.

She recalled with much laughter Frank's insatiable thirst for tea and her efforts to keep him supplied in his journeyings back and forth from Tanera; she felt that it must have some connection with Frank's intellectual prowess for she declared him to be very brainy! This chimes with an incident in the Sudan in 1961. Frank drank tea so copiously that the Dinka woman asked if any other white man could drink as much tea as Frank. The interpreter told her that Frank was the 'greatest tea drinker of all men'.

Again, Abie recalled going down to the shore with a female visitor from the south to meet Bobbie whom she spied rowing the two miles across the sound from Tigh an Quay. On seeing Bobbie turn to meet the shore and climb out, the visitor was astounded at such a feat of courage and endurance, and asked, 'What's your husband doing letting you row all this way by yourself?' 'Talking to a man on the quay over there,' replied Bobbie, regaining her breath with a nod of her head towards Tanera. Rowing by oneself across the sound could be regarded as routine; it was occasioned by need and only in good weather. It was one of the tasks in the island life which the ever resourceful Bobbie took in her stride and which demonstrated the great moral and physical strength she possessed and which stood her in good stead in the last months of life at Tigh an Quay. Frank rarely offered endearments to Bobbie in his diaries and books but he admired her 'business as usual' attitude in the most outlandish and exacting conditions. This was apparent on the landings of the family on deserted islands usually after painful voyages; we read plenty of Frank's sea-sickness but never a word about Bobbie, good sailor though she was, except on that first expedition to Chleirich; only that she was ashore organising the home and producing fine fare come storm, come sunshine. When Frank broke his leg returning from milking the cow on Tanera, she took the emergency without fuss.

> Bobbie can always be depended on to be efficient on such occasions. She did not sit looking at me with a long face and asking what we were going to do: she got me a cup of tea in no time and carried on making the steamed pudding at which she was busy when I came creeping in. Margaret Leigh [a visitor] has since said that her most vivid memory of that day was Bobbie's production of a hot dinner (complete with steamed pudding) dead on time and the fact that we all ate well and heartily. That is as it should be.[97]

I read *Island Farm* in 1944 while in the R A F. It left me with a great desire to visit the Fraser Darlings on Tanera on my next leave; a week later my life was changed by a posting to Canada and by the time I returned the island farm had gone. But this was not so with many others.

> During that winter of 1940–41 we got the idea that we should have a quiet summer barren of the joy of friends. The war was not very old and all of us were still in the serious mood of the past summer when holidays were not things to be associated with the present. But when spring came folk were tired with air-raids and overwork and needed just that break of remoteness which Tanera could give. Letters from friends came increasingly often, asking with some hesitation whether they might come to see us during the summer. There were also letters from people we had never seen who would like to call. Well, it is difficult to 'call' in the Highlands: in peace-time a call meant lunch and tea in our part of the world, and it was common for us and our acquaintances to make the double journey of twenty to fifty miles to pay such a visit of courtesy. An island is more difficult to reach than even the scattered households of the North-Western

mainland, so when we say we shall be glad for anyone to call, it usually means that our open house extends the traditional Highland hospitality for forty-eight hours. Whether chance acquaintances stay beyond that time is for us to say. Our family has no piper who, on the second morning can play *Lochiel's Farewell to His Guest* before breakfast, but there are equally courteous ways of achieving the same object . . .[98]

Thus has our house been full each summer from March or April till October, and I believe Tanera has had its place for these few in healing war-worn bodies and minds. We have had fresh food in plenty for them from garden and dairy; we have seen lines soften in their faces and frames toughen, and it has been joy for Bobbie and me.[99]

That joy was of a high carat known to people who have earned it the hard way, through pain and privation. After all that Frank and Bobbie had been through together and the joys they had shared, it did not seem likely that such an overtly natural partnership should end. Yet end it did on the age-old rocks of estrangement. They needed help with the farm and were also divided on who should provide it. Bobbie saw the need for an able-bodied man who could tackle the full range of tasks, particularly the handling of the launch; Frank saw the need met by a girl from the Women's Land Army, who might mix farming with secretarial and research work. The land girl was Averil Morley, a young ornithologist from the Edward Grey Institute in Oxford, whom Frank knew before she arrived at Tanera in 1943 and with whom he fell in love in 1942 and married in 1948. Bobbie left Tanera for the last time in March 1944 and went on to do lecture tours on island life, mainly to the Forces; she went as far as Malta with the Royal Navy. Later she worked for the Scottish Association of Youth Clubs as an organiser in the Highlands and from there went to Kilmory Castle, Lochgilphead, for ten years as Warden when it became a Youth Club Holiday House. Until the break-up of the family with the great sadness, inevitable bitterness and estrangement which it caused, Frank's life had been one of several sharp changes of scene; the island life had for him run its course and though he was unsure of where it was to take him, he had to quit Tanera. Despite these events and to some extent because of them, the story of Fraser Darling and his islands remains one of the most romantic in the North-West Highlands this century. *Island Years* possessed a romantic spirit which

164

Island Farm lacked. The former was full of promise; the latter had the feeling of a dream not wholly realised. In a letter to Francesca in 1971 he wrote: 'I myself have written a good deal of ephemeral stuff, but for what it is, it is done with the same care as I would write anything else. My worst book is *Island Farm* which made more money (for Alasdair's education and buying some furniture) than anything else I have written.' Just when the aspirations of earlier years were about to be fulfilled the war intervened.

Perhaps, in the longer-term, technical and economic failure of the island farm was inevitable, but it is a pity that the objectives of the husbandry which Frank propounded so effectively were not tested more fully on the ground and that today the land he and Bobbie worked does not bear better witness to their efforts. Would that the soils of the garden and big park were as durable as the rocks of the quay and their bonding, the farm might yet be a fit place to mark the advent of a fine effort. Yet, there are still signs of green pasture on Cnoc Glas which bear tribute to the tons of slag and 'coral' sand carried up there on Frank's back. However, the influence of the Tanera experience was spread far more widely to other hillsides by his advisory work and the West Highland Survey, which was a logical succession to both the practice and ideology of the reclamation of Tigh an Quay.

I could stay no longer in Coigach. My visit to Tanera in the rain had been a reunion with Frank. It seemed as though he had been waiting to show me around. With a full heart I rushed back to Inverness to attend a meeting about a new nature reserve in the Old Caledonian pine forest of Abernethy in Strathspey. As I sat at the head of the table in the Conference Room in the NCC's North West Regional Headquarters, I had behind me on the wall a fine colour photo of Frank and, on the wall opposite, his Rona stone under glass. Before I left the room I read again on the plate under the portrait the citation which I had composed in 1976 when the building was named Fraser Darling House in his honour.

Sir Frank Fraser Darling Kt, DSc, PhD, LLD, FRSE, Conservationist, scientist and philosopher who pioneered nature conservation in NW Scotland and later became Vice-President of the Conservation Foundation, Washington DC, USA, and worked with distinction in North America and tropical Africa.

165

9

Letters from Tanera

Frank Kendon was an editor at the Cambridge University Press with whom Frank Fraser Darling worked on the publication of *Bird Flocks*, *Wild Country*, *The Seasons and the Farmer* and other works until the early fifties. He was also a poet. They had a close friendship based on an inspired, often passionate correspondence and occasional meetings in the south of England. Frank drew comfort and inspiration from Kendon. He admired his intellect, praised his work and his family life in the English countryside, and envied his gifts as poet and artist.

In reading the correspondence I am reminded of Shelley's *Defence of Poetry*: 'Poetry is indeed something divine. It is at once the centre and circumference of knowledge; it is that which comprehends all science, and that to which all science must be referred . . . Poetry is the record of the best and happiest moments of the happiest and best minds'. Frank would have agreed, but he wrote no poetry and declared it difficult to conceive and even to interpret.

> My appreciation of poetry is so poor that my opinion has no value. Averil Morley quite despairs of me at times when I don't see what the poet is getting at and how he is doing it. For me, *The Time Piece* [an anthology by Kendon] is too disconnected not only in its component poems, but within each lyric I find too much of the staccato. This is because I have not trained my mind to read post-Hopkins as I should have. There was a time when you wrote poetry very much as Bridges did in *Testament of Beauty*, and I found myself entirely at home with it.[100]

The letters date from 1938 and have their origins in the business of publication and literary criticism but soon assume a much deeper and more personal level of thought and

166

feeling. The two men seemed eager to expose to each other the basic elements of their respective, physically different yet spiritually similar lives. This exchange revealed much of the true character of Frank through a spontaneity and honesty of expression which Kendon evoked in him.

For example, Frank in his writings and dealings in public life projected himself as a man of science; but this correspondence shows him more as a man of letters:

> I am interested and glad you should say that my book [*A Naturalist on Rona*] seems to convey the spiritual and authentic quality of Rona in no uncertain fashion. It is to this end of true interpretation I am always striving, whether in science or letters, and being the primitive animal I am – deeply affected by physical and mental environment – I find that I can interpret best when I am actually feeling. Your first rate mind could probably have written my book from the poverty of a London attic or from the security of a well-furnished and book-lined study in deep English country. But for me; I must light my prose from the intensity of present experience . . .[101]

The letters span the war years, the creation of the island farm at Tigh an Quay, the break with Bobbie and Alasdair, the West Highland Survey, the second marriage to Averil and the move south to The Old Rectory, Lilley, near Newbury. They provide a true and sensitive record of life on Tanera and a remarkably vivid impression of the kind of person Frank was in himself.

When war broke out, gone were Frank's plans for a national survey of seals, which he saw implemented some thirty or more years later by the Natural Environment Research Council with the use of permanent scientific staff, fast and powerful inflatable boats, a landrover and aircraft. As with his work on red deer, he was ahead of his time with the seals and, following the disruption of the war years, it took the up-and-coming generation of biologists – and the politicians who funded them – at least twenty years to begin to take up where he left off. Much the same could be said of his plans for the study of reindeer in Labrador and elephant in Uganda in the thirties. His intellectual gifts and tremendous motivation were explosive and the question of what to do at the outbreak of war worried him greatly; he was thirty-six, able-bodied and hardly yet a farmer in a reserved occupation.

The advent of the war taught us much. We found our normal life and means cut from beneath our feet and it did not seem to matter at all. I hardly felt regret for the loss of the research I had hoped to do and which enthusiasm of years had built up. Grief enveloped me; grief, not gloom or anger. Perhaps I was slightly bitter a little later on when I found that a man of thirty-six was a young man no more and not immediately required for service if he had had no previous military training. Worse still, the kind of knowledge I had seemed to be of no value, even my agricultural knowledge, which was probably deeper and sounder than in the wide field of biology in which I had delved in recent years.[102]

I have not found further mention by Frank in his writings about his disappointment in being rejected for military service. However, Iain Grant of Rothiemurchus tells me: 'More than once Frank tackled me about his having at the outbreak of war forthwith volunteered to join the Army and was turned down somewhat brashly, which certainly was one of the hurts which rankled with him throughout his life. I told him quite plainly that the military were right to decline his services . . . he was then doing a far more useful job . . . than he might have got (at 36 with no previous Army training) as the Railway Transport Officer at Fort William!'

Frank may have volunteered for the Army without the knowledge of his family, but I think that is unlikely. He volunteered for the Home Guard, but it seems that he was turned down because, living on Tanera, he would be unable to attend for training on the mainland when required. The letter which Frank wrote to Kendon from Tanera on 4 September 1939 makes no mention of military service, only agricultural service.

My Dear Kendon,
  It seems as if the light has gone out entirely and I am heartbroken just now. In these first moments of dull shock I can't see my own dear land and sea quite the same and yet it is one of the loveliest of early autumn days. Last week I was at the British Association and saw the sorrow of a selected class of the population. It was plain sorrow in our best trained minds. Since then I have met many ordinary men or women both high and low in our society and once more I have struck sorrow – never anger nor flag-wagging patriotism.
  Till now, I have felt it my duty to refrain from any activity

168

whatsoever directed towards war – even so-called safety preparations, for I have felt them all to be a lack of faith. Now
the calamity is upon us I feel I must do something towards
the general good of the people and to this end I shall take part
in any work of agricultural organisation to which I may be
called. I suppose you and I cannot influence governments,
but with the calamity upon us we can think no more of the
past but do what we can to end it soon . . .[103]

On 13 September, he continued to Kendon:

Dear Frank [K.],
I am heartily glad to get your letter. Since I wrote to you
last I had hardly written a word but have occupied almost all
the daylight hours in hard work . . . we are terribly short of
young men and this week practically all of them have gone,
eighteen from a total population of two hundred . . . just
before our late harvest is ready to cut. So this week I have
been mowing corn with the scythe for an old lady whose sons
are away. (There are no self-binders or mowing machines in
this district.) Her daughters, wives of doctors and other
professional men, are here in the fields also, tying and stook-
ing what I have cut. Bobbie is with me as crew of the boat and
helper in the harvest. So you see the trappings of a sophisticated society fall away and we are today in the same position
as innumerable forefathers. These girls have sung old Gaelic
songs of labour which they thought they had forgotten and
all of us felt a sweetness from the social quality of this work
in the fields. And like some Ceres, has sat the old lady under
the rowan trees, minding a host of babies and small grand-
children from Glasgow.
I feel, then, a little less stunned than when I wrote last, but
none the less acutely aware of the misery which is being piled
up. How difficult it is to hold to a conviction in the face of
propaganda! This crusade, this holy war; if we speak of not
fighting we are not considered as cowards this time so much
as men utterly devoid of the elements of decency. It is going
to be very hard to stand against and I am not yet certain of my
own strength. If I take some job in an agricultural organisation, or remain on my croft as a very poor man, I shall at least
be following a task of peace, but it might be too easy (as a way
out of intellectual difficulties). My family is temperamentally
one of great fighters. So to take the easy way out may not
satisfy me; and yet again may that be my hardest battle – to
take what appears the easy path? These are the sort of doubts
and questions which run through my mind. I have a feeling
also, that the likes of you and me who have the ability to

169

Plate 9.1. Frank Kendon, May 1952. (photo Mrs C. Kendon)

write, and who have something of the seer within us (do not let us be mock-modest) have a very special responsibility at this time. We can write not protagonistically or in any partisan spirit, but as we would wish to, of the things of peace and the good life, objectively . . .

Yours ever,
Frank F. D.[104]

From people who knew Frank at the time, I gather that he was shocked by the awful drain of young and talented men from the Highlands by the war. Early on, he saw his role as a rebuilder of the Highlands *after* the war, when good men would be scarce. However, these were heroic, if disappointing times for him as a sensitive man caught in a *cul-de-sac* of his own making. The broken leg of autumn 1939 – in his own words, a 'relatively slight accident' – need not have delayed unduly his joining up if the will had been there to do so, as it initially seemed to be but, as the weeks passed, was no longer.

> . . . within a fortnight of my accident the Russo-Finnish War broke and resolved all my doubts about the rights and wrongs of wars and their causation. I burned to go to Finland and cursed my helplessness. Once more the Chamberlain Government appeared to be slow-timing (though for once they were right). The sense of frustration worked in me throughout the winter until that war ended and Germany had entered Scandinavia. By then I had grown accustomed to lameness and knowing my physical limitations, had finally made up my mind to stay where I was, to put everything that was in me into making this farm from scratch, to demonstrate that in which I had faith – that this wild and neglected country could grow things as well or better than elsewhere if one could but lay aside tradition and think out a husbandry afresh, and that this was worth doing now. War is not the time to drop all that is creative, because man needs a field for creation to toughen the essential quality of hope, and to give reality to the faith which is beyond hope and which says, 'This shall be because it is good.' I could produce more food for my labour elsewhere, but in starting from scratch on Tanera I was going to work on faith in a principle, and its influence could go beyond the few acres of this island.
>
> But for a broken leg, then, got when doing such a simple homely task as going to milk the cow, there would have been no Island Farm.[105]

These words from *Island Farm* were written in 1943 in hindsight. Those written at the time in letters to Kendon show him searching for a leading line to the future and in need of time to settle his mind and conscience. The outbreak of war found him unprepared, confused and remorseful, obtaining considerable comfort from Kendon. The broken leg gave him the time he needed to assert himself upon the course of his life, coming to terms with conscience and

171

pacifism. Bobbie has always felt that the factor which influenced him most not to join the Army was not the fear of war itself but the rough and tumble of sharing life with his fellow soldiery. By 1941 the tables seemed turned; Kendon seemed to be receiving comfort from Frank. Gone was the uncertainty in Frank's mind that his decision to remain on Tanera had been right, justified by hard labour in reclaiming a small derelict farm; a harder lot, I would judge, than that of many who joined up.

Frank was not a conscientious objector, though the letters to Kendon show how close he might have come to being such and of how he fought and won the battle within himself. Bouts of introspection are mellowed by informative accounts of life at Tigh an Quay, which glow with the pride of achievement in the island farm and wholesomeness of life as epitomised by the home-grown potato, dug from newly created soil, cooked in its jacket and peeled hot on the end of a fork. The two Franks derived joy and strength from each other and one relished greatly the other's erudition, philosophy and literary prowess. They had an exciting, common purpose in the publication of a series of children's books on *The Seasons*, *The Young Traveller* and an ambitious *Book of Knowledge*; only the first materialised. More than anything the letters reflected the gossamer fabric of civilised life in sequestered places against the tumult and barbarism of war.

Isle of Tanera, 5 October 1939

My dear Kendon

Your letter and poem were good to receive. I collected them at the Post Office where they had been lying for a few days and I sat outside on a dry-stone dyke reading them, oblivious of my wife's efforts to get me on the move. It is almost uncanny to read the thoughts and feelings running through your head and find them almost wholly my own and in very much the same order. There is that terrible tiredness and yet the knowledge that the spirit must act in individual fashion. I have written a large number of letters to people in many walks of life in these last three weeks, people to whom I might never have taken the immediate trouble to write in the ordinary way. Several of these people have been scientific colleagues and acquaintances, men who, in the abstract and academic contemplation of war, are completely and unreservedly against it. Some, I know, have changed their views in the actuality, others have not made their feelings known.

172

Kendon, I feel so wretchedly lonely, and you can imagine how much your friendship means at this time. In this isolation of the spirit I am far more lonely than ever on Rona on nights of December gales.

This is where I must apply my own medicine so glibly set out in the preface to my little book. I have felt spiritual loneliness before because, after all, the number of people with whom you can exchange the depths of thoughts and conviction are few, but now it is different. We are not dealing with our fellow men in their normal tranquility of thought, men who proffer good will and hold to the scientific outlook, but with the very best of our friends who seem to have been hoodwinked out of these convictions . . . To love universally and not selfishly is the hardest of all things to learn and attain – and in a wave of nationalism it passes for treason. God knows I am no lamb; my great sin and temptation of quick temper, the natural arrogance I have inherited and the common human desire for vengeance on those who do cruel things – all these are within me and many times asking to be let loose. But the island years have, as I believe, brought me to the threshold of truth and clear outlook. Now that I see my natural sins I do not bewail them nor indulge in remorse. They are seen objectively – as St Francis said, 'Little brother, sin'. But if I am wide-eyed in seeing human emotions and the results of their actions unrestrained, it is quite impossible for me to cloak this war in holy vestments and join the reverent throng. If I do that I know that I sin cold-bloodedly and that, after all, is the essence of meanness. All of us sorrow at the devastation in lives, property and social integration which war causes, but what hurts me most is the way people fall before the not-so-very-clever jingoism of a government and press at war. To hear folk you thought were intellectual rather than emotional, talk the stuff the politicians have said as if it were their own goes right to your heart – and as I have said, I feel very lonely then . . .

I don't think I shall be wasting my time here on Tanera; you do not know much of our home life, but I may tell you that we keep open house. From the middle of May until the beginning of October we were never alone – even when we were on Rona this year there were friends in our house. I cannot tell you of all the good talk carried on in that atmosphere of timelessness which is the gift of this West, of the new meetings of like souls, and of the changes in some folk between their coming and going. Many faces have been new to us. Bobbie and I have had a rich and unexpected reward in learning that Tanera, an extension of the old Dundonnell,

173

but with more opportunity for work and play together with the stream of those who pass through, stands for something in these lives. Tanera goes with them. We feel now that it is our duty to strengthen the bond and outlook of Tanera . . .

Our pier and harbour are really beginning to look again what they were in 1820 when William Daniell made his print of 'Pier at Tanera, Loch Broom'. One of those prints hangs over the mantelpiece here in my study. Much of the parapet had gone, as well as a lot of the main body of the pier, but it is coming back now and I get immense pleasure from looking at the pattern of the wall I have built – a job done as well as I could do it. Some day I shall send you a photograph of the pier on the before and after principle. We have got a twenty-foot pole supported by four strong guys and to this we attach an endless chain block and tackle for lifting the really big stones – about 5 cwt to half a ton – from the harbour floor, and when smaller ones come along we substitute a simple rope and pulley and haul them up directly.

7th October. The days have gone by and I of all people have been laid up with a severe attack of mumps! This complaint does not give one rose-coloured spectacles, but having had long hours when I could not read or do anything else, I lay and thought over afresh the deeds of recent years and what you might call the ethos of groups of years since the last war. In the early years we were just content to be sure there would be no more war, then there came a scornful, rather academic outlook towards war, a period when the professional soldier tended to be derided. You remember the period of the famous Oxford motion. And then, I thought, after the slump of 1931, when many of us received a bit of a shriving, there grew a widespread and sincere analytical period when the folk of all ages began to think why and attained to fairly satisfactory reasons why they should not fight their fellow-men. For myself, during all this time, I found I was unable to say there were no conditions under which I would go to war; for I felt if men were risking their lives to feed me and mine, it was not for me to refuse to risk mine alongside, however much I might disagree with war. Now you know how I feel, but I wonder if you can understand me when I say that I can still imagine myself joining the army as a private soldier, not in order to foster resentment against war but to give some of the serenity of my island years in war. Meanwhile, I am a small nobody on a croft who is glad to find that his particular sort of writing is wanted. That I can do and shall. . . . Goodbye till next time,
Frank [F. D.] [106]

Kendon's reply much resembled in scope and intensity the character of Frank's outpourings of heart and mind. The correspondence seems to have given an opportunity to both men to vent their feelings and thoughts in the sure knowledge of a sympathetic hearing and philosophical response. Their relationship had been secured by candid but respectful discourse over several years; they had intellectual identity; their friendship was unlikely to be sullied by honesty of utterance. To some extent therefore, the frame of mind which gripped Frank at the beginning of the war and which so much affected his actions at the time and his outlook thereafter, was probably strengthened by his liaisons with Kendon. Take his reply on 4 February 1940; it identifies very closely with that which might have come from Frank's own pen.

> Beechcroft, Harston, Cambridge
> 4 February 1940
>
> My dear Frank [F. D.],
> . . . You ask me for an account of what in the circumstances I would do, or advocate, and that has worried me almost as if it were an accusation, for I don't know, or at least whatever I might answer as possible action – steps towards the world as just to the common man as I would like to see it – is so intolerably open to the materialist objection 'impracticable and unpractical' that I cannot bring myself to formulate it. Moreover, every day of the war gets us deeper into the maze, the suffering is silenter than it was in 1914–18, but it goes on growing. To make peace now, which I know is the sensible thing, seems much more like a betrayal of the Polish refugees and the Finns. It needs a faith with a quality of steel in it. Yet the evidence is that as war ages both suffering and hardness of heart in us and in our opponents increases. To stop the rot now is a thousand times harder, and harder to justify, than it was a month ago, and will, one must suppose, continue to get harder . . . Could a statesman possibly arise, and get support, who would, in spite of what might be insinuated of cowardice and defeat, have the courage to sum up to the moment the follies and ills complete, and say 'I will sue for peace, for peace is more amenable; peace is better than this'? The end can only come by a decision taken by one side or the other *not* to continue, the reason for such a declaration must be either defeat, or magnanimity that is sure to be sneezed at as defeat. Yet that, I feel, is what I would wish done; it is what, I believe would, more speedily than violence, eventually re-

175

establish justice. In any event, by war or by a well-lived and sacrificing protest, the defeat of the unjust in power must be a process, not a blow. Properly and sincerely and (so to speak) rashly done would it not tremendously draw together those countries that are now looking on and make them delight to bestow their moral support on the nation that had the foresight to do such a thing? I dare say it might; but I cannot think that any statesman would hold his authority a day who had the pluck to announce such a policy – a mad prophet might get a following, but not at Westminster, where 'interest' keeps its head pocket-sane, and prefers another kind of sacrifice in the name of ideals. As you can imagine I have threshed this matter out, back and forward, down this road and up that, at the invitation of all sorts of arguers, and every time I find myself 'home' in nothing short of a revolution. The wrong interests everywhere are to be found in politics, perhaps inevitably. Nothing can be done suddenly. Nothing can be done heroically on a grand scale . . . The only immediate action that I should hope for politically, the magnanimous gesture, seems by all arguments to be impossible, and the best and most effective and only course is for *persons* to exemplify social love and peaceability and goodness and sacrifice and magnanimity, both as a policy and as an act of faith. This ought to leave us with the consolation that, though our single efforts are entirely insignificant and atomic, they are yet by far the most powerful of all available forces for what men mean by progress. I don't think you will impatiently dismiss this as a getaway, or even as a counsel of despair.

Strangely enough, we, like you, have had several people lately who came to spend a day or so with us and found rest and some sort of strength in our way of life to such a degree that they have said as much. And I want to copy out for you and Bobbie a poem that is one of the best rewards we have ever had. But first of all, I wonder if you remember my colour slide of a live dragonfly? He settled on our yew hedge just as the poet walked in under the beech tree, and stayed there, incredibly, while I took nine close-ups of him. Now here is the poem; it was sent to me from London two days later:

> Living in London, with the fear of wings
> Looming upon us from an open sky,
> I could recall, like all unlikely things,
>   Your dragonfly.
> Still I could see the yew-hedge and the garden,
> The children running and the door ajar,

176

And you, whose harvest smile would never harden
    With hate or war.
Summer pinned up this brooch upon your hedge,
The badge of God's achievement and of yours,
Time's insect, gleaming on the narrow ledge
    Of life's good hours.
It rested, in the royalty of quiet,
Perfectly settled; for of any home,
Yours was the one, remotest from all riot,
    Where peace might come.

You have given me your evidence; this, and the quite unexpected words of other friends, especially lately, is mine. It is the only positive thing, a lived spirit, that is entirely out of the reach of all dictators; it is easy to see that it is the one antidote they fear, and that they hope mass propaganda is a remedy. It is, of course, the philosophy (not the religion) of Christianity. In spite of the leaders, the owners, the popes, the ranters, ideals directly derived from Jesus and supporting philosophers are, in the quiet heart of a majority of men, accepted almost as self-evident nowadays. Trace these back to their obscure and humble source, and then I think there is right and reason to claim the lived spirit as the most powerful of all causes of human progress. You know, Frank, I don't preach at you in this, any more than you preach at me. I am glad I began to write to you today, because I have had some hefty doubts in my own mind, and self discouragement, and a month of dull and despairing inactivity, but to have written to you seems to have dispelled it a bit . . .

I am busy compiling – or rather acting as an opportunity for poets to bring poems to – a book of poetry written by living poets in the last 5 years. We thought we had indications that all kinds of people were vaguely feeling the need at this time of poetry. That poets are by their practice trained contemplators, capable (as far as man is) of facing themselves in search of a grain of general truth. That the fact of this war is, man is now faced with himself, his greatest problem. That poetry was perhaps unconsciously sought because it exemplified a mode of thought requiring much bravery and much practice but most particularly necessary now if Man is to get out of this muddle and save himself from ruin and Barbarism. That anything written at his utmost by any competent and mature poetry in the last five years must bear in its grain even if not in its subject a special relevance to the times. Lastly, we thought that if the poetry were published entirely without names, this anonymity, besides being a sort of guarantee of good motive and belief in poetry, would reveal a unity in the poetic approach to life and its problems and help readers to read . . .[107]

Life on Tanera was dominated by hard physical work purposefully created to overcome the psychological stresses of war, isolation and loneliness. Nonetheless, Frank had much time for contemplation, and as he walked the island he no doubt turned over current dialogues again and again in his mind. The pros and cons of his decision to remain on Tanera weighed heavily on his mind throughout 1940. A year after the outbreak of war he was still struggling and had not yet put the cause and effects of the war behind him. From Tanera on 12 September 1940 he wrote to Kendon:

> You are in my mind every day and I often wonder if you suffer the bewilderment that I do. Perhaps not quite, because you have not abandoned the attitude you adopted before the war. If I were to live this year through again I think my mind would take the same course as it has done. The barbarians are at our gates and I cannot see that good can come from letting them in, for they have not the simplicity of primitive men. Sometimes I wonder if there is such a thing as absolute evil and not just distorted good and then again I think that defeatist thinking. I am bewildered as a man and would-be Christian and am dissatisfied with my own reactions and development at this time.[108]

The winter of 1940–41 was a hard fight against the elements which ended in a good deal of storm damage but with a much improved morale. The blighting of all the early growth by the cold and salt spray brought a spirited bounce back from Frank and Bobbie to make good their losses and build their defences. There was also an evident settlement of mind regarding the war and his occupation as a crofter and writer on agriculture. In hindsight he saw his tendency to pacificism at the outbreak of war as over-reaction, but was by now much more reassured that he had done right in sticking it out on Tanera for an honourable cause in a society at war. This is evident from the following excerpts from a letter to Kendon written on Tanera between 5 March and 28 July 1941:

> My dear Frank [K.],
> . . . When I began writing this particular letter I had the idea we were pulling through the winter and I was going to tell you something about it and us and the place. The winter

178

seems to have been a bad one all over: our version of it is different from yours, our little hardships of a different kind from yours. Last summer and autumn were the wettest and most dreary we have ever known, day after day of rain and usually high south westerly wind. Happily we had got our hay in before the weather broke and the things growing near the ground were not troubled. Our apple crop was exceptional for quantity and, according to old folk on the mainland, for quality also. These apples were from the four 150 year old, closely grown and unpruned trees which grow in our garden, formerly known as the little Irish park because some of the soil therein was brought as ballast from Ireland towards the end of the 18th century. Tanera, or at least our bit of it, was famed for its garden and its fruit in those days. Even Daniell mentions the garden of our place in his notes of 1820 which describe his lithographs. I believe we bought our place because of the pier, the stone archway and these four apple trees. Trees are scarce enough about here anyway and fruit trees almost non-existent. Here there were four with their thick trunks about 18 inches high and all their branches driven eastwards by the south-westerly gales. But those branches are so strong that I can walk along them far away from the trunk. They form a bower or arch of branches beneath the trees. Some folk say I ought to support these branches by cleft stakes but these old trees have been independent so long that their support is within them, like that of a good man. You ought to prune them, say some, but I prefer the dense foliage and the shelter the trees give the garden.

What I have done is to carry stones and raise the wall which is immediately to the south-west of the trees so that they can make a little more height before being swept horizontal by the gales. You can imagine what these trees mean to me and how I watch the minute development of their growth. The south-westerly winds which blew until Christmas did the trees no harm because they had grown themselves to carry this wind and after all there is no poison, but the softness of the ocean in the south-west. Then in January after the snow and cold calm the weather broke with violent winds from the eastern half of the compass and they blew more days than not until well through the spring. The easterly blizzard of snow of 18th–19th January was truly terrible, our main fear being the launch in our harbour which is sheltered from everything but due east. I was out several times in the night to keep an eye on her. Then on 22nd January we had a hurricane which rose to the full of the neap tide about three or four o'clock in the afternoon and then subsided to an ordinary strong gale – all from due east. The cold during this affair seared our windpipes as we fastened extra ropes to the launch and made her as safe as could be. We were also wet through in the first few seconds with the clouds of spray which stung worse than hailstones. We would come in after that and warm ourselves with tea, but we were thinking of our merchant sailors, some of whom would be adrift in the North Atlantic at that moment through German cruelty. Gale after gale blew until about the time I began this letter to you. Then we entered upon a spell of weather even more glorious by contrast with the misery of the winter. The sun shone its full span, day after day, there was no wind and the very earth seemed to warm. Grass began to grow and all our soft fruit bushes came into leaf. The buds of those old apple trees swelled and those on the fruit spurs got ready to break and let forth the blossom. Everything was extraordinarily early and we hoped. But it was a vain hope. The east wind came again and on the night of 26–27th March did tricks which I hope I may never see again. Crabs, starfish and a ballan wrasse weighing 1½ lbs were thrown as far as 200 yards up our ground from the sea. The grass was blackened – the soft fruit bushes were killed back to ground level. Some of the outer branches of the old apple trees were shredded of their bark, like velvet coming off a stag's antlers in August. All through this gale the spray drove – there was no rain then nor for a fortnight afterwards. The result was that all the buds dropped off the apple trees – the fruit spurs then looked like the handless wrists of little children. It was terrible. A nine inch wave of gravel was thrown up at the mouth of our harbour just where I had taken great trouble to make a good clearance of stones. Many of the shrubs and trees we had planted during the winter were killed. I found myself deeply depressed by the general havoc. This state continued for several days or even weeks until the trouble resolved itself within me. After that I felt able to tackle the works which that gale had shown me were necessary. We must get our acre of garden walled on the east side to ten feet in height, i.e. 4–5 feet higher than it is at present. It will mean taking down the existing wall and widening the foundation to carry a 10-foot wall in drystone. We have plenty of stone for the job not very far away. There must also be a terrace built at the head of the harbour and on that another high wall to form part of a walled garden we have planned. A year ago I would not have thought to tackle these jobs; too much of a task I would have said, but then the challenge comes in no uncertain terms and the soul gathers the strength from it. For me it is always a

180

matter of gathering the initial energy for a job; then I can direct it and the work itself is more pleasing than toil. The reflective side of me ponders sometimes on the struggles of this fellow Fraser Darling. I see him in eagerness by this ruin and in his first enthusiasm fall upon its dereliction to clear it away. Then he steadies a little, going more gently and getting more methodical. He begins to love the place differently from his first liking and joy in ownership and he finds his mind and his hands not being used separately as in the past (both to some purpose but nevertheless separately) but that an integration of his whole personality is taking place. The challenge of this last winter found the chinks of his armour. This fellow came, perhaps with some arrogance, to make this place of Tanera. Perhaps he is making it, who knows, but I have a fancy the place may really be making him.

At this moment we are deriving some pleasure from our work in the past two years. The garden is looking like a garden now. Places which were just docks and nettles or heaps of rubble are now good black earth bearing the orderly arrangement of crops which is part of the delight of a garden. We have made good stone paths about this acre of ground and planted hedges here and there. I double-trenched a good deal more ground in March from the old turf and it is now bearing a superlative crop of potatoes. Our heavy use of basic slag has had its effect in helping all our plants to make good root systems and withstand the unprecedented draught of this spring and early summer. The blasted soft fruit trees have put up new growth and the apple trees have made new leaf buds and are green again. All our crops look well. We have had peas and new potatoes since the beginning of July. Bobbie has grown pansies, violas, wallflowers and snap-dragons from seed this year and the first two are now coming into flower in the border under the young hedges where they have been put. Another little bed which was formerly a heap of broken slates is now a blaze of annual flowers and roses. My correspondence with strangers who have written to me about my books is enormous, but it is not all loss to me, chafe though I do sometimes at the time it takes. Some of these correspondents have sent us cuttings and things for the garden and we get particular pleasure now they are growing well.

Since last year I have got a very beautiful collie bitch called Trimmie. She is small, all alertness and a good worker. The first night she came here (her old master having sold up his croft and gone ship repairing on the Clyde) she tied herself on to me and seemed as if she had never been anywhere else. It was strange that she should, so quickly. We have bred a

181

bitch pup from her for she herself is fairly old though still as fast and lively as ever she was. This pup, Beth, was born 1st May and is marked almost exactly like the mother – white snip, black head, white collar, tan cheeks and eyebrows, black back, white tip to tail, white legs and chest. To have this pup growing about the place has been a healing thing to our hearts this spring. There was someone in the world anew, a world which knew not war or heartbreak. We have loved watching her first times of doing things, her absorbing curiosities and findings-out, her growing realization and ready acceptance of disciplines, of things you can and can not do. She is devastatingly pretty but mercifully she is an extraordinarily good puppy in that we hardly ever have cause to be cross with her. I never saw a pup hefted on to humanity at such an early age as she was, for at a month old while she was still being wholly fed by her mother she would prefer to have our company. At that time she would sit quiet on my coat while I worked in the fields. While we watch her we forget the war.

As I look back now I think my attitude at the beginning of the war was a bit precious, or at least academic. It is not reasonable to disagree so absolutely with the German way and do no positive act to prevent it enveloping you . . .

Having now shed the insincerity of the early months of this war and decided to withstand the march of evil, I think we are right to drop the nervous approach which will achieve nothing and to act positively towards a finish . . .

If a machine-gunning German pilot dropped here on Tanera I should probably do exactly what so many of our people have done already to such men – offer him a cup of tea. But I do not think an academic pacifism any good at all. It gets you nowhere. The war is bad, but it is for us all to learn from it. The final result will be bad only if we let it be so. I want to see the war shrive the world as it can well do. It is our responsibility to those who die.

Do you remember my mention of a naval surgeon early in this correspondence? That Christ-like man is dead. He was last seen moving about the deck of his sinking ship, easing the state of wounded men still being machine-gunned from the air. He was our dear friend.

I have a feeling that you and I need the opportunity for talk to get us farther than this correspondence is taking us. What do you think? I do wish you were coming here. I grieve if I am failing you whom I love but if I do not speak with honesty as things strike me at any one moment I fail you worse.

Ever yours, Frank [F. D.][109]

182

This letter found Kendon depressed and drawing some considerable encouragement from his friendship with Frank. Both were by now very fond of each other in a purely Platonic way. I can understand this, for my own relationship with Frank had something of the same personal, spiritual and intellectual complexion. Each letter was something of a confessional. In 1939–40 the flow of spiritual and intellectual strength had been from Kendon to Fraser Darling, but by 1941 that was reversed with Kendon as *il penseroso* and Frank as *l'allegro*.

Cambridge University Press,
28 November 1941

My dear Frank [F. D.],

Your letter has just come to put heart in me. Convention is too often allowed to stop the expression of affectionate regard; I have read through your generous letter twice and for your free gifts of kindness in it I get at once an impulse to try to make words return it, loaded with and lightened with my love . . .

I am just reading Boswell's Journal of a tour to the Hebrides with Johnson. I must send it to you for Christmas, though perhaps you have read it. Boswell has his faults but faces and accepts them; his love for Johnson can include his self gratification at being the companion of the great. He does not know that Johnson is partly great because Boswell loves him. The book is the delightful success it is because of Boswell's generosity. With all his vanity and snobbery and even priggery on board, because they are not foolishly mispretended, but frankly and not mockingly allowed to be there, they not only do not falsify his genuine love for Johnson they somehow guarantee it. As for Johnson himself, he is really wise too, and does not let his mortality handicap him, because he too does not despise it. Johnson's repentance is self-renewing like true love. And I love the way, don't you, that, being presented with a problem he gets right through all that tangles most people, and says the simple essential. Johnson's answers remind me of fingers fumbling through grass stems to the stem of the daisy and picking the daisy stalk blindly but unerringly.

I have been spirit tired and sad and often thinking of various kinds of death lately – don't make this say more than it says; I'm not in any kind of danger. Moreover I am as sure as ever that the only 'chemical change' in humanity that counts is an atomic change involving each unit. But circumstances – not only the war, but family cares, and love of habit

183

and lack of energy or reason or perhaps ability to work at writing down my own creation – circumstances have beaten me lately. I am conscious of doing less than my duty by just doing my duties, and of being weak and middle-aged and material and tender about cold weather, carpet slippers, cups of tea, and above all tobacco! I have been seized by and trying to do a long poem – a Life and Death of John Smith – but it has come out very episodic, disjointed, and sometimes depresses me with a notion (as do other things) that my powers are failing for lack of other minds in my world. There is nothing I would like better than to sit it out with you and regain a little wisdom, but the battle is my own, and the fault is a sort of laziness plus despair. I cannot make the desperate change in physical circumstances that would end it, because of the 'hostages to fortune'.

Frank [K.][110]

Isle of Tanera, 14 December 1941

My dear Frank [K.],

. . . It is a bit of a problem, knowing what to do. I want to know just what I am doing with my life, a life in which I am just as thrilled and interested as ever I was, but now I realize that it isn't just my life. Time is precious and must not be wasted. I start as a child constantly full of the wonder of living things and eventually become a farmer. Then I find I have an inquisitive mind which is not satisfied with the empiricism of the farmer's life, I want to know principles behind observed phenomena, and I find I want time to enjoy some of the other living things of the earth as well as those found on a farm. So I get the name of being a bit of a biologist; and now, largely because of the circumstances of war, I have become a peasant with his bit of ground. I love it dearly and enjoy making it and working it, but where am I going? Am I to carry on now as a farmer with outside interests and contacts, or am I to drop it after the war and go looking at seals again? Perhaps the light will come in its own time, but I do vaguely trouble about it – at times. I have taken the line in life of never following money, yet at the moment of the outbreak of war I was well in sight of a livelihood which would give me a reasonable standard of living, and that is as it should be – the labourer is worthy of his hire. Now it is difficult; I depend on writing for money, and spend it pulling this place from its dereliction. In that I am doing a social service with my pennies and I believe the artist in me is a better artist for the wholeness which this work of my hands gives. But I don't think being monetarily

184

Plate 9.2. The island farm from the south, showing the head dyke, the shelter wood and the improved pasture (pale) set in heather hills (dark). Looking to Badentarbat Bay. (photo Dr A. Fraser-Darling)

poor really suits an artist because he has to deflect too much energy wondering where the next penny is coming from. As I grow older this necessity for pennies will increase and an older man does not find them so easily as a younger man. I suppose I could write a good deal more than I do, snappy articles and all that, but many an artist goes wrong there. He deteriorates and that time he tells himself he is earning in order to write something good never comes. I am quite serious and single-minded about my writing; if it isn't the best I can do it is bad, and I feel bad about it. Somehow, I feel I shall not go back into biological research pure and simple; there is probably a more social job of interpretation and application waiting for me. Tanera is rather like that even now for its significance goes far beyond the immediate amount of food we are getting off the place. To one like myself who may go along one of many paths, the problem of choosing the right one is considerable. It is different for you now. You are the servant of a fine institution for part of your

185

time and that being so you are able to live another life as well which shall be free of the immediate pressure of pennies. You have created such an independent life in your family and home and in your art. You and Celia have made a gracious and liberal home, adorned when I was there last by two of the nicest kids I have ever met. Alice and Adam gave me an impression I have not had anywhere else – they showed me they were not just 'the children', but that they were part of the home; though they could not have phrased it they seemed confident of being integral, contributing to and having an assured place in that home. This is quite different from the dreadful spectacle of parents sacrificing everything to their children and having them ride the place roughshod. Your achievement in this is considerable. Your art pervades and draws from your home and family and you must cherish this knowledge. It is the especial lot of the artist to suffer and you are suffering. The artist suffers from his own make-up and vicariously for all humanity. The quality of the *man* is in his ability to bear the suffering and transmute it. The men who can do that are the great artists. Lesser artists have a tendency to become defeatists or nihilists, but you are not of them. Hold fast to the power within you, to that cell of God that is in you.

> Each tree being good of its kind by self-obedience
> The whole purpose of beech mast being intrinsic.
> To do its living best to be that kind of creature.

And your beech tree, in being that, goes far beyond its own environment, inspiring your poesy, giving me thereby the beauty of the tree, and by its shed leaves helping to grow your potatoes . . .
Yours ever,
Frank [F. D.][111]

The correspondence continued throughout the forties with one or two letters each year. By 1942 the dialogue had moved away from introspection on the war to literary matters, achievements on the farm and the prognosis of Frank's life. On 18 October 1942 he writes:

Our house has been full again this year from March to October and it has done our heart good to see tired faces clear and to hear a lot of laughter and fun echoing through these old ruins. Bobbie and I both feel that this place which so long carried an atmosphere of doom has felt kindlier this last year or so . . . More than ever, we get the feeling that our lives are not our own and once we accept that fact all sorts of things seem to straighten out and puzzling things don't worry as much as before.

There was a mood of optimism engendered by the recognition which he was beginning to receive in Government circles and this put an end to any qualms about his role in the war.

> I shall be spending half my time spreading the principles of crofting husbandry I have unearthed here to the rest of the West Highland coast. Do you know, I thought I was hard-boiled, but I approach this work with gratitude and enthusiasm. It is the logical outcome of my three years toil here and I feel it such a wonderful opportunity to serve. I do not come to these people sentimentalizing them or despising them, but still loving them.[112]

The last letter from Tanera is undated about the turn of the year 1943–44. It reveals that Frank had been asked to stand for Parliament for 'a Highland constituency in place of the present member when he retires' and declares that

> such a course of action will not be necessary now for the work I must do has become plain to me. That is in the rehabilitation of the West Highland countryside . . . it is my hope that I shall soon be able to institute a social and agricultural survey of the West Highland problem on my own terms, when I shall be prepared to accept good money for a good job. Averil Morley will be my right hand man and Bobbie is now being drawn into the network of social endeavour and service in relation to the Highlands. We are folk who know our problem and are being recognised as such. Our hope is to tackle it now. For myself, I want to treat it as a problem of human ecology . . . Because of the growth of the West Highland work, I think we shall have to leave Tanera. This will be hard to thole, but we must not let ourselves be sentimental. If Tanera has done its job, we must be prepared to leave it in face of the bigger job beyond . . . Averil would like me to enclose one or two of her latest poems, and this I am very proud to do.[113]

The land girl of Tanera was a poet with whom Frank had long since fallen in love. The broken family left Tanera in different directions and a year passed before Kendon received an explanation from Frank in a short letter of 30 April 1945 from Kilcamb Lodge, Strontian:

> . . . I envy you your family life and your family ability. It hasn't been my good fortune. Bobbie and I were excellent comrades in work and as long as we kept to working together

187

Plate 9.3. Bobbie at the tiller of the launch.
(photo Fraser Darling Collection)

and not being man and wife and mother and father together,
we got on splendidly. It was on the rock of the family we have
foundered. I was denied children . . . after Alasdair was
born, and in the first half of 1942 I fell in love afresh and
struck away from the old life . . . No man had a finer comrade
than Bobbie was to me and I do not want to forget that . . . I
have no animosity. All that terrible antagonism that was
between us has gone and all the violence of temper. In these
years I have grown up, rather suddenly, and know that I can
tackle that which is asked of me . . .
Yours ever,
Frank [F. D.][114]

Frank never talked to me of the 'denials' of his married life
with Bobbie; neither were they a matter of discussion between Bobbie and me, but Alasdair has explained that Bobbie's story is different. He wrote (28 July 1985): 'Frank's
letter [above] gives only one side of the story. From the time
they came to Edinburgh when I was three months old, they
had no secure income. In fact for a period when they lived in
Portobello, Bobbie herself had to go hungry to ensure buying
sufficient food for me. I believe that despite Frankie Crewe's
backing he did not get the Leverhulme Fellowship at first
188

and it was only after an appeal to Crewe that he was granted it. If he had not got it, they would have been destitute. In those days birth control was an unmentionable subject and Bobbie herself was far too ignorant about it to know what to do as she freely admitted to me.'

Later, Alasdair explained further (27 October 1985): 'She [Bobbie] tells me that she longed for more children but had an absolute terror of further childbearing when they could hardly afford to bring up one child . . . she did say that, in her innocence, she thought that Frank had accepted that if they were to do the work he wanted to do then the sacrifice must be no further children.' Bobbie's side of the story had its own 'denials'; the pain, poverty and privation through which they came in their entire life together meant great self-sacrifice for her for the sakes of both Frank and Alasdair. The transition from one life to another was 'extremely traumatic' for everybody and it took several years to work itself out.

True to form Frank wrote to his mother to give reasons for his break with Bobbie. However, he told them also to two close friends at the time, Frank Kendon and Bob (now Professor Sir Robert) Grieve – who was shaken that a partnership of such overt popularity and strength should come to grief. In the midst of the trauma, Bob Grieve recalls walking the hills of Morven with Frank who declared himself phyloprogenitive by nature and passionately desirous of more children – as, it seems, was Bobbie.

Bob remembers also sitting in the comfortable lounge at Kilcamb Lodge discussing with Frank and Averil Morley the Highland situation and items of much wider human interest. 'I liked their ways with each other' Bob said, 'more like a good-mannered partnership than an association of colleagues. But there is no doubt that she had the kind of scientific outlook that Frank deeply respected; and this he made clear to me. He also had an almost boyish admiration for her skill as a pianist. The overall impression was of a sound and affectionate relationship.'

10

'The West Highland Survey'

There were a number of key persons in Frank's life who
hailed him as something out of the ordinary. Frankie Crewe
saw his intellectual turn of mind; Julian Huxley his streak of
originality in ecology; Michael (now Lord) Swann his gift of
communication; and Fairfield Osborn his sagacious personi-
fication of the conservation ethic. When he left Tanera in
May 1944 to a new life, Frank had still a long way to go to
becoming the 'big personality' of nature conservation of his
days in the Conservation Foundation in Washington DC.
However, he might never have made anything of the new life
had it not at the outset carried the support of that revered
Scottish politican, Tom Johnston, who was the wartime
Secretary of State for Scotland. Johnston saw in Frank a new
evangelism in the use of natural resources at a time when a
messianic figure was badly needed in the Highlands and
Islands. The island life had an attractive inspirational base
and the wholesomeness of Frank's writings on crofting agriculture had an appeal in a society which elsewhere was
ploughing and digging for victory for all its worth.

In June 1942 Johnston asked Frank to see him. There
commenced a train of events which carried Frank from the
confinement of the early war years, when he was in his
self-made *cul-de-sac* on Tanera, to the widening open road of
agricultural advisory work in the crofting areas in 1942–44
and the West Highland Survey from 1944 onwards. The
advisory travels were accompanied by a series of articles in
Highland weekly newspapers, which reached a majority of
crofting households and generated a great deal of interest
and some controversy. These articles are still remembered
by crofters in the islands. But at the time Frank found
himself misquoted on defeatism in the Highlands and in

trouble with meddling in social affairs; economic and technical issues were popular but leadership and the fostering of
community spirit and co-operation were unpopular. 'He has
no right to tell us how to lead our lives; he's an incomer
anyway!' said the bigots. But it took more than the small-
mindedness of his critics to put him off his stride and he
summed-up his impressions of the campaign in two articles
in the *Glasgow Herald* of 7 and 8 March 1944 entitled 'Problems of the West Highlands'.

> When provocative remarks raise a storm of protest it may be
> prudent for the man who made them to lie low for a while.
>
> If, however, the man has no axe to grind and is genuinely
> anxious to get to the bottom of a problem, he can endure even
> the inaccuracy of statements attributed to him and the gross
> misrepresentation of his view.
>
> In the spirit of science, which is nothing more extraordi-
> nary than a conviction of the need for orderly thinking, he
> considers the nature and origins of the protests, reconsiders
> his problem, and tries to assess how far his ideas have been
> changed or advanced.
>
> Certain correspondents in the local newspapers have sug-
> gested that there is no West Highland problem at all, and
> certainly no social one. Economic problems were allowed,
> but the word 'social' seemed to arouse special resentment as
> if it bore an unendurable stigma.
>
> There are social problems in most societies, whether they
> be urban or rural, intellectual or Boeotian, rich or poor,
> simple or over-civilised. Whatever stigma such a problem
> may carry (and not all do), it is largely washed out by an
> honest realisation that something is wrong, accompanied by
> a desire and an attempt to set things right.
>
> The West Highland problem is one which should give
> Highlanders themselves no inferiority complex so long as
> they are ready to find out what is wrong. There was certainly
> never a time when there was more good will on the part of the
> State to make the West a place of content – content in living,
> in staying, in working, and in the natural leisure of life.[115]

He was criticised for his history of the social disruption
which followed the collapse of the clan system

> I do not deplore the break-up of the clan system, because, in
> my opinion, such exaggerated patriarchalism is a definite
> check to progress unless it can adapt itself to a changing
> world. Nevertheless, the fact is that for the Gaelic society as
> it then existed, the clan system did work and produces ex-

amples of co-operative behaviour which would adorn any modern social economy.

What I do deplore is that the disruption of the system was not accompanied on the part of the Government by any constructive social policy which could take its place. Eighteenth century political opinion was not sufficiently advanced to extend the hand of friendship and co-operation to a broken countryside.[116]

His desire to see a reinstatement of leadership was misinterpreted by his critics as a suggestion of dictatorship, when he meant only that local councillors and prime-movers in the movement of the young farmers' club should be drawn from among the crofters themselves and not from lairds or incomers. However, the heaviest criticism came when he meddled with domestic economy and particularly, the deficiencies of oatmeal! The criticisms, he felt, were partly justified because he had not taken enough trouble to explain himself fully as he did in the *Glasgow Herald* of 8 March 1944.

There are certain things the crofter's wife cooks pre-eminently well, and, as a nutritional survey by Professor Cathcart and his colleagues showed, in the remoter parts of the section studies of the Outer Hebrides, the diet of the people was adequate and there were no signs of malnutrition.

My own comment on this point is that that diet, though excellent, is made up of a very few staple components – oatmeal and barley meal, potatoes, milk, and fish. The loss of one or two components and the substitution of processed foods immediately unbalances it.

Oatmeal and fresh milk together are an excellent food, but if the milk is dropped or condensed milk substituted a large intake of oatmeal is bad because the oat contains a substance called phytin, which makes heavy demands on the body calcium in the absence of Vitamin D which results in physical troubles such as rickets.

To drop fish from the diet will probably result in a deficiency of the calcium-phosphorus intake. Potatoes cooked in their skins in a closed pan provide a considerable amount of Vitamin C, but this may be largely lost if they are peeled or boiled open to the air, or fried. It is usual for potatoes to be exceptionally well cooked in the West.

Fish is not so plentiful on the West Highland mainland as it should be, and milk is in many districts extremely scarce in winter.

Until very recently, the art of pickling eggs was not gener-

192

ally followed. The winter diet, then, has to be filled out by goods bought in and which are often not as good as the home-produced food they replace.

The standard of cooking, as well as the standard of nutrition, inevitably falls. It is my belief that a well-stocked vegetable garden to every croft and a store cupboard full of potted summer butter, pickled eggs, and home-made jam and bottled fruit, and a cheese or two, would go far to adding to the content of the crofting life.[117]

Frank's comments on Highland diet have been borne out by the researches of Denis Burkitt in East Africa, particularly on the influence of dietary fibre on health. The good West Highland diet is high in fibre (oatmeal and barleymeal) and potatoes, and has adequate protein in fish and milk. He was appalled when he first went to the Highlands at seeing a diet consisting of baked beans and steamed bread. Bobbie baked all their bread, wholemeal and good! Like Tom Johnston, Frank saw a great future in new development of hydro-electricity. His thinking was of the ecological factors linking housekeeping with agriculture, energy resources in peat and locally generated hydro-electricity. He had a vision of a new age: the high, rain-soaked, torrential land would yield a new wealth through water and gravity at the blast nozzles of turbines, and this would in turn enhance the yield of soils and the prosperity of the people. In the kitchen, electricity would provide new opportunities in self-sufficiency in cooking, particularly in the use of the oven for baking of yeast bread. The reduction of peat heating could be accompanied by cleaner houses, less back-breaking labour in winning peat and more time spent in winning winter keep for the general-purpose cow: the well acclimatised Highland–Shorthorn cross.

Such a vision referred to the mountainous mainland and islands with great rainfall catchments, but not to smaller, lower islands without natural, perched reservoirs. Even West Highland mountainous catchments can dry out in summer and the capital expenditure needed to win the water-power crop to meet summer drought from winter flood was enormous.

This was not taken into account fully by Frank though many of his innovations are now built into the croft house. The baking displays at the 'shows' are still fit testimony to the widespread use of girdle and oven, but the art and science of housekeeping envisaged by Frank was not realised. After the 1939–45 War the self-sufficiency of the crofting township did not return to its erstwhile strength. The home-grown, home-made, home-baked tradition is still gradually disappearing even with reliable supplies of electricity, bottled gas and fuel oil to provide a much higher plane of efficiency and achievement than in the day of peat or coal heating and paraffin.

His enthusiasm for crofting as a part-time occupation depended on the complement which he saw in forestry in the glens and fishing on the seaboard and islands, but his vision has not been realised in the events of the past forty years.

> Forestry is due for considerable expansion, and the Commission always prefers, I believe, to employ existing crofters on the three-days-a-week basis than to establish new holdings. Afforestation is probably the only solution for bracken-infested land which cannot be tackled by machines.
>
> Our fishing is in a bad way, but observations lead me to believe that fisherman-crofters often have the best-kept crofts. One of the finest constructive steps a British Government could take in the West Highlands would be to close the Minch to trawlers, build a good number of small, solid, L-shaped quays with local stone and local labour, and thereafter make long-term loans available for buying small line-fishing boats. There is a market for the fish in the West itself, especially in summer when the tourist traffic is large.
>
> I remain, then, an optimist as to the possibilities of the future of the West Highlands. Young men and women will come back after the war if we can show we are in earnest, and that natural resources are present in fishing grounds, grazing grounds, and supplies of lime.[118]

The work which Frank did among the crofters in the north-west Scotland was probably the most sincere and selfless he ever did. It was his biggest single effort. He was employed for thirteen years by the Conservation Foundation in Washington, 1959–72, but during this period was 'thinly spread' over a global field of interest and activity with little in-depth personal involvement in any single issue. His grounding in employment and training was in agriculture and, while the crofting scene may have been different from farming in the Pennines and there was little about crofting at college, his essays in agriculture in the Highlands and Islands have a ring

194

of self-assurance not possessed by those in pure science and philosophy. *Crofting Agriculture* is a beautifully composed little book which is now more of a collector's piece than a manual; techniques have changed but the basics of agricultural conservation in the ecological setting of the West Highlands remain intact. Though he was to become more famous later in life, Frank was at his intellectual best during his Edinburgh, island-going and crofting days between 1930 and 1950; yet it is interesting to note that no direct reference is made by him to this great formative period of his life when coming to write the Reith lectures in 1969. However, there is ample indirect reference through Frank the consistent impassioned matchmaker of nature with human nature. In 1944 in *Crofting Agriculture* we find this:

> What we are seeking in the West Highlands and Islands are not necessarily big cash profits, but the good life, a satisfaction and content of being in the land we love. The good life means a cultural content of the mind as well, and I hold that physical surroundings of greenness, and healthy, thriving crops and animals are a necessity, if that content is to grow and be maintained in a rural community. Our heads may be above the clouds, but our feet are still on mother earth. The earth has to be tended with toil, love and wisdom if she is to give us our content. The toil and love I take for granted in Highland folk, and in this book we will keep to the subject of knowledge applied to the very distinct set of conditions found in the West Highlands and Islands.[119]

and in 1970 in *Wilderness and Plenty*, this:

> This pragmatic man, typified by too many of our politicians and those considered to have their feet firmly on the ground, has his head in some world of illusion of his own making. What is the use, he asks, of all that forest if it cannot be brought to the service of man? The answer is that it is already in the service of man if he is willing to accept fellowships with the world of nature. The forest is generous: it can spare him some trees for his timber, and all the time the silent forest is busy, giving us our oxygen, taking away the surplus carbon dioxide, helping to remove the pollutants. The hedgerow trees of England were never more valuable than today – nor the hedgerows – yet a misguided government department can give 50-per-cent grants for clearing what is called scrub. Even visually the trees are beautiful and stress-relieving, but in their silence they do much more. Their only voice is the

Plate 10.1. Strath na Sheallag and Beinn Dearg Mhor in the Fisherfield Forest was one of the great wilderness areas in Frank's life, forming in his mind the impression of the 'wet desert'. (photo Tom Weir)

wind; they have no vote and are defenceless. The practical man (who Disraeli said was he who could be depended upon to repeat the mistakes of his ancestors) can remove what is the nation's heritage and nature's tool to allow the easier passage of some mechanical Moloch.[120]

The former passage is fine brush work and the latter a broad brush in a different setting; yet the message is the same and both carry Frank's own, strong, personal brand of didactics.

Whatever the separation from Bobbie and Alasdair may have contributed, it was the increasing involvement in national issues and ultimately the West Highland Survey which took Frank away from Tanera. It was not possible for him to provide the time and facilities necessary for these activities at Tigh an Quay. The incessant to-ing and fro-ing to the island and delays caused by weather and tides were an added burden and anxiety to one whose primary focus of interest was no longer in the island farm. He found a new location at Kilcamb Lodge, Strontian, on the shores of Loch Sunart, which, though still isolated, allowed direct road access to many crofting townships, to ports of call for the Inner and Outer Isles mailboats, to the railhead at Fort William and to St Andrews House in Edinburgh. There was available, close-by, land for demonstration purposes and though this was not used on the same scale as had been done with Bobbie on Tanera, Bruce Campbell remembers vividly Frank's toil at Kilcamb during the heatwave of August 1945: 'On a very hot morning he had scythed single-handed a half-acre patch of hay and came in from the field dripping with sweat from his thatch of black hair, a figure of physical and intellectual power, practising what he preached'.

Frank's mission among the crofters was accompanied by another event in his life which was to carry him far from the glens and the isles. In 1943–44 he was appointed by Tom Johnston to a Scottish National Parks Survey Committee under Sir Douglas Ramsay. It is salutary that even in the dark days of the war, the concern for what was happening to our countryside was very much a live issue. The name of Fraser Darling was attached to its earliest moves and has survived within the conservation movement when almost all the others have been forgotten.

The Committee were in Frank's opinion 'an innocent bunch of idealists' who differed widely on what national parks should be and had little capacity to reconcile these differences. The Committee was enlarged later to take in a wider range of expertise and it also became necessary to have a sub-committee under James Ritchie (and later J. R. Matthews) on Wildlife Conservation. The Report of the Wildlife Conservation Committee has a strong flavour of Fraser Darling; his ideas and views were probably somewhat *avant garde*; but was not the whole idea of national parks in Scotland the same?

A similar committee was working in England and Wales under Sir Arthur Tansley. This group was ahead of that in Scotland and the former was to a considerable extent dependent upon the latter. In 1946 he wrote to Kendon:

> I am on the Secretary of State's committee in Scotland and have been sitting in on the English deliberations. For once I feel that this kind of committee stuff is important. We are

197

fashioning something new and which should have lasting effect, both for the wild life and civilisation. Most of us on the committees seem to be imbued with this earnestness with the result that the meetings are eager and not boring occasions. All of us are short of time but are giving much of it to this business. it is really grand to work with a bunch of men, who, though in middle or later life, feel the enthusiasm and urgency which youth feels. The eagerness coupled with the intellectual capacity of middle age, should get something done.[121]

Tansley and his colleagues provided some basic definitions in nature conservation which were relevant in Scotland and were not bettered by the Scottish group. Take, for example, the Tansley purposes for national nature reserves as compared with those of Ritchie:

to preserve and maintain as part of the nation's natural heritage places which can be regarded as reservoirs for the main types of community and kinds of wild plants and animals represented in this country, both common and rare, typical and unusual, as well as places which contain physical features of special or outstanding interest. These places must be chosen so far as possible to enable comparisons to be made between primitive or relatively undisturbed communities and the modifications introduced by varying degrees of human interference; typical and atypical physical conditions; distinctive characteristics imposed upon communities and species by differences in geographical position, physiography, climate geology and soil, both within the main physical regions and in the transitional zones between them; the behaviour of species or communities living within and at the margins of their geographical distribution or their ecological tolerance. The series as a whole should take fair account of the varied requirements and interests of the several different lines of scientific approach: the systematic study of particular groups of species; studies of communities or species in relation to their environment; of the rise and fall in population numbers; of breeding stuctures of populations and the way in which inherited variations are distributed; of geographical distribution; of plant and animal behaviour; of the climate and microclimate conditions which so largely govern the distribution of organisms; of soils; of the rocks and the fossils they hold; and of the physical forces which shape the surface of the land; as well as general evolutionary studies. Considered as a single system, the reserves should comprise

198

as large a sample as possible of all the many different groups of living organisms, indigenous or established in this country as part of its natural flora and fauna; and within them the serious student, whatever his bent and whether he be professional or amateur, should be able to find a wealth of material and unfailing interest.[122]

The academic excellence of this definition stands out against the less polished but more pragmatic treatment of the Scottish Committee, considerably influenced by Frank's thinking of a decade on a State Biological Service:

By nature reserves we understand areas delimited for the express purpose of safeguarding and perpetuating the natural assemblages of plants and animals which they now contain, plant and animal assemblages which might settle there under more favourable conditions, and special features of geological interest. Such reserves would offer invaluable opportunities for scientific study. Broadly speaking, three types of nature reserves will be required.

At the outset we wish to make it quite clear that the reserves which we envisage will be National Reserves which, while adding to the amenity, will not conflict with the good management of adjacent properties. It should be realised that the success of nature conservation depends largely upon co-operation and the pursuit of a 'good neighbour' policy.

It is useless to declare an area a nature reserve and then to leave it to its own devices. Lack of adequate control speedily defeats the objects for which the reserve was intended. If nature reserves are to be successful, it is imperative that they be managed scientifically, and that they be used as observational areas for gaining new knowledge about plant and animal fluctuations under natural conditions.[123]

This separate discussion of nature conservation within the national park debate led to the creation of a separate government agency (The Nature Conservancy) for the administration of national nature reserves. The outcome was the establishment of national parks in England and Wales only and a system of national nature reserves and other statutory sites in Great Britain as a whole. This meant no national parks in Scotland and that the administration of nature conservation in Scotland was vested, not in the Scottish Office, but in the Privy Council. Since that time this responsibility passed to the Natural Environment Research Council (1966–73) and is now with the Department of Environment. The decision of the government of the late forties not to establish national parks in Scotland Frank saw as sardonic, and it was a deep disappointment to him.

> The shortsightedness and wrongheadedness of that decision becomes the more apparent as the recreational function of wild lands is realized as an urgent and proper form of land use.[124]

Sadly, stemming from the public debate of the late forties, the words 'national park' have become almost unmentionable in the Scottish establishment. In my many years of work in nature conservation in Scotland I have had to exercise the greatest care in the use of the term, which could stun or even kill discussion. This I found to be in contrast to its use abroad where people generally find the Scottish situation difficult to understand.

The answer lies mainly in the notion that the establishment of a national park system in Scotland is unnecessary, since the function of such is already carried out by a number of bodies acting together to the same end. National parks would create another tier of administration to add to that of central and local government and could compromise the aims and functions of a plethora of voluntary bodies, professional associations and private interests. Implicit in all this shared responsibility and joint action is the need for consensus and co-ordination in policy-making, planning and functional programming, particularly in the rehabilitative use of land and sea.

When Fraser Darling was in the thick of the national park debate he had a friend and admirer in Sir William Robieson, the editor of the *Glasgow Herald*, and was one of a group of columnists on Highland affairs. An article on 13 January 1947 by one of them, A.M. Weir, drew attention to the problems of setting up administrative machinery to deal with the type of overall planning and management of natural resources similar to that required for national parks in the Highlands and Islands.

> Over the past 30 years (going back to 1917) there have been a dozen commissions, inquiries, reports, and investigations, all of them unanimous in the conclusion that something must be done and all of them advocating innumerable things that ought to be done. The conclusion is, therefore, that *what* requires doing is established . . . Yet little has been done. In

200

Plate 10.2. Loch Beinn a' Mheadhoin in the Glen Affric hydro-electric system. Frank saw hydro-electricity as a great advantage to the Highlands. He also saw in areas such as Affric great opportunities for the creation of National Parks in Scotland. (photo North of Scotland Hydro-Electric Board)

truth from the aspect of co-ordinated and all-round planning and development, nothing has been done . . . The difficulty lies in building a new authority charged with the duty of effective action into the existing framework of local and central government . . .[125]

That Frank was seized of these difficulties, is clear from his expressed wish to see the integrated planning and co-oper-ation of agriculture, forestry and hydro-electricity in a High-land version of the Tennessee Valley Authority. He did not suggest that the whole of the Highlands and islands became a national park, but he saw the principle of planning and management of national parks in the Scottish idiom extend-ing to other areas of rehabilitation outside the parks. In the *Glasgow Herald* of 26 December 1947, a 'Special Correspon-dent' (Frank or someone very close to him) wrote an article on the proposed national park in Glen Affric under the headline 'Common-sense Method of Rehabilitation in Affric Suggestions – Model Plan for Similar Regions':

Briefly, the plan for this National Park – and for the four others which have been proposed – would be based not merely on the recreational and educational facilities which such an area ought to provide but on the life and work of the glens.

So forestry would be 'married' to agriculture. Hydro-electric development would be so contrived that the new dams would put an end to flooding in Strathglas, the power-houses would supply current to a variety of new workshops and small factories (most, if not all, engaged on processing farm and forest products) and the roads and hydro-electric installations would serve, too, for the tourists and for the resident population which would be increasing steadily in numbers.[126]

The West Highland Survey was Frank's idea. In 1943 he proposed to Tom Johnston and two of the Development Commissioners, Dr. W. G. S. Adams of All Souls and Sir Hector Hetherington of Glasgow University, 'in the spirit of scientific enquiry', a study of the causes underlying the depopulation and economic decline in the Western Highlands and of extending advisory work and demonstration. What could be a more logical sequel to the Tanera experiment and a more suitable outlet for Frank's ecological evangelism? The proposal succeeded not simply on its paper commendations but because there was nothing airy-fairy about this fellow Fraser Darling; he had backed his ideas with action on the ground! A grant from the Development Fund to the Department of Agriculture for Scotland saw the survey off in September 1944 with Frank as Director and Averil Morley as Research Assistant. Grant-aid covered the period 1944–50 and increased over the years to a maximum of £4000 per annum. In all, nine persons were employed and at the time of peak activity (1947–8) all nine (one part-time) had to share that sum which is testimony to the devotion of Frank and his team to the work. Averil had some hand in the drafting of the plan and also had a big hand in getting the survey under way. In the first year she was Frank's only assistant and worked full-time until their marriage at Kilmonivaig on 24 March 1948, and part-time until the birth of their first child, Richard, in March 1949.

In the Preface of *West Highland Survey: An Essay in Human Ecology*, Frank gives a potted version of the problem which the survey was set to solve.

Plate 10.3. (*Right to left*) Averil, Richard, James
and 'Peggy' at Shefford Woodlands in 1954.
(photo Miss F. Fraser Darling)

What is generally called the Highland problem may be said
to be 200 years old, although its roots reach farther into
history. It developed when the patriarchal clan system of
government was finally broken after the Rising of 1745;
when a new way of life had to be found; when the natural
resources of the forests were being depleted for purposes
beyond the needs of the people within the area; when sheep-
farming on the extensive system replaced the indigenous

cattle husbandry; and when the advent of the potato, and the decline in smallpox and biologically expensive internecine warfare, allowed the population to swarm as it had never done before, and at a rate far greater than in well-settled farming districts even as near as the eastern side of the Highlands. The problem has continued to deepen through periods of gross mismanagement, and of increasing differences between the simple social culture and primitive agriculture of the Highlands and Islands on the one hand, and the highly urbanized, commercial civilization of the rest of Great Britain on the other. The Highlands and Islands have had no buffer from the raw effects of these great changes of two centuries. Had Britain been physically three parts Highlands, the problem would not have arisen, because the nation would have developed with this particular environment as a major part of its being instead of as a sore little finger. The population concerned is 1/400th part of that of Great Britain.[127]

The survey starts with the optimism that the problem was in fact soluble. Failure in the past was due to a piecemeal, sectional approach by politicians and developers who aspired to cure a collection of ills by a breakthrough improvement in one of them. Two popular misconceptions were the beneficial effect which improved communications would have upon industry and the improvement in self-sufficiency in crofting townships by hydro-electricity. Frank believed that none of these antidotes would have the desired effect outside of an understanding of the wholeness of the problem, and of a linking of the socio-economic factors to the widespread, protracted misuse of the land. His notion of the total ecology of the situation as the baseline for planning and decision-making was before its time. He saw that a data-bank and information system was required and set out to acquire the approval of the sponsors of the survey to publish the tabular data in full – but failed. It is perhaps of little consequence that those data were deposited 'at certain accessible centres'; it is of the greatest consequence, however, that the survey was published as one of the first attempts at rural regional planning in Europe.

No-one had so far attempted to bring together in a single work such a corpus of knowledge and experience of the area. What effect would such an analysis of the whole natural and human situation have in creating new perspectives and pathways for remedial action previously unseen? What intellectual and practical opportunities would be obtained for a synthesis of local and regional conditions? What options for solutions to the Highland problem and its constituent problems would flow from the new state of knowledge? These questions were the fuel which propelled the survey but behind it all was Frank's conviction that having gathered the pieces together the jigsaw would fit and the picture of a new prosperity in the Highlands and Islands might stare him in the face. Yet he was not without his doubts.

> The desirable completeness of knowledge is probably unattainable, for historically we can infer only from that which is recorded intentionally or fortuitously in word, stone, soil, or artefact; in examining present conditions we are limited by the stage of development of research methods and our ability to apply them; and the problem involves the states of mens' minds to an extent and depth we cannot scan or fathom.[128]

The approach of the survey was novel then and remains novel even today. His idea of an essay in human ecology was born from his obsessions with man the animal, not man the human being. Of course, he acknowledged that man was human and subjected to an ecosystem which he had taken a hand in creating; yet, to him, man had a common denominator with the red deer he had studied in the Gruinard Forest, the gulls of Chleirich and the seals of Rona. He acclaimed the survey as a logical follow-on to his studies in animal ecology and behaviour into human affairs. He was always quick to point out man's wisdom in working *with* nature as, for example, in the use of shells and and seaweed spread by man further than the sea and the wind was able to carry it, to ameliorate the peaty soils; or the folly of working *against* nature, for example, by the over-grazing by rabbits (a man-introduced species) and domesticated stock, of sand dunes and sandy grasslands beyond the point of physical integrity with the destruction of great areas of pasture by rutted and blown sand. This interdependence of man and nature Frank saw as a covenant which had been betrayed by man in the Highlands and which had to be restored if any enduring solution to socio-economic problems was to be found.

> The foundations on which this Survey has been built are the soil, the sea, and the natural resources on which the human population is finally dependent if it is to be self-supporting biologically and economically. The interactions of human

205

behaviour, ideas and practices, of the growth and decline of population and their consequences on the terrain and the present generation of folk are the substance of this report. And finally, the bald unpalatable fact is emphasized that the Highlands and Islands are largely a devastated terrain, and that any policy which ignores this fact cannot hope to achieve rehabilitation.[129]

The covenant holds good in the self-supporting, self-regulating situation with no 'outside' influences. For example, the flocks of Soay sheep at St Kilda live in the absence of any interference by man; the populations are regulated by a natural mechanism. The survival and prosperity of the sheep population depends entirely on it utilising the limited pasture and shelter in such a way that in perpetuity the pastures and shelter are not destroyed. The covenant between the sheep and their islands may not be a conscious one in the minds of the animals but it is programmed genetically within them and locked into their behaviour patterns. The annual cycle of summer plenty followed by winter poverty sees the sheep having lost in March up to half their body weight of the previous September; the regime is severe but successful. This simple, basic dependability seldom, if ever, occurs in human societies because of provisioning from *within* and support from *outside*. The challenge of Tanera was that of self-sufficiency and the story of the red deer - like the Soay sheep - epitomised that natural state of self-sufficiency which is expressed so beautifully in the wild animal but which has been substantially lost by man. Perhaps it was an adherence to an ideology of natural resource management and nature conservation rather than of agriculture, fisheries and forestry for their own sectional interests, which prompted the subtitle *An Essay in Human Ecology*. Frank took a perverse delight when learning of natural disasters around the world – devastation by tornado in the USA, flood in Bengal or famine in Africa – in slamming man for bringing tragedy upon himself by living in areas prone to drastic elemental changes, or by abuse of the land by deforestation and overgrazing. He had pity on those who suffered; they were innocents in the hands of inept and often exploitive regimes. He was impressed, for example, by the dry-farming of the Hopi Indians on their arid mesas in Arizona; they cultivated in watersheds, but made no attempt unnecessarily to increase their numbers

206

by extending the area of cultivation of natural soils through irrigation and hoarding of water.

'Human ecology' exclaimed Mr Bowler-Hat. 'Whatever's that?' There is little doubt that the ideology employed by Frank in the Survey resulted in the work being non-conformist in the agricultural lobby and disregarded as a serious basis for policy and planning in the Highlands and Islands. In America the idea of a new prosperity for a finite area of country by integrated development of natural resources on ecological lines had been demonstrated by the Tennessee Valley Authority. Minds of the type which created TVA scarcely existed among Scottish decision-makers of the late forties and early fifties. Tom Johnston had the inspiration and vision for integrated development and Fraser Darling had both of those gifts plus the ability to put it on paper for the West Highlands and Islands. About the same time Bob Grieve was doing the same in the Clyde Valley. In later life, Frank mentioned frequently to me how inspired he had been by the TVA, how lacking in any imagination was the establishment in Scotland, and of how his Survey was far better known and appreciated in America than it was at home. 'Do you know that I never received an acknowledgement when I sent the final report of the Survey to St Andrew's House? Six years' work and not even an Official Paid Post Card in reply!'

Whether or not the Department and Frank were estranged in the course of the Survey is uncertain; in later life he expressed to me a personal dislike of the man with whom he worked in St Andrew's House. Certainly he would not find it easy to co-operate with the agricultural Civil Servants of the day at St Andrew's House; to them he was probably professionally outrageous and an administrative maverick. Iain Grant of Rothiemurchus remembers, from personal acquaintance at the time, how unwelcome Frank's writings were in the Department of Agriculture and the National Farmer's Union, and, later, confrontation between Frank and St Andrew's House staff during all the discussions on the proposed Deer Act! In an Introductory Note to the published report in 1955 the Development Commission on behalf of the Department stated (my italics) that

> Dr Darling and his colleagues *should be allowed* full scientific freedom in presenting and interpreting their results and in

expressing their opinions and conclusions. It follows that in this report on the Survey the conclusions and views are their own, freely expressed, without regard to Government policy or doctrine, and that *they carry with them no official implications or endorsement.*[130]

That is the standard disclaimer provided by the establishment when wishing to distance themselves from actual or possible alien opinion and information. No doubt those words were chosen with great care in the Scottish Office, yet not with sufficient care to avoid the impression that 'scientific freedom' was given in compensation for the lack of Government recognition of the Survey. The Commission and the Department also paid a handsome tribute to Frank in publishing the West Highland Survey directed by

> . . .one who makes a new approach to it [the West Highland problem] not only from the point of view of the ecologist but as having qualified himself deliberately for the task by long residence in the West Highlands and Islands. In this Survey Dr Darling has examined the history and physical and biological characteristics of the Highland area; he has studied the ecology of land use, the rise and decline of populations, the agricultural background, and the social conditions. His primary aim was to find the causes of existing conditions and thereafter to suggest how the crofter's resources can be rehabilitated and more fully used and his standard of living raised by the right care of the land, and also by having regard to its past and the changes brought about by the practices and customs of man, wise or unwise.[131]

In fact the Survey was never officially recognised nor used by Government. It has been a mine of information for the student of the West Highlands and Islands for thirty years, and though its statistics, social and economic conditions and assessments of natural resources are long since outdated, the basic ecological processes and many human values and attitudes are still the same.

Soon after the Survey, Frank went to America and met Paul Sears, the author of *Deserts on the March*, which awakened America to the ideas of conservation and population control, and recorded his feelings about the Survey which were released by his travels with Sears in Ohio.

> Paul has one of those cultivated minds which must yet have close contact with the land. He farms himself in Ohio and
> 208

sees with a farmer's eye. As we drove and walked the next morning through the good land along Lake Erie we got the feeling of having known each other for a long time. For me I had found a master as well as a friend. Paul gave me that day what I badly wanted – assurance. My mind had been running along a train of ideas about land use for several years, and the more I had felt the truth of what I was finding, the lonelier a man I was becoming. To one who likes a mountain black-face ram as well as I do, there is no pleasure in coming to the decision that extensive, i.e non-agricultural, pastoralism eventually devastates a country, wherever it is.My work of the West Highland Survey, which I was then just finishing, had brought this out as a central theme or chain – deforestation and its consequences, pastoralism with a lack of balance between cattle and sheep, the sheep always taking more than they could give, the gradual deterioration of the habitat, with the economic and sociological collapse of the West Highland region. I found myself going dead against the political and administrative trends and against the pseudo-scientific opinion of the agricultural advisers. Unless you are some sort of exhibitionist or professional awkward fellow, there is no particular happiness in this kind of career. But I could not forswear trust as I saw it.

I went to America shaken, not as to whether I was right in the conclusions to which I had come through a long period of time, but socially, as how one was to go on living and earning a living in an environment where hard thought and – as I thought – well worked out conclusions were considered unreal and unrealistic.[132]

The West Highland Survey stands as a milestone in environmental science in Britain. It was twenty-five years before its time. Had the work been done today it would have been immediately relevant to the Integrated Development Programme for the Western Isles, which the Department of Agriculture and Fisheries and other agencies are operating with financial support from the EEC, and to programmes of the Highlands and Islands Development Board, Forestry Commission, Nature Conservancy Council, Countryside Commission for Scotland, the Regional Councils and Comhairle nan Eilean, none of which were in existence when the Survey was ready for use, but which the Survey helped to create and activate. The organisers of any future Agricultural Development Plan for the Scottish Highlands would do well to read the *West Highland Survey*, imbibe both its knowledge and spirit and, with its help, generate a new vision. The organiser of a Highland ADP would also profit from reading one of Frank's articles contemporary to the Survey in the *Glasgow Herald*; the individual and corporate will to make short-term sacrifices for sustained long-term benefits is crucial.

One of the truths that hurt and one which arouses a good deal of antagonism when mentioned in Britain is that marginal land under agriculture is often in the hands of people who are running on a shoestring and hopelessly under-capitalised. The same phenomenon is evident in America and that is why you will see lots of badly beaten-up land in Georgia and the Carolinas. Land use by these people is headed the wrong way, but because they have to live and that happens to be their place, they have to go on misusing the land to get their short-term but diminishing dividend. We feel in this country at present that marginal land, because it will not pay agriculturally, must be made to pay somehow or other, if only on paper, so vast sums are going into subsidisation of modes of land use which have shown themselves unable to be perpetuated. Eastern America is primarily a cellulose-growing area – via timber – and a yielder of water. Much of marginal Scotland is just that also.

I know quite well that I am talking heresy in this country at the present time. If we don't pour money down the drain or scatter it on the bare hill sides for an uneconomic return, what are we to do for food? It is quite a problem, but this question is a diversion from the old theme that it is easier to let blind necessity allow continued misuse of land than it is to start expensive, long-term rehabilitation towards right use, which may temporarily cut down the yield of food.

My own view is that a switch in the management of marginal land will have to be faced up to within the next century. The area under agriculture will decrease, but that which continues to be farmed will be farmed better altogether. Forestry will increase because forest is the right cover for most of our slopes, and the existence of forest growth will enhance the workability of the lessened area under agriculture. The high grazings remain, and we shall have to use these as our forefathers did, by herding the cattle in the corries above the tree line in summer. Life up there in weekly shifts is not half so bad as it looks from down below, and high-ground herding might be an attractive long-vacation employment for the right type of undergraduate and older schoolboy.

In short, we shall ultimately accept the dictum of Dr Paul Sears, Professor of Conservation at Yale, 'The soundest ecological apportionment of the landscape would be represented by a minimum of carefully selected, skilfully operated ploughland with a maximum of natural vegetation', except that much of our natural vegetation has gone from our marginal lands and it will take time to regenerate it. The ultimate off-take in food and cellulose from marginal Scotland if the land were ecologically integrated, and therefore building up in natural wealth, would certainly be greater than at present when we are attempting to bolster a deteriorating habitat under continued misuse.[133]

These words are even more relevant today than they were in the mid-forties; the agricultural surpluses and quotas of the mid-eighties, with accompanying forecasts of vast areas of marginal land to be taken from agricultural production, offer a whole new opportunity for rehabilitation along the lines envisaged in this article. The socio-economic ills have persisted despite Frank's message of atonement for centuries of misuse of the Highlands. His key point has not been accepted, that depopulation can only be cured by placing the use of the land on a sounder footing. Fishing boats, home industries, tourism, better communications, electricity and water supplies are important but not seminal to solving the Highland problem in the long-term. The solution lies in land use and by atonement Frank meant that the land should be rested for a century or more from sheep which, in many areas of the West Highland, he would have replaced by cattle, from large stocks of red deer and from muirburn. For proof one only requires to look at the spontaneous growth of woodland which occurs throughout the Highlands where sheep and deer are fenced out and burning stopped. He thought that, in the West Highlands, the cattle-sheep ratio should be narrowed from existing stocks of up to 1:78 to well below 1:10 and that numbers of red deer be halved. He espoused the conservation of woodland in the Highlands by greatly reducing grazing and burning and envisaged a more efficient agriculture over a much reduced area of improved land. He favoured conifer and broadleaved afforestations well-proportioned with each other and with arable land and open hillside, in the make-up of Highland country. His views, I am certain, would be little changed today. These days strong objection is taken in the Highlands to the land being termed 'wilderness'. It smacks of the primitive and a lack of civilised respect. Yet, in its origins of use by John Muir in the Sierra Nevada, wilderness was conceived not as a place of savagery, not a curse upon the civilised world; rather was it the opposite: an asset to humanity, a noble and civilising influence upon mankind dating from the book of Exodus. However, wrong as popular Highland reaction to 'wilderness' may be in the eyes of the ecologist, it is broadly understood as having bitter roots in Highland history; the desolation of mountain and glen possesses a macabre quality different from Muir's 'country of light'. Much of the wild land north of the Highland Line is *not* true wilderness; it is a man-made wilderness which in Frank's mind should be managed back to a semblance of its former character as wildland for the people as a whole. This he envisaged as providing employment in the areas greater than the present regimes of hill-farming and sport, a concept which comes close to other ideas he had of the establishment of national parks in Scotland.

After leaving Tanera and during the first three years of the Survey, Frank wrote his *Natural History in the Highlands and Islands*. This provided a fine outlet for his wealth of knowledge and experience gathered over ten years' continuous residence in close proximity to wildlife and in contact with almost all the Highland naturalists of the day. Among these was James Fisher, ornithologist, island-goer, and one of the editors of the New Naturalist Series of Collins. It also provided a ready repository for new information which came his way through the Survey and gave an opportunity to describe in a more popular way some of the content of the Survey which related to the conservation of nature and natural resources.

Some of the chapters of his *Natural History* were in fact trailers for parts of the Survey, though it must be understood that the former covered the whole of the Highlands and the Hebrides and the latter the West Highlands only. Parts I and II of the *Survey* relate to chapters I to 3 of the *Natural History*. Chapter 4, entitled 'The human factor and remarkable changes in populations of animals', relates the saga of human devastation of the Highlands and Islands and prepared the reader for a habitat by habitat review of what now remains. Two chapters deal with the life histories of the animals he loved the most, red deer and grey seals, and recites a good deal of *A Herd of Red Deer* and *A Naturalist on Rona*.

Frank illuminated the *Survey* with many insights into the working of both man and nature separately and together and comes to conclusions which are often of more inspirational than pragmatic use.

> The question which no one has yet carefully analysed in order to make any convincing answer concerning the Highland problem is, Where are we going and what do we want to do? It seems to us that there are three ways to go: first, Gaeldom as a culture can be ignored altogether and every effort made to crush it out, or absorb it into the undifferentiated magma of Western Civilization so that any distinctive character is lost; second, Gaeldom can attempt cultural resistance to pressure by reaction, adopting rigidity, looking back over its shoulder and refusing to change; third, it can accept change and evolution in the conscious poise of its own strength and its own values.
>
> The first course was followed as a policy in the eighteenth century, greatly aided by such evil influences as the Society for the Propagation of Christian Knowledge. Such action failed though it crippled Gaeldom.
>
> The second course implies death from within, because it means in effect that the culture is refusing the challenge of proximity of the dominant culture. An organism which declines challenge and attempts passive defence is doomed. It can no longer evolve, but becomes encysted.
>
> The third course is by far the hardest for all of us, because we do not fully know how. It would be a great test of human behaviour between man and man, and our knowledge of integration of scientific and political action on an ecological level is as yet dim. We do not have enough administrators trained to the notion that technological advance will not solve the Highland problem without imaginative tolerance and a capacity to foresee consequences.[134]

Those were conclusions taken from 'The social situation'. I close on the Survey with the following, perhaps the most incisive of Frank's conclusions from 'Ecology and landuse'.

> The greatest value the mass of Highland land could give to the nation would be as a continuing productive wild land in which perhaps twice as many people could live than are there at present. The very fact of successful growth would be a satisfying thing, helping to keep a forest population happy

213

living there, cropping the wild lands but not mining them as they have been mined. This ecological continuum, nobly bearing its character of wilderness, would yield more to the nation than the subsidized devastation, rendered the more macabre by imposed mechanical industries which, as we saw in the chapter on population, have a habit of concentrating population and destroying the desired dispersal over the countryside. Man-made devastation is no environment for psychological health in a people as a whole. There is nothing unrefined about the wilderness, nothing unmodern or outmoded.[135]

11

Visit to St Kilda

During the course of the Survey, Frank visited most of the parishes in the West Highlands and Islands and, having an eye for country and people, gained an immense amount of knowledge. No one had made the same journey with such interest in the natural make-up of the area and insight into the ecological processes which bound man and nature as a unity. In 1946 he was delighted by a visit to Sutherland.

> Have just returned from a week in the extreme N.W., the emptiest and remotest-feeling corner of Britain. Nowhere else are there such vast slopes, not necessarily steep, but going on and on, and as you cross the horizon there are miles and miles more, and sometimes a shepherd's house or shooting lodge tucked in the corner of an alluvial fan from a hill stream. There are a few crofts hanging on to the coastal strip of Archaean gniess, like white currants on a grey bun! Nowhere else in the Highlands are the colour effects so vivid. Then I joined a flight (in a 'Sunderland' flying boat from Invergordon) to see the Scottish Atlantic seal nurseries with James Fisher, Brian Roberts and a few more. We wound about through the Orkneys and Shetlands and then swung across to North Rona, Sula Sgeir, the Flannans and St Kilda and back again to the Sound of Harris and up to the Butt of Lewis and Cape Wrath. Magnificent, but I was very ill (with airsickness), and all in one day.[136]

That was Frank's first, rather miserable sight of St Kilda which, following the evacuation of the people in 1930 was then uninhabited and had become the symbol of depopulation and dereliction. He wished to visit St Kilda as a member of the Scottish Wildlife Conservation Committee and Director of the Survey and to add his weight to the scientific interest being expressed in the islands.

Placed in the solitudes of the wild ocean 64 km west of

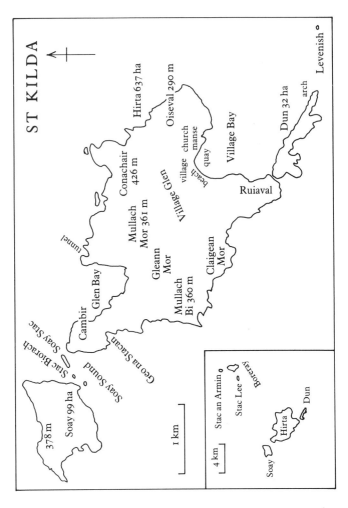

ST KILDA

Levenish

Hirta 637 ha

Oiseval 290 m

Conachair 426 m

Village Glen

village church manse

beach quay

Village Bay

Ruiaval

Dun 32 ha

arch

Mullach Mor 361 m

Gleann Mor

Claigean Mor

Mullach Bi 360 m

tunnel

Glen Bay

Cambir

Geo na Stacan

Stac Biorach

Soay Stac

Soay Sound

Soay 99 ha

378 m

1 km

Stac an Armin

Stac Lee

Boreray

Dun

Hirta

Soay

4 km

Griminish Point in North Uist, this freakish archipelago is a little world on its own. There are four cliff-bound islands and many spectacular stacks. The great precipices rise, sometimes vertically, sometimes with spacious terraces. Conachair, the highest cliffs, drop plumb 390 m to the sea. The dark pinnacled bastions, pitted with sea-filled caverns, pierced in

216

natural tunnels and built with buttress and arches, take the full force of the Atlantic. Stac an Armin (190 m) and Stac Lee (163 m) are two magnificent spires dwarfed by the 375 m western face of Boreray, and all are covered in summer with solans (*Sula bassana*), as if plastered with snow. Nineteen species of sea-bird breed there of which puffins, fulmars, kittiwakes and guillemots are the most numerous. There are sub-species of wren and field-mice (see p.100) unique to St Kilda and a primitive variety of sheep: a living 'fossil' similar to the early domesticated sheep possessed by Neolithic farmers in Britain, the Soay breed.

Soay sheep take their name from the Isle of Soay at St Kilda and it is thought that they were taken there by early settlers, some of whose artefacts have been found. The sheep were probably already there when the Vikings arrived in the ninth century to give the name 'Soay' (meaning 'sheep island') to the most inaccessible island of the group. There are many accounts of the human and natural history of St Kilda available. The literature of these well-documented yet ever mysterious islands is listed in the *Handbook of St Kilda* published by the National Trust for Scotland.

When I was appointed as the Nature Conservancy's first Regional Officer in NW Scotland in 1957, I wrote to Frank asking advice on what I might do. In these days the job specification was almost *carte blanche* and there was great scope for personal preference which now hardly exists for my successors. One of the suggestions made by Frank was an ecological study of the Soay sheep at St Kilda and another – almost to be expected – the continuation of his studies of populations of grey seals at North Rona and elsewhere. As it happened, I followed both of these suggestions between 1958 and 1970 with separate teams of colleagues. The seal work resulted in a few papers, the most important of which was with R. Niall Campbell who was also a personal friend of Frank's of long standing from his days at Kilcamb Lodge; the sheep work resulted in the monograph *Island Survivors: The Ecology of the Soay Sheep of St Kilda* with sixteen authors. At the suggestion of Professor Peter Jewell, who joined the Soay sheep research project in 1959 and is still continuing the study today from the Department of Physiology, University of Cambridge, I asked Frank if he would write the Foreword to *Island Survivors: The Ecology of the Soay Sheep*

Plate 11.1. Soay sheep at St Kilda, one of the most primitive sheep in the world. Frank saw the flocks at St Kilda as offering an outstanding opportunity for research in ecology and animal behaviour. (photo J. Morton Boyd)

of St Kilda. He did and gave vent to his knowledge and nostalgia for islands, sheep and people who had played such an important part in his earlier life.

The second millennium BC is an immensely important era in the human history of the Mediterranean and north-western Europe: the early middle-eastern civilizations were getting ideas sorted out and written down. People were on the move and – a fact of primary significance – western European weather seems to have had a good spell. Mediterranean island peoples made great voyages and set up structures which are objects of wonderment today, Avebury, Stonehenge, Callanish, Stenness, Maeshowe and the rest. We know all too little of those first civilized cultures of our islands and of what the people brought with them, but we have one *living* remnant so little changed from them, the Soay sheep . . . I have known them intimately for over forty-five years, since that other romantic James Cossar Ewart retired from the Chair of Natural History in Edinburgh and left us his handful of Soay sheep, at the Department of Animal Breeding. When we became the Institute of Animal Genetics in 1930, Frank Crewe made a fine gesture in asking the aged Cossar to open the new building. Cossar was splendid, telling us of his

218

Plate 11.2. The village of St Kilda in a similar state to that in which Frank and his expedition found it in 1948. (photo J. Morton Boyd)

meeting Darwin and Tyndall. It was a great day, but in the afternoon Cossar got tired of the fuss and came to me, asking if I would take him to the Soay sheep and Celtic ponies. He asked me because I was newly returned from the northern isles, tracing types of sheep.

Cossar took off his lum hat and claw hammer coat and put them carefully on the gatepost, undid his cuff links and folded back the cumbersome starched cuffs. He felt some hind legs for callosities and we more or less cornered a few sheep. Those who know how these sheep behave will understand my qualification of more or less. The old man was happy.[137]

The crucial date was 30 August 1930; on that day the St Kildans, at their own request, were evacuated and resettled on the mainland. Their homes on the main island Hirta (638 ha) were left full of their possessions which they could not carry with them. Some of their sheep on Boreray and Soay were left also, but those on Hirta were removed. And so, the islands which had for centuries been inhabited were then deserted. The chattels of the vanished race of hardy, cliff-climbing, sea-fowling islanders fell in ruin, but there was at

219

the same time an awakening of scientific interest in St Kilda. In 1931 an expedition from Oxford and Cambridge visited the islands to carry out an ecological survey one year after the evacuation to serve as a datum for future comparison. It was in this spirit of scientific enquiry that students from Edinburgh University, keen to monitor ecological change, asked Frank if he would be leader of an expedition to St Kilda in 1948. Frank agreed, but wisely said that James Fisher, who was the most knowledgeable person of the day on St Kilda, should come as co-leader and nominate one or two others. Apart from Frank's undoubted leadership qualities in island-going, the students had another reason for asking him. He was a friend of the Scottish Office and might arrange for a fishery cruiser to transport the expedition.

Frank wrote a disappointingly meagre journal of this expedition which he sent to me in November 1972 when he was moving home from Berkshire to Moray. The following are interesting excerpts from this journal, which peters out after a few days.

> Darling asked the Scottish Home Department for transport in the Fishery Cruiser. The s.h.d. replied that before this could be granted the Scottish Wild Life Conservation Committee should give its blessing to the Expedition. This was given, but with no great enthusiasm, at the Committee's meeting on June 7, 1948. Lord Bute had given permission for the Expedition to work on St Kilda, towards the end of April, on condition that no specimens of any kind whatever should be collected and removed from the island. Towards the end of June the Expedition was asked by Lord Bute to bring some live gannets and gulls from St Kilda for the Glasgow Zoo. Darling declined to do this (a) on personal grounds and (b) because he could not involve his Committee (the s.w.l.c.c.) which had advised the Scottish Home Department to transport the Expedition.
>
> The party gathered at Oban on the afternoon of July 8, to join F.C. *Vaila*. A northerly gale was blowing, hard enough to prevent sailing that night, but all except Darling went aboard. Next morning, Friday, the wind had abated to a fresh breeze and the Cruiser sailed at 10.30 a.m. The route was by Sound of Mull, Cairns of Coll, Sound of Pabbay, Monach Isles to the Village Bay, Hirta, reached at 5.15 a.m. July 10. The party came ashore 9.15–9.30 a.m. and decided to occupy the Manse, which house was in very bad condition. The whole place was cleaned and the range got into working

220

order. Many windows and doors had been broken. Occupancy of the Manse was decided upon in order to clean it up and put the place in better order.

Tuesday, July 13. A short morning. We got the boat down yesterday, launched it and put her on a mooring. It is a poor thing, a *quondam* motor boat with heavy engine bed, a leaky stern plastered with cement and with high coamings. We pulled her in again today as the weather is so bad and she had leaked a good deal of water. I pottered round the village examining the cleits. Many of them are of excellent rough workmanship. They are in the same style as the cell on Rona, built dry and tapering to the roof across which slabs are laid. A thickness of 18 inches of turf and soil is put on the roof and they are quite waterproof. As the purpose of the cleits is drying various things, the walls outside are left uncovered with turf. Odds and ends of things such as boat rudders and old chairs are still in the cleits. The cottages have largely fallen in, but they mostly had board floors, matchboarded rooms and a small loft lit by a skylight. Bedsteads, some bedding, chairs, tables and dressers are still in the rooms, mouldering to decay. The corrugated-iron and matchboarded post office still contains remnants of official notices and there is a bottle with a label showing it contained s.o. red ink. Life on St Kilda as it must have been lived latterly cannot have been very primitive. Scarpa, Harris, or Smerisary, Moidart, are much more primitive today . . .

Wednesday, July 14. Still N. and S.W. and the whole island was blanketed in mist by evening. Most of the party got as far as the Cambir today. This is a most exciting place. The top beyond the neck has a flat, meadow-like area of good grass. The cliffs are most spectacular, and full of puffins and fulmars. There were 56 Atlantic seals hauled out in Geo na Stacan. Only one was a yearling and two or three were two-year-olds. The rest were adults and I was surprised to see the general darkness of this sample. There was one dead-black bull among them. One cow had a white belly with no spots apparent, and another bull was battleship-grey all over with no white marks. The view of the stacs and Soay from the Cambir is fantastic. The cliff is almost sheer for nearly 700 feet, yet on the few grassy ledges below were several sheep. Stac Biorach (236 feet) is an unscalable pinnacle, the top covered with guillemots. Soay Stac is long, almost as high, and pierced by the sea. Soay rises, cliff bound, just beyond, to a height of 1,225 feet. Sheep were visible on Soay. I had reached the Cambir by going down into Gleann Mor past the shielings. These were nothing more than the ring-huts of prehistoric times. On the other side of the Glen is a great hollow littered with enormous rocks and outcrops. The herbage was particularly green and the puffins had invaded the knolls thus far inland. We came home by Claigeann Mor and brought the long piece of anchor chain from the [air] wreck. Thick mist all the way . . .

Friday, July 16 . . .We fished from the boat in the late evening round the Bay and caught enough mackerel for the party. A ship appeared as we were out and on coming up to her found she was *Explorer* the Fishery Board Research Ship. Capt. Sandison was aboard and we exchanged reminiscences of his visit to Rona ten years ago when he brought the derelict coble. One of the officers of *Vigilant* was also on board, and some of the scientists from Torry. They gave us some more fish, enough for another big meal.

Sunday, July 18. Beautiful morning with light breeze from s.e. A party went out in *Lady Elspeth* [yacht] to round Boreray and possibly the whole group. They did get round Boreray and the Stacs and were well buffeted. I went to the Cambir intending to establish a camp for tonight. D.P. and V.R. came and we hoped to make a series of profiles of soil conditions. As it happened the weather came dull, wind blew up strong from s.e. and then rain. We dug into a small green flat just above and south of the neck of the Cambir. There were three feet of peat and we had not reached the bottom. The peat is soapy and brittle like fen peat. It is possible this is not acid peat at all. D.P. took samples at 1, 2 and 3 feet for analysis and will get advice from H. Godwin when he returns to Cambridge. The weather got worse and the chaps hurried on home, being clad only in shorts and shirts. I descended into the bowl of Gleann Mor to poke around the Shielings. The mist came down low and very thick and I had some difficulty in getting home. The wind was all over the place at the head of the glen and I could not get my bearings. Eventually, I worked by wind on the cliffs, slope and nature of vegetation and finally found myself coming to the bed of Amhuin Ruiaval which was not too bad. Had a glorious hot bath. After dinner walked with James [Fisher] and the Polwarths [from *Lady Elspeth*] into the village where James showed us the earth house, almost the only Pictish remnant, which is long and narrow and has been very carelessly excavated. The beehive shieling, known as Calum Mor's House, is large and high, but very rough and has lost all its outer coat of turf. The job is so rough that one wonders how on earth it stays up. The chocking of the roof stones is very well done.[138]

When the Expedition returned from St Kilda, Frank

222

Plate 11.3. Thrift on the lichen-covered rocks
of the ungrazed island of Dun, St Kilda.
(photo J. Morton Boyd)

found in his pile of mail the latest copy of the *Scottish Naturalist*. It contained a scathing review of *Natural History in the
Highlands and Islands* by V. C. Wynne-Edwards, the recently
appointed Regius Professor of Natural History at Aberdeen
University. The weakness of Frank's make-up as a scientist
without a classical scientific training was suddenly exposed
by one whose scientific pedigree was beyond question. However, Wynne-Edwards' attack was not focused on Frank
alone but on the Editors of the New Naturalist series for their
assertions in the Editors' Preface that 'every care has been
taken . . . to ensure the scientific accuracy of factual state-
ments'.

> They [the Editors] must therefore share the blame for the
> surprising number of half-truths and errors in the book,
> some of which at least are apparent to every discerning read-
> er. The author has not been deterred by them either from
> embracing topics with which he has had no opportunity of
> becoming fully conversant.

Plant ecology is one of these. One might surely expect something more than a flourish of scientific names and uncritical lists . . . Marine and fresh-water biology are no less unfortunate. The yarn handed out about the migration of the herring was the latest thing in the days of Thomas Pennant's *British Zoology* (1761–66); it has long been regarded as an illusion . . . the little bivalve *Pisidium* masquerades as a 'snail' . . . There is no attempt to throw light on conditions in Scotland by comparing them with those elsewhere, even in the rest of the British Isles, let alone Scandinavia . . . Among the curiosities of the book are the passages referring to scent and the olfactory sense . . . I [V.C.W.-E.] cannot follow the supposed relation between irritability and humidity, even with the help of the surrealist graph [see p.51], in which these two variables rise together on the same axis . . . It would do no good to carry this uncharitable dissection further. Clearly a book like this is exceptionally difficult to write, and most of us would not have the courage to attempt it. Fraser Darling's views on conservation I most heartily endorse; his passionate love of his chosen land, and ability to inspire it in others I admire and respect. All human authors err (and I hope in this respect that reviewers are as inhuman as they seem); we might well have been worse off with the opposite extreme, a prosy compendium of incredible dullness, richly documented with footnotes. At least this book has warmth and personality and an infectious appreciation of the good things of life. Indeed, I feel merciless only towards those who dared to say that 'every care has been taken . . .'[139]

This review deeply wounded Frank and angered the Editors of the New Naturalist books who were of scientific pedigree much more akin to the reviewer than to the author. In a letter to me dated 30 May 1986 Vero Wynne-Edwards wrote warmly of Frank with some lingering regret of these distant events: 'It [the review] is a reminder of a painful episode – my own remorse being of course less grievous than the wound I had inflicted on Frank. What I said was no doubt true, but saying it did more harm than good. I did not know Frank personally then, but it soon brought us together. Big-hearted as ever, he soon forgave me, and we remained on the friendliest of terms for the rest of his life.'

Fortunately, there were many favourable reviews which placed his work among the most popular books on the Highlands and Islands ever written. I know; it was I who revised it in the early sixties and can testify that the errors and

224

inaccuracies which I dealt with, though real enough, were minor when compared with Frank's achievement in having attempted such a task and of having done it as much as a work of art – a literary masterpiece of its kind – as a work of science. The licence which Frank adopted in his interpretation of one of the most exciting areas of wild country in Europe clearly irritated his academic contemporaries (as many of his other writings did), who were less than charitable, particularly in criticism of detailed errors of fact (which are corrected easily in new editions), when the magnanimity of the total work apparently passed unnoticed.

In 1949 Frank was asked to be a representative of UNESCO on the occasion of the concurrent conferences on conservation of natural resources of the United Nations and the International Union of the Conservation of Nature at Lake Success on Long Island. In his own words, Frank saw himself as a cosmopolitan remote from his own countrymen. He had the 'pleasant and wholly warming honour' of finding himself on his first visit to America made a vice-president of conference. This must have been for him a considerable boost to morale after a year of trouble and disappointment in Britain. Three months before Lake Success he wrote to Frank Kendon:

> The country here (Berkshire) is restful and giving and I have been grateful for it because in the way of affairs I have had one of the most trying years in my life. You know how it is – there are times when all sorts of arrangements go wrong. Things began that way last May with a review of my *Nat. Hist. H. & I.* book. All manner of nastiness followed and the matter isn't cleared up yet. Then a secretary cleverly pinched £50 and possibly more, though he showed no brains any other way. He has disappeared. The Gov't in Scotland has also acted in a cynical and dishonest way towards the Survey I ran and I come away rather broken hearted, whatever I may say to the contrary. Lastly, things have gone very differently personally than I had hoped in connexion with the Nature Conservancy. In such a turmoil of events in which personalities have acted in ways to make one sorrow, I have found difficulty in keeping a really steady keel. My new married life has been a great help. I know I have been mentally sick because I haven't settled to steady work, despite constant business with small things. And I know that I am not in a position where anyone else is going to put me right. It will have to be my own strength and objective detachment.

225

Nothing is surer than that God helps those who help themselves. I am, therefore, trying to school myself, to avoid like the plague any self pity or sense of persecution. These latter are sure killers. I don't indulge in them and in many ways can meet things with acceptance, but there are odd moments when some new bash comes along, and one finds events hard to bear. It has been an extraordinary year and one which will not have been spiritually unprofitable if I can overcome. Of course, I have no doubt that I shall overcome, but that does not make the battle any easier while it is going on. I hate meanness, speciousness, dishonest thinking and jealousy, Frank, and it is the expression of these things in the past year which has upset me so, in people I did not expect it from. At the same time may I say what a lot of good a good act does – not necessarily to me, that's by the way – but when one comes in contact with active goodness, its influence is very great, very comforting and healing.[140]

In the late forties Frank dropped temporarily the 'Fraser' from his name. He tried on some occasions to distance himself from the 'Fraser' which was given to him by Bobbie by calling himself plain 'Frank Darling'; on other occasions such as in authorship of *Natural History in the Highlands and Islands* (1947) he still held to 'Fraser Darling'. However, as he explained to me later when he had finally adopted the full style 'Frank Fraser Darling', he was so widely known in public life as 'Fraser Darling' that whether he or any others of the family thought differently, the public was prepared to accept nothing less than 'Fraser Darling'. Bobbie never remarried. Alasdair, who greatly cherished the Fraser connection, has adopted the style 'Fraser-Darling' but Christina and Averil's children hold to the unhyphenated style, as Frank did in his entry in *Who's Who*.

Frank was now forty-six and was to live for another thirty years. However, his life was undergoing a rapid and fairly radical change which was to take him to America and Africa with the same banners of conservation which he had raised and carried in Britain in the thirties and forties. His island life was behind him and, though he was to maintain his contacts in the Scottish Highlands throughout his life, the fifties and sixties were to be spent in new scenes with new associates in climes far distant from the isles and glens of Scotland; that, I hope, is the subject of another book.

226

Epilogue: Lochyhill

In November 1972 I received the following letter which was
my first contact with Lochyhill.

My dear Morton,
   Home again from Washington, possibly my last trip. I am
suddenly feeling much better after 2¼ years and after the
doctors telling me I can now expect no improvement. If I am
truly to get better, it won't be a Christian Science triumph
because I had resigned myself to unsteadiness evermore. But
again, if I am getting better I am going to follow it up and try
to get as fit as the angina will allow.
   The big news is that we have decided to give up Shefford
Woodlands House. It is too much for Christina and me to
keep up, with the children growing up and going away. We
hope to sell in the summer of 1973 and to move to Lochyhill
in the autumn of that year. What a job! As a start to clearing
a desk I feel I can't chuck out the enclosed [St Kilda Journal]
without your seeing it first. It is of no value, except just a
little sentimentally. Many of us are still together. I saw Philip
Hugh Jones at the cocktail party launching the Matto Grosso
book and David Gifford is in Edinburgh. Duncan [Poore]
and Vernon [Robertson] are close to us.
   Come again this winter if you can. The US Department of
Interior have given me a Yellowstone Medal, one of six
to 'Elder Statesmen'. Makes you think! The Conservation
Foundation has given me a large silver bowl, a copy of one
by Paul Revere the early American silversmith. Absolutely
lovely, with the Foundation emblem engraved along with a
nice inscription. When I clapped down these silver offerings
on the Customs bench, the officer said 'tokens of international good will' and let me through. I felt quite a feller.
Love to Winifred and yourself, Frank.[141]

   The last stretch of the road from Edinburgh to Forres
crosses the rolling moorlands of the watershed between the

227

Spey and Findhorn valleys. It is beautiful, spacious country which still possesses a sprinkling of native pine trees. I always stop on the high point of the road to look for raptors and, in season, the white hares sitting proud in a stark, dark land. Beyond are the beautifully forested estates of Darnaway and Altyre and the Laigh of Moray upon which is the farm of Lochyhill, hard by the eastern boundary of the well-kept little town of Forres.

Frank and Christina's attitude to Lochyhill was similar to that at Shefford Woodlands. The house stands on a hillock above and out of contact from the biggins of the farm. It was sheltered on the west by trees and has an attractive garden of about 0.25 ha with ample room for peafowl, bantams and goats. The house was in good order but was put right with the building of a sun room, two bathrooms and a well-equipped kitchen. The place was not large enough to take the large pieces of furniture from Shefford but in walking into the house for the first time I could not but admire how well the furnishings of their Berkshire home had been fitted into the archetype of Scottish farm houses; much of the atmosphere of the former had also been transferred to the latter. There by the front door a peacock, in the hall the Daniell print of Tanera harbour, in the sun room the curled leopard cub in the block of serpentine, in the drawing roonm the rococo clock, in the sitting room Russell Flint's Spanish ladies, in the kitchen the oak table with the brass candlesticks; warming by the Aga vent a charged decanter of claret. Everywhere I turned I felt that little or no break had taken place in Frank's retirement to Lochyhill; all the old familiar charm was still there in a different setting.

The noise of the car tyres on the gravel drive would set the three Pekinese a-barking and before I could gather together my things Frank and Christina were at the door extending a welcome which, over the years, had become ever more affectionate. Frank's massive frame towered above us and seemed more massive against the smaller scale of farm house in comparison with the manor house of yesterday. Translated also was Christina's cuisine and the candle-lit dinner served upon the polished oak table in the little kitchen. From the north-facing dormer windows there was a splendid view of the Moray coast, the Firth and the distant hills of Easter Ross and Sutherland.

228

Plate I. Frank with Christina (*right*) and Francesca in
Glen Affric in 1970. (photo Miss F. Fraser Darling)

They sat together in a double spoke-backed chair in pale
wood and I looked across the table in the soft flicker of the
candle flames. Ten years previously at Shefford Woodlands
in the same setting I had thrilled to Frank's accounts of his
travels; now with him in retirement at Lochyhill and unable
to travel far because of failing health, he was eager to hear of
my travels. In the seventies great changes were wrought in
the Nature Conservancy of which Frank was a founding
father, following the Rothschild Report. There followed the
devolution debate in which the newly created Nature Conservancy Council was close to the eye of the political storm.
Through this troubled time I was caught up in the running
of the NCC in Scotland, from London as well as from Edinburgh, and travelled the country continuously to visit places
and people in an endless round of meetings. Abroad, my
work at that time took me to East Africa, the Middle East,
the Soviet Union and Scandinavia . . . All this was manna to
Frank, stimulating his memory, evoking his humour and
making him forget his debility.

229

On 17 September 1975 at the General Assembly of the International Union for the Conservation of Nature and Natural Resources at Kinshasa in Zaire, there was a poignant moment for me. In his absence I was asked to receive, on Frank's behalf, the John Philips Medal, IUCN's highest award. The President, Professor Donald Kuenen from Leiden, made appropriate remarks in the brief ceremony, quoting one of Frank's pithy sayings which states the obvious with a pregnancy of meaning: 'Don, you know, we must never forget that today is the present!' In my own Journal I record the great thrill this was for me, the shiver in my spine and the deep feeling of affection for Frank in my remarks to the hushed international audience receiving instant translation into other languages.

> Sir Frank Fraser Darling's life has turned full circle. Almost half a century ago he started his work with the red deer of the Scottish Highlands and the grey seals of the Hebrides. Since then he has come to influence us all in the conservation movement, particularly in Europe, North America and Africa. Now, as it were, he has come home to roost in Scotland and lives in retirement in the beautifully wooded lands of Moray.
>
> Mr President, I am sure that Sir Frank would wish me to convey to you, Sir, to IUCN and to this distinguished Assembly, his humble and most grateful thanks for this outstanding acclaim of his work. Thank you!'

Applause. 'Well said, just right!' said Sir Peter Scott as I resumed my seat beside him in the audience. I could hardly have felt better had I received the award myself and it gave me a good reason to go and see Frank at Lochyhill soon after I returned to Scotland.

Throughout the seventies his health gradually deteriorated. The trouble with his middle ear affected his balance and the inability to walk straight, coupled with angina, made him increasingly housebound and cut him off from his worldwide circle of friends. In September 1971 he came with me on what was to be his last journey to the islands, to Orkney where we met his life-long friend of island days, Malcolm Stewart. We visited Hoy and journeyed to Rackwick, where Frank stood among the deserted crofts on a grey, cold day and pronounced upon the plans of the Hoy Trust to bring life back to the Island. His tall craggy figure standing beside the little stone-built cot at Sandybraes was reminiscent of the Old Man in the sandstone pillar, unsighted behind the Culags.

At Glen we talked to Jack Rendall, the last surviving crofter, and looked across the unkempt fields to the lip of the bay, a curve of thrashing breakers and a back cloth of red perpendicular sea-cliffs. Frank might have been back on Mingulay or Hirta of years long ago. He looked frail and ill as the stormy blast tugged at his clothes and his melancholy look seemed to match the occasion perfectly. He told of how he had thought of buying Gairsay when recently the island had come on the market. This was not to be, not only because of cost but also because it was the incarnation of the island farm and that was a stage in life already lived and never to be relived. Gairsay with its fine hill and ancient, fortified Norse drinking hall at Langskail was a grander spec than Tanera with its 'ten acres Scots or thereby' and the ruined fishing station. In all his island days as ecologist and historian combined, Frank's mind's eye saw the longships come through the Sounds and we fell to talking of the Vikings in Hoy, depicted later so vividly by George Mackay Brown's vision of their arrival.

> The crags of Hoy at first light towered above them,
> pillars of fire. Towards noon they came to Rackwick.
> > Beach shineth in blackness,
> > After hard voyage a hidden valley,
> > Hills for bees to be hived in,
> > Beasts kept, a cod-hungry boat,
> > A comfort of fire in the crofts.
> > We furled sail, set firm our feet,
> > Stone laid against stone,
> > Laboured long till ebb of light,
> > Hungry men round a dead hearth.
> > Dreamed I that darkness
> > Of horse, harp, a hallowed harvest.[142]

In this sort of verse there is a wealth of natural and human ecology in the idyllic setting of Rackwick which we relished on that bleak day without overcoming our pessimism – such days of prosperity of a hardy people would not be other than legend in Rackwick for a long time to come. Frank cast a weather eye for the last time upon the roofless cottages and the slanting storms on the Pentland Firth, climbed into

Malcolm's vintage Austin and was homeward bound. Later we made plans to go back together to the Hebrides but his health failed; however, it was not until 1978, almost within a year of his death, that Frank had his last personal contact with the Hebrides when his daughter Francesca went to Barra for five months to do field-work there for her degree in social anthropology at Edinburgh University. Two stories of drowning in the isles told to her by Frank sometime before were the starting point; they served in providing a call to her to identify with the island folk in the struggle for survival. She came to me for advice; I suggested Barra and she went with two pieces of additional advice from her father: 'Never ask questions, and always make sure you have something to do inside as well as outside and don't be anxious about finishing a task at one go. You've got to be prepared to move from one to another depending on the weather.' He wrote many letters of encouragement and reminiscence to her at this time and they shared a closeness of this discovery and rediscovery. Later in December 1979 Francesca returned to the Western Isles to work with community co-operatives, but Frank had died six weeks before, on her birthday. She wrote that, in a curious way, his release was his last birthday present to her. Now Francesca works for the Council for National Parks; this appointment would have brought great pleasure to Frank.

In 1977 Frank and Christina came to Inverness to the unveiling of his photographic portrait and the naming of the NCC's North West Scotland Office, *Fraser Darling House*. I had the great privilege of giving a short appreciation of Frank in his own hearing. I described his life as an Odyssey in three parts: Britannica, Americana and Africana. He stood to reply and, though bent and unsteady, his mind was razor-sharp and his speech erudite as ever. He was touched by the occasion, the more so since the Regional Officer was Niall Campbell, whose wife Moira unveiled the portrait and whose father, Colonel Ronald Bruce Campbell, was Frank's supporter and mentor when he most needed help in the days of the West Highland Survey. Bruce, Niall's elder brother, recalls how Frank and his father talked to members of a youth club from South Wales in camp at Salen and of the lasting impression which the two pioneers made on these young people and their attitude to the countryside. Frank wrote of Colonel Campbell:

> It is the human being you remember and love. Elderly, boyish, rugged, and wise in his own way, I kept having the feeling I knew him [Bill Mann, Director, Washington Zoo] well or that he was like someone else. Then I got it. His counterpart in Britain is Colonel Ronald Campbell, *quondam* Master-at-Arms at the University of Edinburgh, world champion fencer, scout, and good companion. They have the same slightly rascally smile, the same insight into character, the same utter selflessness.[143]

He spied the Rona Stone (see p.121) displayed in its glass cowl and retold the story of its finding by the altar in St Ronan's oratory in 1938. 'Thirty-nine years I have had the stone in my care. A safe harbour for it seemed far away then.' This little ceremony was to be his last public appearance and where better than in a place which bears his name and with people who revered him in a way no others did.

My words were much appreciated by Frank. He talked to me about his journals and papers, and asked if I would edit and have published his African Journal covering his visits to Zambia, Kenya and Sudan; that I promised to have done. I knew him well, perhaps better than any other outside his family circle. He hinted broadly once that he would trust me with his biography, but I responded by charging him with his autobiography even though I believed him too frail. I was puzzled at the time why someone of his literary gifts, motivation, sense of destiny and depth, and variety of life never made time for his autobiography. What kept him back? The three-part feature which he wrote for *The Countryman* in 1972, entitled 'The Way I Have Come', is proof enough if such was needed of a life-story worthy of the full telling by himself. His books provide a stage-by-stage autobiography, but I am certain that Frank was not slow to comprehend that an autobiography written in later life would be a consummate and revealing work. Something deep within him may have prevented him from doing so. To the end of his life, he was very sensitive about his birth and boyhood, and the great influence of his mother who died in April 1966 aged 91; his accountability to her was dominant in Frank's life.

Francesca has her own window upon her father's life:

> Bobbie and his mother almost merged as a female influence on him. They got on very well and he felt 'managed' by them

233

and almost given into Bobbie's capable care by his mother. It was only when he left Bobbie and lived with Averil that he lost his stammer, and it went almost overnight. From then on I think the birthright and its origins faded somewhat though it remained very central to his understanding of others' lives. I'd say a lot of his compassion for humans, as opposed to the natural world, stemmed directly from his knowledge that 'he could have gone to the bad so easily', and that if it hadn't been for his overwhelming passion in natural history, he probably would have done so. The other reason why not, of course, was his mother's decision to keep him in disregard of conventional practice at the time. Usually babies from bourgeois single mothers were farmed out and discreetly hidden, to be forgotten later. Her stand to keep him was central. To us he made more of this repudiation of the conventional, pragmatic and sensible by his mother in her act than of the nature of the conception.[144]

Frank was also sensitive about his marriages, the relationships of his children and his standing as a scientist. It was Bobbie who told me that Frank would never come to accept himself *as he was*; his life had to be proof to himself that he was *not* as he was. The effects of single parenthood and upbringing deeply imprinted in youth stayed with him all his life and drove him to excesses of self-assessment; in boyhood, these produced the maverick; in early life, the man of great physical and intellectual drive; later, the 'big personality'; and in old age, the melancholy sage. His knighthood was proof enough to his peers that he had reached that high point of fulfilment. Sadly, it was not proof enough to himself; after all, he *was* as he was.

These and other disincentives to autobiography were upon him in the late sixties when the time was ripe for autobiography and he was busy in America and with the Reith Lectures, *Wilderness and Plenty*. In the seventies his strength had gone for a work of such magnitude. James states that 'after the Reith Lectures my father was bombarded by requests for book forewords, articles and lectures. He was too kind a man to refuse these piecemeal impositions. He even dissipated his energies one summer as an external examiner for the New University of Ulster at Coleraine (where he received an Honorary DSc). I remember in 1972, at Shefford Woodlands, that he was unable to concentrate on an article that had to meet a deadline. He moved about the house trying to find a

Plate 2. Bobbie: Marian Fraser-Darling in 1982.
(photo J. Morton Boyd)

place to settle, then went out into the garden to see if an
hour's scything of nettles would clear his mind. He said to
me "I'm written out. I've already said everything I have to
say. Why can't people read my books and leave me alone?"
Part of his problem was that his illness did weaken his

intellectual drive, his ability for sustained work. He might have been able to reminisce interestingly with a cup of tea in hand, but such a major project as an autobiography (along with the feeling that it would have been presumptuous of him to have written such) would probably have been beyond him after 1970.'

Yet, on the other side of the coin, these were for him the very incentives which drove him on to overcome the handicaps with which he felt he was born. Those who knew his stammer at its worst would not have thought the same man capable of delivering the Reith Lectures with such fluency as he did. On the introduction of Richard, then a diplomat in Helsinki, to Prime Minister Harold Wilson, the latter spontaneously enquired about his father; the same occurred when Alasdair was presented to Prince Philip; the 'nobody' of the island farm had travelled a long way on great incentives which were essentially spiritual.

In October 1977 the Royal Society of Edinburgh and the Nature Conservancy Council held a joint symposium. It was to be honoured by Frank's presence. His health prevented him, but he was able to write a Foreword to the volume *The Natural Environment of the Outer Hebrides*, his last published work.

When I was a little boy the Garden of the Hesperides, Hy Brasil and the Hebrides had a curious oneness in my mind. Two of these places are mythical; the Hebrides are real, but they reach into a legendary past and the limbo of my own mind and so, the western isles, the Outer Hebrides, however romantic they may have been in their beginnings in me, became a country which had to be trodden. The people were an entity to me as well, an extraordinary amalgam of hard-bitten practicality and high spiritual indifference to commercial prosperity and I knew their folklore. There was also a regard to the creatures of land and sea, completely unsentimental, and yet accepting an identity with the whole environment which reminded me of the early Columban Christian association of people with those other denizens of land and sea. The Outer Hebridean gathered a store of young gannets for winter food and killed seals for sea boots and oil but he did not kill for fun.

But that was yesterday and far beyond, into a prehistory when Pytheas circumnavigated the islands of Northern Britain, when some Mediterranean folk had already raised the Callanish Circle of great stones and set the fact of human

236

occupation. Yesterday when we were very young, the natural resources of land and sea were, with the six-rowed bere, the bread grain, the staff of life, but history had upset any golden age of our imagination. The Vikings had come and stayed, adopting the Gaelic as their tongue but making over two-thirds of the place names Scandinavian. Gael and Mediterranean were so much themselves that the physical type persists today almost as a genetic segregate; the first question to a midwife was often as to whether the baby was a 'Spaneach' or not. The folk had culturally become one and the wild resources of land and sea supported them. Even North Rona, when visited by Martin Martin in the 17th century, had its 30 people paying their proper respect to the environment in their own religious way. But the 19th century was an era of development – the sacred word which we are even now scarcely questioning – though I truly believe this Symposium is asking the question in a new humility and desire for co-operation with nature . . .

The Outer Hebrides by their position and environmental limitations present a fairly simple ecological system for study, which should attract the scholar. For myself I can claim no such high falutin' reasons. I just loved the place and the people, as much for the 'backwardness' of everything as for the surging beauty of land and sea and of wildlife. It took time to see that if one had any intellectual notions, they must be ordered and applied. Not being a very good scientist, nor an historian nor archaeologist, but one extremely conscious of the necessity of all these disciplines, I became an almost 18th-century style of dilettante, interested in so many things. In such fashion was the West Highland Survey conceived . . .

Island life, as I know, needs special gifts which the environment can develop. One is living near the edge so that, like the Eskimos, a multiplicity of physical possessions can be an embarrassment. Richness can accumulate in social achievement. Language as a means of communication, the arts of music and poetry making, are part of the cultural heritage which radio and sound recording can enrich – and they can impoverish. Which is it to be? Science is discovery and impersonal. Technology is personal and science-using. They *can* achieve a harmony.[145]

So wrote Frank when in old age he described his earliest recollections of the Western Isles of Scotland. His inward vision was of the awe-struck faces of the first Hebrideans – these Mesolithic people of dark Mediterranean stock – as they beheld the Hebrides stretching north-westward into the

237

sunset. He saw the milestones of human kind through the ages from the Callanish stones to the missile-launchers of West Geirinish today. They were reflections of a people in a golden age of plenty sustained by the seemingly endless resources of land and sea. Seasons of winter poverty were offset in summer plenty by an indigenous culture of provisioning of food and fuel harvested within sight of home. The spirit of the earth was that of regeneration and renewal: the spirit of man that of eternal youth. Frank had his own passport to *Tir nan Og*, the Gael's legendary land of the ever young; yet, he knew that the golden age of the Hebrides when man and environment were a harmonious whole is more of the imagination than of fact.

The pensive sage, melancholy of look, bowed but yet raven-headed, saw in his meditation the grand relationship of the elements of air, land, sea and people in a setting of isles with great drifts of shell-sand and blankets of peat. Shadowy figures of yesterday, men, women and children, break the undulating skyline of the sandhills with creels of seaweed on their way twixt shore and the life-supporting patches of potatoes and oats. Others haul drift nets in the half light of dawn; herring splutter everywhere, their silver bodies reflecting the new day's glare from behind Ben Mor Coigach.

My visits to Lochyhill might have been better employed by recording conversations with Frank or by making notes and no doubt I let some opportunities go a-begging. Yet at the times that I tried to record and write, Frank did not react well. He became suddenly formal and far less naturally articulate than in normal conversation. When I delivered the John Phillips Medal to him, I took with me another distinguished conversationist, Dr Joe Eggeling, who knew Frank well. He was my predecessor in the Nature Conservancy and had been for twenty-five years in East African forestry. He was now retired and I listened to them re-running the events which led to this failure or that achievement in wonderful places. Both were personally involved in the establishment of the Conservation Area in the magnificent Ngorongoro Crater in the northern highlands of Tanzania, and for an hour we were back on the spacious floor of fifteen-kilometre-wide caldera with its herds of wildebeeste, zebra, gazelles and buffalo; its families of elephant, prides of lions and countless flamingos.

In his retirement to Lochyhill, Frank returned to the part of the world he loved more than any other in his far-cast life. He was, however, denied peace and enjoyment as month by month and year by year through the seventies, his physical faculties gradually failed him. Those of his friends, like me, who saw him only occasionally for a few hours found him dispirited and preoccupied with self and death; he seemed overcome by his own debilities and the illnesses of Francesca and Christina. The man of great fortitude seemed to lack a strength which faith and prayer can bring. However, there was much more to it which I would have discovered had I been longer with him.

What was going on in his mind as he talked of death? Francesca shed light on this in a recent letter to me:

> . . . his meditations on death were not so much to do with himself and his concerns, as with what untimely death destroys and what an overlong stay in life also destroys. For him as he said, 'the best legacy you can leave your children is to die at seventy', a half facetious remark that became more ironic to him when he failed this precept. At seventy-four and failed in health, he felt it was perverse and problematic that he should be unable to leave life as he desired, whilst others were plucked out before their time. In coming to my side when I was dying (in India) and his presence being so instrumental in giving me the succour to live, he felt he had been given an understanding of what 'God's' intentions had been in keeping him alive to seventy-three. Christina's peril (cancer in 1976) upset the balance and his almost obsessive thoughts on death were more to do with trying to penetrate the mystery of this rather than morose and morbid cogitations on the unfairness of his lot. That is how I saw it . . .[146]

In 1972, though soon to have an operation himself, Frank left home to be with Francesca who had fallen seriously ill in India. He sat with her all day for six weeks and in the end felt that his life of handicap made sense. Although unable to nurse Averil to life, he had done so for Francesca and saw that his physical degeneration had not stood in the way of giving strength to others. But throughout the years, as I saw it from outside the family, Christina was the anchor which never failed. The strains of the move from Shefford Woodlands to Lochyhill and of the illnesses of Frank and Francesca were immense; she also had her aged mother living at Lochyhill. When Francesca was well enough to travel, she went to India alone and brought her home to recovery and good health. In 1976 Christina's health broke seriously and she was admitted to hospital in Edinburgh for radiotherapy. During this period Francesca lived at home with her father and came to understand more the mystery of his mind. Christina made a fine recovery and returned to Lochyhill to convalesce and later to attend to Frank in the last months of his life.

Many of his friends from all stages of his life made pilgrimage to Lochyhill to see and talk with Frank. He was respected by a multitude, held in affection by many and loved by a few who would not be separated from him.

Shortly before he died, Frank showed James the copy of *Origin of Species* (1917 edition) which he had had as a schoolboy of fourteen. He said how bored he was by his French lessons in school. He used to read *Origin of Species* under the desk. One day the master became aware of Frank's inattention and angrily grabbed at the boy's elbow, expecting to find some trash adventure story. When the man perused the volume, he was taken aback, saying, 'I don't understand you, Darling!' Frank was not punished. Charmed by the story, James asked if he might leave the grubby, little volume to him. The old man duly wrote a note to that effect and put it between the pages; James has gifted the book to me. I also had the privilege of sitting with him from time to time looking again at the great canvas of his life recalling vignettes of An Teallach, North Rona and Tanera, of the Great Smokes, Yellowstone and Yosemite, of Tsavo, Amboseli and the Serengeti. Even on my last visit two weeks before he died, his recall of island days was sharp.

In the summer of 1979, Frank had difficulty in speaking owing to a stroke earlier in the year. However, he did express himself with his eyes. One could talk to others in the room and know that he included himself in the conversation, even though he spoke little. Sometimes he was left alone too long and to correct this James would go especially to talk, but sustained conversation would tire him utterly. James writes 'he could not read at this time, so I read to him – for example, the epilogue of David Cecil's *Lord Melbourne* with its nostalgic back view to the subject's youth in the great aristocracy of eighteenth-century England, where the Hall, the Great House, was the centre of a pre-industrial land, the centre of

240

Plate 3. Red deer hind with calf in June in Wester Ross: Frank's favourites. (photo Tom Weir)

civilisation as opposed to the grimy cities of the 1840s onwards. I also read Lord Tennyson's *Death of Arthur* remembering how he looked to that legendary period as the ideal of the Golden Age. How else could I console the dying man?'

For ease of nursing Christina had Frank's bed moved into the drawing room. I found him awake, propped up on pillows and exhausted by a painful rasping cough. He looked straight at me with an incisive stare which seemed to disarm me completely of words I had momentarily prepared. He held out his great hand, now skin and bone, and I stifled my grief. His voice was weak and my words were few and hard to come by. I talked about the seals and for a moment his eyes sparkled with life and he was once again with Old Tawny on Lunga's shore. We sat in silence and I observed the wisdom in his dark eyes. What were his thoughts?

Were they of the Hebrides – the vivid frontier, half legendary, half real? Were they of the Gaels whose roots he saw like those of marram grass, and whose attachment to their islands he likened to the holdfasts of the seaweeds and shellfish on their stormy shores? His last letter written to Francesca in late August 1978 before she left Barra ended: 'my love to you, and my love to so many of the folk I have never met and who are yet not unknown to me. Remember that the line of the Hebrides has been the other shore to me.'

Later I searched his writings in the hope that a divine hand would lead me to the last thoughts of nature which dwelt with him to the last days of consciousness of the world. I think that I found them in the book which brought us together.

> The deep and precipitous corries and the spiry summits may cause awe, but the high grasslands on a summer day have an idyllic quality. They are remote and quiet. They are green and kind to the eye. They are ease to the feet. The flowers have great variety and a new beauty, and the very pebbles among which they grow have a sparkle and show of colour. To climb to one of these alps of grass and descend again in a few hours is not enough. Take a little tent and remain in the quietness for a few days. It is magnificent to rise in the morning in such a place. The only sounds breaking the silence, if you get the best of the early July weather, will be the grackle of the ptarmigan, the flute-like pipe of the ring ouzel, and perhaps the plaint of a golden plover or a dotterel. See how the deer, now bright-red-coated, lie at ease in the alpine grassland. Listen, if you have stalked near enough, to the sweet talkings of the calves who are like happy children. Of your charity disturb them not in their Arcadia.[147]

Frank died at Forres Hospital on 22 October 1979.

Sources of Quotations

Frank Fraser Darling

PIJ: 1936-7 *Priest Island Journal*, MS

TJ: 1937 *Treshnish Journal*, MS

HRD: 1937 *A Herd of Red Deer*, Oxford University Press

BF: 1938 *Bird Flocks and the Breeding Cycle*, Cambridge University Press

NRJ: 1938-9 *North Rona Journal*, MS

SF: 1939 *Seasons and the Farmer*, Cambridge University Press

NR: 1939 *A Naturalist on Rona*, Oxford University Press

FFD/FK; FK/FFD: 1939-49 Letters to and from F. Kendon, MS

FFD/RM: Letter to Dr R. Martin, MS

IY: 1941 *Island Years*, Bell

IF: 1944 *Island Farm*, Bell

GH: 1944 Articles in the *Glasgow Herald*

CA: 1945 *Crofting Agriculture*, Oliver and Boyd

NHHI: 1947 *Natural History in the Highlands and Islands*, Collins

US&M: 1951 *An Account of Journeys made in the United States and Mexico in the course of Rockefeller Special Fellowship, June-December, 1950*, TS

WHS: 1955 *West Highland Survey*, Oxford University Press

PW: 1956 *Pelican in the Wilderness*, Allen and Unwin

FDAJ: 1956-8 African Journal, MS

FFD/JMB; JMB/FFD: 1961-2 Letters to and from J. M. Boyd dated 27 April 1961 and 29 September 1962, MS

H&I: 1964 *The Highlands and Islands* (jointly with J. M. Boyd), Collins

W&P: 1969 *Wilderness and Plenty*, The Reith Lectures, BBC

TC: 1972 'The Way I have Come', Three articles in *The Countryman*

243

FFD/JMB: 1972 Letter to J. M. Boyd dated November, MS

ISStK: 1974 Foreword to *Island Survivors: The Ecology of the Soay Sheep of St Kilda* (edited by P. A. Jewell, C. Milner and J. M. Boyd), Athlone Press, London University

FFD/AFD: 1977 Letter to A. Fraser-Darling, 24 January, MS

NEOH: 1979 Foreword to *The Natural Environment of the Outer Hebrides* (edited by J. M. Boyd), Proceedings of the Royal Society of Edinburgh, Vol. 77

Other Sources

SN: V. C. Wynne-Edwards 1948 *Scottish Naturalist*

OT: George Mackay Brown 1978 *An Orkney Tapestry*, Gollancz

Fca/JMB: Francesca Fraser Darling 1984-5 Letters and notes to J. M. Boyd, MS

AF-D/JMB: Alasdair Fraser-Darling 1984-5 Letters and notes to J. M. Boyd, MS

JFD/JMB: James Fraser Darling 1985 Letters and notes to J. M. Boyd, 1 and 9 April, MS

JPG/JMB: J. P. Grant of Rothiemurchus 1985 Letter to J. M. Boyd, 29 May, MS

LKS/JMB: L. K. Stewart 1985 Letter to J. M. Boyd (April) undated, MS

Notes

Prologue
1 : FFD/JMB, 1961
2 : JMB/FFD, 1961
3 : FFD/JMB, 1962
4 : AJ, p.4
5 : US & M, I
6 : PW, 224-5
7 : PW, 372
8 : IY, 300
9 : NRJ, 8
10 : AJ, 257
11 : US & M, 43-4
12 : AJ, 54

Chapter 1
13 : TC, p.28
14 : PW, 226
15 : PW, 239
16 : FFD/AF-D, 977
17 : TC, 30
18 : PW, 256
19 : TC, 32-3
20 : TC, 34-5
21 : TC, 36
22 : IF, 11
23 : IF, 12
24 : IF, 13
25 : IF, 14
26 : IF, 14
27 : IF, 15
28 : IF, 16
29 : TC, 66-7
30 : TC, 67
31 : IF, 17

32 : IF, 18-9
33 : IF, 17
34 : IF, 21
35 : IF, 21
36 : IF, 22
37 : IF, 23
38 : TC, 70

Chapter 2
39 : HRD, p.23
40 : HRD, 2-18
41 : HRD, 27
42 : HRD, 114-6
43 : HRD, 79-80
44 : TC, 72
45 : IY, 5

Chapter 3
46 : TC, p.72
47 : IY, 7
48 : IY, 8
49 : IY, 28-33
50 : PIJ, 1-2
51 : PIJ, 8-12

Chapter 4
52 : BF, pp.33-4
53 : BF, 37-8
54 : PIJ, 36
55 : BF, 67
56 : BF, 109
57 : PIJ, 41
58 : PIJ, 44-5
59 : IY, 72-3

60 : FIJ, 48-9
61 : PIJ, 48-9
62 : IY, 35-6

Chapter 5
63 : TJ, pp.18-21
64 : IY, 179-80
65 : TJ, 54
66 : NR, 103
67 : TJ, 16-38
68 : TJ, 58
69 : TJ, 92-4
70 : IY, 189-91
71 : TJ, 117
72 : IY, 199-200

Chapter 6
73 : IY, pp.223-4
74 : NRJ, 33
75 : NRJ, 6-16
76 : NRJ, 20-4

Chapter 7
77 : NRJ, pp.30-1
78 : NRJ, 17-18
79 : NRJ,
80 : NR, 78-9, 84
81 : IY, 279-80
82 : IY, 283-5
83 : IY, 297-8

Chapter 8
84 : IF, p.136
85 : IF, 140

246

Index

247

248

251